A CELEBRATION OF POETS

ATLANTIC
GRADES 4-6
SPRING 2009

creativeCOMMUNICATION
A CELEBRATION OF TODAY'S WRITERS

A CELEBRATION OF POETS
ATLANTIC
GRADES 4-6
SPRING 2009

AN ANTHOLOGY COMPILED BY CREATIVE COMMUNICATION, INC.

Published by:

creativeCOMMUNICATION
A CELEBRATION OF TODAY'S WRITERS

1488 NORTH 200 WEST · LOGAN, UTAH 84341
TEL. 435-713-4411 · WWW.POETICPOWER.COM

ISBN: 978-1-60050-258-3

FOREWORD

Earlier this year I received a phone call from an individual who was sending in a poem written by a friend's son. Through the conversation it was revealed that the person I was talking to was the author, poet and playwright, John Tobias. His poem, "Reflections on a Gift of Watermelon Pickle Received from a Friend Called Felicity" is one of my favorite poems. Starting with the line "During that summer, when unicorns were still possible..." his poem takes me back to all the magical summers that I had where anything could happen. I was given a treat in that Mr. Tobias recited his poem and related the story that inspired it. What I gained most from the conversation was that the inspiration for any writing may seem to come from an event, but it is really written from a lifetime of experiences.

I also received a letter this spring from a young lady who was published in one of our anthologies in 1999. Now a published author working on her second novel, she took the time to write and thank Creative Communication for giving her the start for her writing career. The poets in this anthology are beginning writers. Yet, as they continue in their writing, the experience of being a published author will hopefully be an inspiration to them. As they gain a lifetime of experiences, I hope they will continue to write and share themselves through poetry.

As you read each student's poem, realize that every famous author started somewhere. I hope that I will continue to receive letters from authors who relate that we were the first place they were published. Will one of these authors become famous? Anything is possible.

I hope you enjoy this anthology and the poets who share their lives through words.

Thomas Worthen, Ph.D.
Editor
Creative Communication

WRITING CONTESTS!

Enter our next POETRY contest!
Enter our next ESSAY contest!

Why should I enter?
Win prizes and get published! Each year thousands of dollars in prizes are awarded throughout North America. The top writers in each division receive a monetary award and a free book that includes their published poem or essay. Entries of merit are also selected to be published in our anthology.

Who may enter?
There are four divisions in the poetry contest. The poetry divisions are grades K-3, 4-6, 7-9, and 10-12. There are three divisions in the essay contest. The essay divisions are grades 3-6, 7-9, and 10-12.

What is needed to enter the contest?
To enter the poetry contest send in one original poem, 21 lines or less. To enter the essay contest send in one original non-fiction essay, 250 words or less, on any topic. Each entry must include the student's name, grade, address, city, state, and zip code, and the student's school name and school address. Students who include their teacher's name may help their teacher qualify for a free copy of the anthology. Contest changes and updates are listed at www.poeticpower.com.

How do I enter?

Enter a poem online at:
www.poeticpower.com

or

Mail your poem to:
  Poetry Contest
  1488 North 200 West
  Logan, UT 84341

Enter an essay online at:
www.studentessaycontest.com

or

Mail your essay to:
  Essay Contest
  1488 North 200 West
  Logan, UT 84341

When is the deadline?
Poetry contest deadlines are August 18th, December 3rd, and April 13th. Essay contest deadlines are October 15th, February 17th, and July 15th. Students can enter one poem and one essay for each spring, summer, and fall contest deadline.

Are there benefits for my school?
Yes. We award $15,000 each year in grants to help with Language Arts programs. Schools qualify to apply for a grant by having 15 or more accepted entries.

Are there benefits for my teacher?
Yes. Teachers with five or more students published receive a free anthology that includes their students' writing.

For more information please go to our website at **www.poeticpower.com**, email us at editor@poeticpower.com or call 435-713-4411.

TABLE OF CONTENTS

STATES INCLUDED IN THIS EDITION:

DELAWARE
NEW HAMPSHIRE
NORTH CAROLINA
RHODE ISLAND
SOUTH CAROLINA
VERMONT
VIRGINIA
WASHINGTON D. C.

Spring 2009 Poetic Achievement Honor Schools

* Teachers who had fifteen or more poets accepted to be published

The following schools are recognized as receiving a "Poetic Achievement Award." This award is given to schools who have a large number of entries of which over fifty percent are accepted for publication. With hundreds of schools entering our contest, only a small percent of these schools are honored with this award. The purpose of this award is to recognize schools with excellent Language Arts programs. This award qualifies these schools to receive a complimentary copy of this anthology. In addition, these schools are eligible to apply for a Creative Communication Language Arts Grant. Grants of two hundred and fifty dollars each are awarded to further develop writing in our schools.

Atkinson Academy Elementary School
Atkinson, NH
Maria Vanderhoof*

Bensley Elementary School
Richmond, VA
Maria T. MacLaughlin*
Satonya Perry

Berry Shoals Intermediate School
Duncan, SC
Sheila J. Dobbins*

Blaney Elementary School
Elgin, SC
Beth Granger*

Boiling Springs Intermediate School
Boiling Springs, SC
Susan Lyda*
Melissa Slater

Buffalo Elementary School
Buffalo, SC
Pam Gault*

C Hunter Ritchie Elementary School
Warrenton, VA
Mary Cicotello*

Cape Henry Collegiate School
Virginia Beach, VA
Tina V. Howard*
Hilda Roe

Chapin Middle School
Chapin, SC
Shannon Allonier*
Martina D. Fox*

Clover Hill Elementary School
Midlothian, VA
K. Geczi
Carol Marable*

Cool Spring Elementary School
Cleveland, NC
Aimee Adkins*
Tonya Cassidy
Kelly Collins
Jessica Duncan
Tricia Freeze

Cooper Elementary School
Hampton, VA
Marci Miles
Mrs. Schrage*
Shirley Sypolt

Courthouse Road Elementary School
Spotsylvania, VA
Mrs. Abramaitys*
Brenda Nettles*
Michelle Sims
Natalie Warren*

Crestwood Elementary School
Richmond, VA
Diane Bivins*
Christine Guerci
Mali L. Hart

CrossRoads Middle School
Columbia, SC
Cynthia Furr*

East Mooresville Intermediate School
Mooresville, NC
Julie Keelan*
Amy Smith*

Edwards Elementary School
Chesterfield, SC
J.P. Watson
T. Watson

Fairforest Middle School
Spartanburg, SC
Mrs. Hayes
Kathy Stevens*

Floyd T Binns Middle School
Culpeper, VA
Charissa Hollyfield*

Forestbrook Middle School
Myrtle Beach, SC
Stephanie Necessary*

Four Oaks Elementary School
Four Oaks, NC
Wanda Lee*

Grace Miller Elementary School
Bealeton, VA
Susan Aylor
Amy Costanzo
Sherri McMillon

Heron Pond Elementary School
Milford, NH
Kathy Melconian*

Holy Cross Elementary School
Dover, DE
Cathi Bolton*

Homeschool Plus
Norfolk, VA
Carol Martin-Gregory*

Hope Valley Elementary School
Hope Valley, RI
Richard C. Macksoud
Jennifer Ricci

Linkhorne Middle School
Lynchburg, VA
Angie Bryant
Jeanie Templeton*

Main Street Middle School
Montpelier, VT
Stephanie Drew*
Lisa Moody

Manchester Elementary School
Spring Lake, NC
Mrs. Abraham-Johnson
Christy Thomas

Manchester Elementary/Middle School
Manchester Center, VT
Rachel Mark*
Anna Nicholson*

Maple Wood Elementary School
Somersworth, NH
Jennifer Landry*

Mary Walter Elementary School
Bealeton, VA
Patricia Baker*

Monelison Middle School
Madison Heights, VA
Mrs. Saunders
Lynette Smith*
Sarah Thomas

North Windy Ridge School
Weaverville, NC
Christopher Schmidt*

Northside Elementary School
Seneca, SC
Cathy Nutt*
Lyndsey Sullivan

Oak View Elementary School
Fairfax, VA
Alyson Eaglen*
Cynthia Unwin

Olde Providence Elementary School
Charlotte, NC
Lynn Allen
Colleen Bill
Jill Boyajy
Mary Gath
Susie Henry
Mary Marcinkiewicz
Jane McCall
Maureen Nappi
Cheri Powers
Beth Smith
Helen Vahamikos
Linda Wahl
Murdice Willie
Kristen Wysocki

Pine Tree Hill Elementary School
Camden, SC
Ms. Faulkenberry*

Pocalla Springs Elementary School
Sumter, SC
Ureka Hilton*

Prince of Peace Catholic School
Taylors, SC
Mrs. Martinez*

Queen's Grant Community School
Mint Hill, NC
Tiffany Dunagan*
Ms. Williams

Queens Creek Elementary School
Swansboro, NC
LeAnn Henry*

Riverview Elementary School
Spotsylvania, VA
Chris Andrews
Bevin Arnold
Cindy Barsanti
Barbara Bollman
Barbara D. Brown
Karin Cameron
Abby Capaz
Ginger Carey
Kim Cartoski
Christy Clark
Cheryl Croyle
Renee Gauvin
Missy Howard
Dara Lee
Cheryl Nichols
Melissa Parker
Kirsten Slade*
Diane Smart
Nolan Speichinger
Amber Williams

Rye Elementary School
Rye, NH
Doris Gianforte
Phoebe Guarnaccia
Rosalind Robichaud
Eric Ross

St Christopher's School
Richmond, VA
Cynthia Brown
Linda DiLucente
Deborah Epes
Renee Fraine
Margaret Frischkorn
Marion Halladay
Margaret Hunter
Paula Jones
Glorietta Jones
Cabell Jones
Susan Kirk
Ms. McAdams
James Morgan
Mrs. J. O'Ferrall
Sandra Oakley
A. Pava
Ellen Sands
Mrs. D. Suskind
Wanda Vizcaino
Christie Wilson
Nancy Young

St Helena Elementary School
St. Helena Island, SC
Christina Johnson*

St John Neumann Academy
Blacksburg, VA
Rachael Beach
Patricia Kesler
Mrs. Leece
Jenny Mishoe

St Mary School
Cranston, RI
Jane Bowry*

St Rocco School
Johnston, RI
Judy Carroccio*

St Thomas More Catholic School
Chapel Hill, NC
Linda DiGiovanni*
Jennifer Sullivan

Tabernacle Elementary School
Asheboro, NC
Mrs. Maness
Ms. Perryman
Laura Popp

Trinity Christian School
Fairfax, VA
Mrs. Adams
Vicky Butler
Sue Datema*
Penny Gale
Melissa Knaus
Margaret Locke*
Mrs. Procter
Katherine Rickwald
Jennifer Silva
Susan Tyler

Vergennes Union Elementary School
Vergennes, VT
Elaine Pentaleri*

Vienna Elementary School
Pfafftown, NC
Mary Pat Cowan*

Wakefield Forest Elementary School
Fairfax, VA
Karen M. Hickman*

Waller Mill Fine Arts Magnet School
Williamsburg, VA
Sherrie A. Geyer*

Language Arts Grant Recipients 2008-2009

After receiving a "Poetic Achievement Award" schools are encouraged to apply for a Creative Communication Language Arts Grant. The following is a list of schools who received a two hundred and fifty dollar grant for the 2008-2009 school year.

Acushnet Elementary School, Acushnet, MA
Benton Central Jr/Sr High School, Oxford, IN
Bridgeway Christian Academy, Alpharetta, GA
Central Middle School, Grafton, ND
Challenger Middle School, Cape Coral, FL
City Hill Middle School, Naugatuck, CT
Clintonville High School, Clintonville, WI
Coral Springs Middle School, Coral Springs, FL
Covenant Classical School, Concord, NC
Coyote Valley Elementary School, Middletown, CA
Diamond Ranch Academy, Hurricane, UT
E O Young Jr Elementary School, Middleburg, NC
El Monte Elementary School, Concord, CA
Emmanuel-St Michael Lutheran School, Fort Wayne, IN
Ethel M Burke Elementary School, Bellmawr, NJ
Fort Recovery Middle School, Fort Recovery, OH
Gardnertown Fundamental Magnet School, Newburgh, NY
Hancock County High School, Sneedville, TN
Haubstadt Community School, Haubstadt, IN
Headwaters Academy, Bozeman, MT
Holden Elementary School, Chicago, IL
Holliday Middle School, Holliday, TX
Holy Cross High School, Delran, NJ
Homestead Elementary School, Centennial, CO
Joseph M Simas Elementary School, Hanford, CA
Labrae Middle School, Leavittsburg, OH
Lakewood High School, Lakewood, CO
Lee A Tolbert Community Academy, Kansas City, MO
Mary Lynch Elementary School, Kimball, NE
Merritt Secondary School, Merritt, BC
North Star Academy, Redwood City, CA

Language Arts Grant Winners cont.

Old Redford Academy, Detroit, MI
Prairie Lakes School, Willmar, MN
Public School 124Q, South Ozone Park, NY
Rutledge Hall Elementary School, Lincolnwood, IL
Shelley Sr High School, Shelley, ID
Sonoran Science Academy, Tucson, AZ
Spruce Ridge School, Estevan, SK
St Columbkille School, Dubuque, IA
St Francis Middle School, Saint Francis, MN
St Luke the Evangelist School, Glenside, PA
St Matthias/Transfiguration School, Chicago, IL
St Robert Bellarmine School, Chicago, IL
St Sebastian Elementary School, Pittsburgh, PA
The Hillel Academy, Milwaukee, WI
Thomas Edison Charter School - North, North Logan, UT
Trinity Christian Academy, Oxford, AL
United Hebrew Institute, Kingston, PA
Velasquez Elementary School, Richmond, TX
West Frederick Middle School, Frederick, MD

Grades 4-5-6

Note: The Top Ten poems were finalized through an online voting system. Creative Communication's judges first picked out the top poems. These poems were then posted online. The final step involved thousands of students and teachers who registered as online judges and voted for the Top Ten poems. We hope you enjoy these selections.

Top Poem Grades 4-5-6

Nature's Calling

Nature's bells are ringing,
slicing through the breeze.
They're louder than any church bell,
but softer than the moonlit peace.

Nature's limbs are swaying,
rattling as the cold wind blows
They reach down to caress my hair,
but really they're touching my soul.

Nature's heart is leaping,
frolicking through the sky.
Her air flows through my body
like an icy river passing by.

Nature's calling, speaking,
she wants me to join her fun.
But I cannot go up to meet her,
for the time has not yet come.

Tori Breen, Grade 4
Bethlehem Elementary School, NH

Top Poem Grades 4-5-6

The Wind

It's as large as a river 100 miles long,
    yet it takes up no space at all.
It sometimes tickles my nose and cheeks,
    and other times it burns my eyes and tosses me around.
Sometimes it cools me during the heat,
    and other times it adds to the cold.
It may be an addition to a thunderstorm,
    or it may enhance the beauty of a rainbow.
Is it an enemy or a friend?
That's your opinion.
It is the wind.

Jacob Cashour, Grade 6
Berry Shoals Intermediate School, SC

Top Poem Grades 4-5-6

Family Is Like a Flower

Family is like a flower.
It continuously grows, and grows, and grows, and grows,
Finally, resulting in the blossom of a green clover.
Similar to a clover, a family begins as a small fragile seed.
After a while, the seed starts to sprout.
It later begins to develop a thin, delicate stem topped with four silk petals.
After an extension of time together, a breeze sweeps in and carries
The four petals in separate directions.
Of course, in the growing of a flower there are weeds.
In the life of a human "weeds" are friends.
Friends come and go.
Weeds are tossed into a pile of dirt by the gardener.
That is the only difference between a flower and a family.
Flowers die, weeds are tossed aside, and friends drift apart.
But family is forever.

Madison Donohue, Grade 6
Chapin Middle School, SC

Top Poem Grades 4-5-6

Hatching

The warmth of my mother
sends an urge to my body
that lets me know
it is time!

I slowly but carefully
crack the egg
letting a trickle of light
flow into this dark, lonely room.

The comforting "cluck, cluck"
of Mama
helps me gather the strength
to move on.

Then to my surprise
the pitch dark room bursts
and I see the world
for the first time.

Lori Hart, Grade 4
Buffalo Elementary School, SC

Top Poem Grades 4-5-6

I Wonder if Grass Feels

I wonder if grass feels.
I suppose they do.
They have family roots around them.
They laugh when the wind moves them.
They're tickled when picked and played with.
In the winter, they feel trapped among walls of white.
In the spring, new neighbors — flowers — surround them.
In the summer, they're full of laughter.
In the fall, they're covered by change.
I wonder if grass feels.

Lauren Hawkins, Grade 6
Oakland School, VA

Top Poem Grades 4-5-6

Emotion Pocket

Poetry is an emotion pocket,
Which holds your sad, mad, funny and happy moments
So you don't have to.
It will never betray you,
but help support you.
Never tell,
Your worst moments.
Never tell,
Your love moments.
But instead,
help you hold
that moment,
secretly,
Forever.

MacKenzie Jones, Grade 6
Boiling Springs Intermediate School, SC

Top Poem Grades 4-5-6

Green

Grass and leaves blow in the breeze.
I walk outside to see
crickets staring at me.
I sit in clovers that cushion my fall.
I listen carefully to the low ribbet of a frog
and soft melody of a cricket's chirp.
I come inside to taste mint ice cream
and a green lollipop waiting for me.
And the smell of lime chills my spine
Green is delicious!

Katherine Milson, Grade 5
St Mary School, RI

Top Poem Grades 4-5-6

Without a Sound

Without a sound
ever darkening
enchanting
shadows casting over crisp golden leaves
beams of light piercing the darkness
to show forlorn grass
the poetry of the trees pulling you
closer and closer
to the lush sacred emerald grounds
that are only to be revealed on sorrowful days
silent
calm and peaceful
a place that seems like another world without a sound or sorrow
but only peaceful silent melodies humming in your ear
without a sound

Kyle Radigan, Grade 5
Daniel J Bakie School, NH

Top Poem Grades 4-5-6

Swim Race

Waiting waiting waiting,
For the sirens to start the race,
As the siren screams go,
We swim face to face,

Like jumping into an ice bucket.
Your senses start to clear.
Swimming through the water,
With anxiety and fear,

You're in the lead,
The clock is ticking,
The water is cold,
And the people are screaming,

The finish line is a few feet away,
Swim swim the trophy is mine,
You win you win,
1.25 is your time.

Piotr Sowulewski, Grade 5
Manchester Elementary/Middle School, VT

Top Poem Grades 4-5-6

Rebirth of Earth

A depressive miserable feeling;
Cold, frosty —
everything feels like nothing, nothing ever to be proud of.
The environment seems to be fading
and a deathly fog fills the Earth.
The plants, the trees
slowly lose their leaves;
the dark shadow consumes them.
Without the glimpse of seeing light again
the sharp feeling of the dark, cold winter.
This occurrence happens to all the Earth;
when the dark depth will be filled with light once again
alive for the rebirth of a new life.
This joyful feeling works its way back to us;
the renewal of life when everything is bright.
Earth is creeping back slowly from its deep sleep
a feeling so great, a feeling so rejuvenating
the feeling of spring.

Christian Stufano, Grade 6
St Rocco School, RI

Hidden

We are called illegal aliens — but really all we want is to be free.
In my old town we didn't have to hide, I could go in the yard and play as long as I wanted.

But here it's not the same, my friends are all gone.
I'm stuffed in a room all day, hiding, and waiting.

Papa and Mama are always scared. Their eyes are wide with fear.
My brother Miguel and I try to be quiet, but whispering isn't enough for me.

I don't understand why we came to this country, if all we do is hide in a cramped room.
I miss my home, I didn't want to leave. In Mexico, I wasn't called an alien.

We are told every day to behave, it's not hard to listen though,
Because in such a small place, trouble can't be made. Trouble is caused if we are found.

Sometimes I hope we will be found, so I'm not stuck in a tiny room.
After all, no one can see my potential, when I'm trapped inside all day.

America is the land of the free, but I am not free even though I live here.
Why did we come here? Papa says that I'll understand someday.

He says that soon we'll have a real life. I'm not so sure of that,
But if I don't hope, I'll have nothing to live for.

Hannah McClellan, Grade 5
Moyock Elementary School, NC

Just Another Day at the Park

The smack of the glove.
 The call strike one.
  The sun beating down on your skin.
   The smell of hotdogs comes to your nose.
    You take a deep breath and step into the batter's box.
    Here comes the pitch you pull the ball to left field.
     Crack! It goes into the sky you run and run.
      As you look at the ball it keeps going until it's gone.
       You run the bases and look at home plate your teammates have it surrounded.
       As you round third you think "I did it!"
        You jump on home plate and your teammates surround you. You've won the game.
         They say "nice hit" and you walk to the car and think
          "Just another day at the park."

Collin Reed, Grade 6
Boiling Springs Intermediate School, SC

I Have Learned That...

I've learned that it's not easy winning a game.
I've learned that there are two roads, one is to victory, and one is to loser town.
I've learned that if you take the right one you would be victorious.
I've learned that if you stop trying and start crying during a game, you could lose.
I've learned that if you don't give up you could win.
I've learned that if you're down by twenty in a game and you don't use your team, you're going to lose.
I've learned that if you don't give up like the little engine that could, you can win.
I've learned that if you ball hog in a game, you have very little chance of winning.
I've learned that always scoring is not good.
I've learned that using your team is better than you being a ball hog.

Braxton Gambrell, Grade 5
Northside Elementary School, SC

Shoelaces

Shoelaces

I dislike them so much

Bending down to tie them

If you don't they will trip you

I'll fall and it will hurt

All their fault

Change to velcro

It's the way to go

Shoelaces
Who needs velcro

Who needs sandals

When you have laces

All we need is sneakers

Sneakers to run in

Sneakers to play in

Shoelaces

Lauren Buellesbach, Grade 5
Oak View Elementary School, VA

White

White looks like a cloud happily floating in the sky.
White sounds like the crinkling of paper.
White smells like powdered sugar on a fresh waffle.
White tastes like vanilla ice cream melting in my mouth.
White feels like the cold snow brushing against my face.

Anna Marie Del Vecchio, Grade 5
Holy Cross Elementary School, DE

I Am Air…

I am air…
I seem to be invisible even when I do so much
I am clear and not to be seen
I am like an ant, too small to see
I am helpful and peaceful
I'm everywhere
I am mist or wind
I am air.

Jasmine Fasold, Grade 5
Wakefield Forest Elementary School, VA

Bright Red Shoes

Shiny and new,
I slipped on my bright red shoes.

I wear them to school every day,
I yell with my friends as I laugh and play.

I love my new car as my shoe hits the pedal,
I take all my friends as I begin to settle.

I walk down the aisle, still wearing my shoes.
I find myself smiling as a baby coos.

I took down the box that encloses my shoes,
Thinking about the memories I will never lose.

Emma Dahlin, Grade 6
Linkhorne Middle School, VA

Shooting Star

A spark of light
A flash of color
Sparkling stars
A trailing tail
A million wishes
Can you afford to fail?
Follow your dreams
Make a wish
Let your heart free
Follow them all through the night
On the tail of a star

Brenda Sprouse, Grade 6
School of International Studies at Meadowbrook, VA

Clouds

Do clouds ever get tired of being in the air?
Do clouds just want to sit in a chair?
Do clouds ever eat?
Do clouds have two feet?

Shelby Troublefield, Grade 5
Pine Tree Hill Elementary School, SC

My Favorite Place

White rapids
The blue branch littered sky
The wetlands
Trickling little waterfalls
People walking, birds chirping, water moving
The sun glistening on the water
So peaceful and quiet
I feel so relaxed
Very quiet, quiet, quiet.

Casey Pridham, Grade 4
Maple Wood Elementary School, NH

Summer

Summer's the time for relaxation and fun,
Laughing and playing in the warm sun,
Summer's the time just for me,
No homework, no school, finally I'm free,
Summer's the time I get to sleep late,
No worrying about the time or the date,
Summer's the time when I hang at the beach,
Surfing, swimming and eating a peach,
Summer's the time I take a dip in the pool,
Splashing and diving while keeping cool,
Summer's the time I celebrate Fourth of July,
With fireworks, parades and blueberry pie,
Summer's the time when I go on vacation,
Exploring the sights of this great nation,
Summer's the time when the days never end,
Spending them happily with family and friends,
Now you know the many reasons,
Why Summer is my favorite season.

Nicholas Stanzione, Grade 6
St Rocco School, RI

Horses

Horses are beauty
They gallop, walk and canter
Saddle up and ride!
Katherine Eminger, Grade 5
Robertson School, RI

Lions

Lions are great,
Lions are fun
Watch out zebra, here he comes!

Lions are dangerous
Searching for prey
Getting hungrier every day!
Luke Stribling, Grade 4
Mary Walter Elementary School, VA

Dropped

Dropped
regretfully
foolishly
accidentally
unfortunately
helplessly
surprisingly
Dropped
before she ate it
in the ice cream parlor
over the floor
over her dress
over her dignity
Dropped
because of her slippery hands
as she was about to eat it
since she is so clumsy
because of her absentmindedness
since she was so jittery
Dropped
Maddy Howard, Grade 6
St Mary's School, SC

A Single Shard

A single shard of sky
Fell down upon the Earth.
The brilliant sun would catch it
And time would have its birth.

A single shard of moonlight
Was blown across the stars
It stopped in the shadowed night
Where it now floats afar.

Remember now, all things start
A single thought, along with heart.
Caroline Wall, Grade 6
Greensboro Montessori School, NC

Darkest Hour

The sun is down. I look around.
We're in our darkest hour.
The Nazi soldiers are so strong.
They seem to drain our power.

With the moonlight on, and the sunlight gone
We're simply very moral.
With the Nazi soldiers talking tall
Our work is very oral.

Why is this Hitler so very wicked, to many innocent people?
The innocent Jews are very quiet so that you can't even hear a sniffle.
This is it, this is it we're at our darkest hour.

The Americans are here, the Americans are here, to truly renew our power.
Johnathan Ross, Grade 5
West Hartsville Elementary School, SC

Dreams? An Endless Question

Many scientists and wonderers want to figure out what dreams are
Some say dreams are illusions of wonder or dismay
Others say another realm to impossibility
Dreams may be dark, mysterious and eternal, yet fake reality
These are a few predictions that people make
There are so many possible answers
I say it's an endless question
People can guess over and over again.
But in reality, there is no definite answer to the endless question, dreams.
Dylan Puco, Grade 5
Rosemont Forest Elementary School, VA

If I Were…

If I were president I would be boss, but it would be hard
If I were a fireman I could put out fires, but it would be dangerous
If I were an astronaut I could go to the moon, but I am scared of heights
If I were a waiter I could serve people food, but I might be clumsy and drop the food
It does not matter what I grow up to be because right now I am a kid
And I follow the number one rule:
    Give it all you got and never say you can't do it
There is nothing I can't put my mind to!
Dylan Spears, Grade 5
Courthouse Road Elementary School, VA

I've Learned That…

I've learned that following God will get you through a black and dirty heart.
I've learned that friendship is a privilege.
I've learned that parents are "life guides."
I've learned that going by the Bible in every decision is the key.
I've learned that the love of money is the root of all evil.
I've learned that praying to God is the best form of communication.
I've learned that heroes aren't people on TV.
I've learned that you can confess anything to God.
I've learned that gossip is a deadly sin.
I've learned that God will forgive.
Harper Abbott, Grade 5
Northside Elementary School, SC

Scissors

Scissors are one of the world's most helpful tools,
They are a tailor's most sacred jewel.
In a whole variety of all different colors,
Some have sharp blades, some are duller.

Without them how could we make a paper snowflake?
Or open the plastic wrapping around a tender steak?
Look at that flawless, straight snip,
The handles on scissors have a perfect grip!

What else could you use to cut the tag off of a new shirt?
Or maybe the tag was on a brand new frilly skirt?
Think about it, aren't they a precious gem?
Just remember, don't run while you hold them!

Neha Goswami, Grade 6
River Bend Middle School, VA

The Great Guiro

I'm the great guiro,
time for me to play.
My music sounds skillful,
every single day.
Scrape Scrape Scrape.
My music's frequency is high.
It's nowhere close to a lullaby.
I'm pronounced wuiro to me,
but I don't know why it starts with a g.
Scratch Scratch Scratch.
I can't be played in a band.
You are supposed to hold me in your hand.
I'm the great guiro,
listen to me play.

Zabih Yousuf, Grade 5
Old Bridge Elementary School, VA

Jonathan Main

Here lies Jonathan Main,
He walked in front of a jet airplane,
From it he thought he would get his props,
All he got was a trip through the chops.

Heath Davis, Grade 5
North Windy Ridge School, NC

When My Dad Went Away

I won't cry if you won't cry
But you saw a tear slip down my eye
And then those tears kept raining down
But then you said,
"I'll be back soon"
Then I said, "It's not so bad"
Just ten more days of being sad
He said, "Hello Yoyo"
And then I screamed and said,
"You are not allowed to go away for the rest of the day."

Johanna Pereyra, Grade 4
Lafayette Elementary School, DC

Where I'm From

I am from my barn,
From the rainbow above,
I am from the sport basketball,
Shooting hoops and running down the court,
The book *Nellie's Promise*,
Dresses and parties,
I am from *Hannah Montana*,
And *That's So Raven*,
From looking up at the sky and playing in the dirt,
I'm from Central Elementary School,
From the 2008 election,
I'm from my cat Dyna and my dogs Molly and Evie.
From the flowers and the wind.
I'm from Jacksonville, Florida
From NASCAR driver, Carl Edwards.
I'm from cookbooks
The cooking and beautiful smells.
I'm from those moments —
They went by so fast growing up.

Shelby Howard, Grade 5
Central Elementary School, NC

Snow Day

All of the children asleep in their beds,
Dreaming of playing in snow over their heads.
They wake up to a world that's all covered in white,
Finding out school is canceled, ooh what a delight!
They rush down the stairs and look out a window,
Seeing all of the trees with the glittering snow.
Eating their breakfasts and putting on all their stuff,
Doing it quickly and eagerly so they could play in that fluff.
Laughing and talking and joking they go,
Down to the hill to play in the snow.
They'll sled down the hill as fast as bullets,
They'll also make forts and snowmen with mullets!
The kids will take breaks for hot chocolate, soup, and stew,
They'll eat it and eat it until they're warm and anew.
The children heave snowballs and make snowmen too,
They'll play all day long until their lips turn blue.
They all head home when they're too tired to play,
Then remember what happened during that pleasant snow day.

Cristina Montemorano, Grade 5
Mary Walter Elementary School, VA

Equal

"I have a dream," he said to me.
"That one day I will be treated equally.
I will go in the same stores, schools, and restrooms.
I will be friends with the whites.
We will have Sunday tea.
I will not be discriminated against."

I look back on that speech and say,
"Thank you, thank you, Daddy."

Abby Peters, Grade 6
Forestbrook Middle School, SC

Sleep

I'm drifting off to dreamland,
On the endless sea of sleep.
My mind is spinning round, and round,
With secrets that I keep.

I'm everywhere but in my bed,
As all the knowledge leaves my head.
I am a coyote howling a tune,
I am a stallion racing the moon.
I am an eagle taking first flight,
I am a child, whispering,
Good night.

Andrea Palmer, Grade 5
Oak View Elementary School, VA

Rafa Nadal

R ocks at tennis
A ctive when playing
F orehand is amazing
A pproves when he is the best

N ever give up
A wesome backhand
D oes anything to win
A mazing player
L oves competition

Coleman Andrews, Grade 5
St Christopher's School, VA

Baseball

B am!!! The ball was hit hard
A boy ran to first base
S afe!!! Said the umpire
E veryone yelled and screamed
B oy that was close said the coach
A ll we need is a triple and we win
L uke you're next
L uke hit a triple and they won the game.

Malik Anderson, Grade 6
Monelison Middle School, VA

Shoes

Shoes are a blessing
Even better than ranch dressing
We wear them every day
Even when we go out to play
I barely know what to say

Shoes come in every color
And we get to pick and choose
The only time we notice them
Is when they come untied
They're there when you need them
And they never run away.

Noah Selig, Grade 5
North Windy Ridge School, NC

Dream

A dream is a tree.
　You can't have too many
　and so it keeps growing.

A dream is an ocean.
　Sometimes it calms you down
　and sometimes it's soothing.

A dream is a heart.
　You can dream all you want
　and it never has to stop.

A dream is creativity.
　You can make it anything you want
　and never have to take it away.

Hannah Seeney, Grade 5
Holy Cross Elementary School, DE

Dance

Just dance on those sweet feet,
　And listen to that beat.

If you can prance,
　Then you can dance.

Don't just sit there and eat,
　Get on those dancin' feet!

Anna Cubbler, Grade 4
Trinity Christian School, VA

Football

Football is the best
There's no time for the rest
You better be ready
Because some of us are heavy
Are you up to the test?

Elijah White, Grade 6
Benjamin Syms Middle School, VA

Kitten/Cat

Kitten
small, fluffy
cuddling, scratching, biting
hissing, meowing, feeding, leading
purring, sleeping, littering
big, furry
Cat.

Tristen Jones, Grade 6
Floyd T Binns Middle School, VA

Woods

Near a spooky house.
Emerald crowns glowing brightly,
While spring fades away

Caroline Mansour, Grade 4
Trinity Christian School, VA

Ninja

I am tall
I am big
Like a ninja
But only one thing stands in my way
My weight
But — I can fix that
I am heavy as a boulder
But I will be light as a feather
I will train like them
Speak their language
I will disappear, then reappear
My meditating is strong; like me
But I never unleash full power
Because my mind is strong
Cruel words won't break me
My enemies can't penetrate me
I have a heart that is pure
And a vigorous mine
I am tall
I am big
Like a Ninja

David Stephens, Grade 5
Manchester Elementary School, NC

Depression

I am hard headed, as well as curious.
I wonder why I am so skinny.
I hear nothing.
I see dragons.
I want a dad that cares.
I am active and smart.

I pretend to be a god.
I feel hollow.
I touch nothing.
I worry about my dying grandmother.
I cry about my grandmother.
I am happy and alive.

I understand math.
I say "say" a lot.
I dream of death.
I try to win.
I hope to win.
I am glad, yet sad.

Alexander Garner, Grade 4
Sangaree Intermediate School, SC

Dogs

Dogs
Cute, awesome
Bark so much
Very loving little animals
Puppies

Metaxia Myseros, Grade 4
Trinity Christian School, VA

Glop

The car that gets
One mile per drop
Is choking and sputtering
And leaking some glop

Buying and buying
More gasoline
The air that comes out
Is never very clean

It drinks and drinks
All of the time
Taking your money
Every last dime

When you have
No more money to spend
Its puttering sounds like
The end

Alex Fry, Grade 6
East Mooresville Intermediate School, NC

Ten Little Walruses

Ten little walruses played on a vine,
One fell off and now there are nine.
Nine little walruses were running from their fate,
One went too slow and now there are eight.
Eight little walruses tried to go to heaven,
Fatty made it now there are seven.
Seven little walruses played with pointy sticks,
One poked his eye and now there are six.
Six little walruses tried to scuba dive,
One hit his head and now there are five.
Five little walruses were slamming a door,
One got stuck and now there are four.
Four little walruses tried to get free,
One got caught and now there are three.
Three little walruses tried to get the flu,
One got it right and now there are two.
Two little walruses wanted to have fun,
One swallowed the ball and now there is one.
One little walrus ate a ton,
He fell through the ice and now there are none.

Kate Shaffer, Grade 5
Blacksburg New School, VA

Dolphin

Little dolphin splash and swim
With your graceful silky fin.
I wonder how it would be if I were you and you were me?
How is it in the deep where the starfish slowly creep
And the octopus who crawls on rocks that sadly never stops?
Goodbye little dolphin around the cove
You had a good day, that I know.

Kaitlyn Hess, Grade 4
Heron Pond Elementary School, NH

Mystery

Circles of wisdom going through my mind
When darkness falls you will be blind
How that you cannot see
We all wonder it's a mystery.

You're better but no one cares
When you leave we all stare.

Heart pounding way too fast
We've been waiting for it to blast
Now that you cannot breathe
We all wonder it's a mystery.

Emily Hayes, Grade 5
West Hartsville Elementary School, SC

Ice Cream Truck

Yesterday I was somber,
And nobody knew why.
When I couldn't go on any longer,
I heard a vivacious cry.
"The ice cream truck's here,"
Then I suddenly lit up.
Now I hadn't a fear,
'Cause I was gonna get an ice cream cup.
As fast as I could, I started to run.
I sprinted right out the door.
When I saw the truck, it ended my fun.
As I stared at the scene in horror.
A hysterical laugh,
Had filled the air.
A figure quite daft,
With grayish white hair.
The truck had been stolen,
By an old grandma.
My heart was never whole again.
I'll remember that day in awe.

Alexander Sawyer, Grade 5
Oak View Elementary School, VA

Friends

Some friends are here for a reason
But some friends come for only a season

One friend may be really kind
And the other may be blind

You should be there for them on their birthday
Just like they are in almost every way

Be there like a guardian angel
Even in a bad angle

Some friends come for a reason
But some friends come for only a season

Madeline Brown, Grade 4
St John Neumann Academy, VA

Birds
B irds
I n their nest
R esting
D own
S o peacefully
Ariana Riselvato, Grade 5
Sanford Creek Elementary School, NC

Horses on the Train
The horses ride on the train
With their long and beautiful mane
They whinny and neigh
Horses need their hay
Often horses like to play in the rain
Courtney Koehler, Grade 5
North Windy Ridge School, NC

Coming Up
It was so, so dark
But it is not anymore
The sun's coming up
Emily Schoka, Grade 4
Trinity Christian School, VA

Ode of My Sister
Sister oh sister you are so cool
You were always there for me
And you always will be
I'll miss you when you move out
I know you're almost 18
Even though we get in fights
We forgive each other and move on
You have your nice moments
It depends on your mood
You are my big sis
And I will always love you!
Sydney Poole, Grade 5
Vienna Elementary School, NC

Dog
Dog
Big, mean
Running, digging, playing
He is big and scary.
Lewis
Tylar Harrell, Grade 5
Pine Tree Hill Elementary School, SC

Jenna
Jenna
Nice, sneaky
Singing, reading, bowling
Honest with her friends
Jen
Breanna Gardner, Grade 5
Pine Tree Hill Elementary School, SC

Dragons
I like dragons
Scary and hairy
Wild and scaly
Is anything
cooler than dragons?
Antonio Franco, Grade 5
St Mary School, RI

Going to a Football Game
I see the strong football players.
I smell the french-fried food.
I taste the salty dog.
I feel the cold air.
I hear screaming, yelling, and cheering.
Quinn Roper, Grade 4
Crestwood Elementary School, VA

Fly Away
I see the birds
Flying outside
I envy them
I want to fly away

I see a plane
Gliding through the clouds
I envy the passengers
I want to fly away

I see a helicopter
Blades slicing through the air
I envy it
I want to fly away

I think I hear something
But when I turn, nothing is there
I see that I am foolish
I will never fly away
Mikaela Billiet, Grade 6
Holbrook Middle School, NC

Ben's Death
Here lies Ben
He died at the age of 10
The reason is he was dancing in the rain
And was hit by a huge train.
Mason Edwards, Grade 5
North Windy Ridge School, NC

Man from New York
There once was a man from New York
Whose favorite food was pork
He went to a farm
But did no harm
He chased the pigs with a fork.
Avery Carson, Grade 5
North Windy Ridge School, NC

Small Steps Over the River
Before me stands a raging river
with the whole world surrounding it.
In it, I see my reflection
and its sparkling waters welcome me.
I place my bare foot on the smooth rock
that lies before me.
Cool water flows under my foot,
but it doesn't pull me in.
I am drawn to more smooth rocks
that make a winding path across
this wide river.
The warm, comfortable wind
blows through my hair
as I make small steps over the river.
Ava Rohacek, Grade 5
Rye Elementary School, NH

Rain
Light as rain,
Dark as night,
The wind drifts by,
Without a fright,
The sky turns blue,
Oh so true,
That the world is light as rain.
Hannah Herter, Grade 6
Northwood School, NH

Cousin Noah
Oh Cousin Noah…
If you have a cousin,
you know how it feels
Oh Cousin Noah…
he is such an outdoor kind of guy
and he's the best.
He's someone you can rely on
great kid
great kid
great kid
He's always there to catch you if you fall,
if you're down he's someone
you can talk to
good heart
good heart
good heart
You need a cousin like him!
Ashley Lyons, Grade 4
Maple Wood Elementary School, NH

Tears
Tears trailing down my cheeks
It hurts so bad I cannot speak
Mental fire coursing through my veins
Oh the pain, the pain
Brianna Ciuffo, Grade 5
Mary Walter Elementary School, VA

Dear Mr. Lincoln

Dear Mr. Lincoln,
How are you?
You've run this country so bold and true
Born in a log cabin
Grew up simple and plain
You were the nation's leader for you experienced much pain.
Sitting down in that huge hard rock chair,
Watching America change and share
Have we made the right choices?
In hundreds of voices,
You watch every person who walks past you
Your eyes following each movement we do,
Are you proud of us, Americans?
Or maybe some things we've done is a total disgrace
Many famous people gave speeches in front of your place.
We are proud of each president who has given so much,
From poor to rich they have a special touch.
But one great president we celebrate each day
is you Abraham Lincoln, famous in every way.

Sarah Young, Grade 5
Cool Spring Elementary School, NC

My Secret Hiding Place

Behind my bed is my secret hiding place
It is warm and cozy
And I feel safe there
I close my eyes
And listen to the sounds around me.
I hear the sound of the shower
I hear my mommy's footsteps
I hear bats and crickets
My mommy's voice sounds beautiful and warm
It makes me feel happy

Tariq Marsh, Grade 6
Children's Studio School, DC

Love My Brother*

Love my brother,
Like a puppy loves to play
I said love my brother
Like a puppy loves to play
Love to call him in the morning
Love to call him
"Hey there, Nathan!"

Rebecca Maguire, Grade 5
East Mooresville Intermediate School, NC
*Inspired by Walter Dean Myers

Chuck

There once was a small duck named Chuck
Who seemed to have very bad luck
He dove in the pond
Of which he was fond
And then he was stuck in the muck

David Castaneda, Grade 5
Vienna Elementary School, NC

I Feel

As I close my eyes and sing a song
It doesn't make me feel wrong
I feel like a Ti note
I feel like a Ta note
I feel like I dance in the wind as it blows through the sky
I feel like I have wings as beautiful as butterflies
I feel like a fairy helping a bird fly
And that's how I feel.

Caroline Hieber, Grade 4
Courthouse Road Elementary School, VA

Ode to My Saxophone

Its golden appearance
Shimmers like the streets
Of Heaven.
It vocalizes the notes when my fingers glide over
The smooth, pearl-like keys.
When it harmonizes with
The other instruments
I feel like I'm apart of the elegant,
Philharmonic Orchestra.
With every note that is
Spilled out of the exquisite instrument,
It ascends higher than the stars,
And lower than the abyss
Of the sea.
People will gaze
With awe
And amazement,
Admiring its flawless sound.
It will sing its songs into the clouds.
My saxophone.

Joshua E. Bristow, Grade 6
CrossRoads Middle School, SC

An Empty Void

Jerry Ray Webb,
at least that's what the gravestone said.
Nevertheless, there are a few things it does not mention.
For example, how your death has caused me so much tension.
Or maybe even how you weren't really my uncle at all,
rather a brother who taught me to always stand up tall.
You taught me that I should never do things in vain,
and when people smile, it doesn't mean they have no pain.
I now realize what you were talking about that day,
how people fake a smile and hope the pain will go away.
When you left us all so suddenly,
I felt as though I had lost a key.
This key opened one of the many doors in my heart.
The door leads to a room that has now been torn apart.
It was a little room of love, thought, and wonders.
It was the room for my brainstorm of lightning and thunder.
However, when you left the room was destroyed,
and in that place now stands an empty void.

Katie Cannon, Grade 6
Belton Middle School, SC

Rain and Sun

Rain
puddles, clouds
dripping, soaking, sobbing
inside, umbrella, rainbow, fun
playing, running, laughing
sleeveless, shorts
Sun

Madeline Mondloch, Grade 5
Trinity Christian School, VA

Dragons

I like dragons
loyal and strong
protective and fast.
Is anything better than dragons?

Joseph Gould, Grade 5
St Mary School, RI

Wishing on a Wishing Star

As I look into space
I star and gaze
At the stars from above
That shift into place
As the story goes
You wish on a star
And hope one day
It will be true from the start

Kyle Goettlicher, Grade 6
Wakefield Forest Elementary School, VA

Started

Started by a key
The engine roared
The car came to life
No one even said, "Yay"
Started by fuel
the fumes flew
Out of the engine
The rocket shot up into space
People watched
And liked it.

Ruslan Thomas, Grade 4
St Christopher's School, VA

Memories

Memories are important
the laughs
and the cries
the time we shared together
even though we were far apart
but the hardest memory
is when you flew above
and took good memories with you
memories

Hannah Lyman, Grade 6
Metcalf School, RI

The Walk

As I grow older I begin to forget where I've been and what I've seen.
So I take a stroll down the path my mom and I would walk down when I was little.
I walk by the river.
Then I go on the bridge.
Then I think what a great life.

Alison Frye, Grade 6
Wakefield Forest Elementary School, VA

Deeply Gone

I can't forget
The time I heard that wonderful voice of yours.
A voice so soft and elegant. I felt like I was under your spell.
What do you want of me? What will you do?
With your eyes as blue as the sky. The eyes you can see from the sky.
Looking, staring at that long gold hair, flowing moving from the wind.
That hair as gold as the sun.

Cameron Carter, Grade 5
Queens Creek Elementary School, NC

Hailey's Life Lessons

I have learned that dogs really don't like to have make-up on.
I have learned that chickens don't always run away from you.
I have learned that some plants are NOT soft.
I have learned that my mom is always right.
I have learned that all 2 to 5 year olds are annoying.
I have learned that some people are just not a people person.
I have learned that cookies and ice cream don't always make you hyper.
I have learned that lying doesn't get you anywhere.
I have learned that you don't need to impress anybody to be their friend.
I have learned that you will always get someone you don't like on your team.
I have learned that you don't need to judge a book by its cover.

Hailey Moore, Grade 5
Northside Elementary School, SC

Race Day

You hear the crowd screaming,
It's race day at Roosevelt Raceway,
The horses are coming out for the Post Parade,
There is tension all around.

And, the horses are off!
Black Diamond is first, out of the brake,
But the others are close behind,
Black Diamond, and Shining Penny are the favorites for today's race.

The horses are coming around the bend,
And the Rookie is in front!
Following is Shining Penny,
Folks, this will be a day to remember!

But wait, Black Diamond is sneaking up,
Wait, wait! Look at the rookie's horse,
"Down Town Brown" has found some new strength,
The Rookie has won!

Juliana Moore, Grade 5
Homeschool Plus, VA

Ronald McDonald Goes to Graceland

I'm Ronald McDonald and I'm a clown
I went around town and ended up with a frown

I have flaming red hair it isn't fair
My nose is big too, but I don't care

Now I'm going to Memphis, Tennessee
I am going to the brand new Mickey D

I can't wait to try a Memphis Big Mac
Hope it doesn't give me a heart attack

After that, I'm going to see the king
It's too bad I cannot go see him sing

I wonder if Elvis would like French fries
If he was here, he could give them a try

Well, home to Greenville, I go on the bus
Another trip to Graceland is a must

Bryce Anderson, Grade 6
Beck Academy, SC

Creatures of the Sky

The birds sing their song,
As they fly through the big sky,
How great a bird is!

Carley Fines, Grade 5
Courthouse Road Elementary School, VA

Green

Green is a feeling of being lucky
Green shouts feelings of confidence
Green feels like a soft clover leaf
Green tastes like a fresh green apple
The feeling of green is luck and confidence
Green skips around finding someone to give luck to
Green is a leprechaun laughing in the meadow
Green is a shimmering shamrock
Green is the luck of the Irish
Green is the freshly cut grass

Corbin R. Norris, Grade 4
Tabernacle Elementary School, NC

Love Is

Love is stealing someone's heart.
Love is not being apart.
It's either you and him or she and she even he and he.
Love is with someone or them.
Love is spreading around.
Love is lying on the ground.
I have love, you have love.
We have love and don't ever give it up.
That is what love is!

Tneia Barrow, Grade 5
West Hartsville Elementary School, SC

Adventure!

I love to go on adventures,
They are so very neat,
When I hear "adventure,"
I have to grab a seat,
When I go on an adventure,
I greet everyone I meet,
When I feel the sun's heat,
I start to feel beat,
I start to wonder why I love adventures,
Then I realize that I love them, because they are sweet.

Courtney Rivera, Grade 5
Rosemont Forest Elementary School, VA

Big Big Fish

Big, blue fish
With sharp, sharp teeth
Got caught on a hook
Bit the man, jumped right in the net
That was the end of the big, blue fish

Then came the big, red fish
With thick, thick scales
Got caught in a net
Scraped the man with his sharp, sharp scales
Jumped right in the bucket
That was the end of the big, red fish.

Isaiah Moore, Grade 4
Angelus Academy, VA

Aquamarine

Aquamarine is always splashing in water.
She is a beautiful gem stone.
Aquamarine can be happy, calm, sad, or relaxed.
She can be found on Neptune and Uranus.
Her best friends are green and blue.
Her enemies are pink and red.
One of her talents is to paint the sky at dawn and sunrise.
She loves to color rubber balls.
She also stains the morpho butterfly's wings as she passes.
Aquamarine always smells like sea water.
Her favorite sport is swimming.
But she hates basketball.
She is different than me in some ways.
And same in others.

Abril Rosales, Grade 4
Youngsville Elementary School, NC

Here Come the Kings

Here come the kings from the animal kingdom.
The lion of the jungle, the bear of the forest,
the whale of the sea, the monkey of the tree.
Don't forget the eagle, that soars in the sky.
They come to fight the enemy, of their world.
The human.

Dawson Taylor, Grade 5
Oak View Elementary School, VA

Friends

Friends are keys.
They unlock your true feelings.

Friends are shields.
They protect you from mean thoughts.

Friends are a tree.
Your friendship grows with them.

Friends are balloons.
They bring you up.
Callie Wheeler, Grade 5
Holy Cross Elementary School, DE

Fall

Red,
Orange,
And yellow.
Falling from the trees.
Faster than falling,
Hurrying.
Swaying with the breeze,
As they float to the ground
Symbolizing the beginning of fall.
Katelyn Connelly, Grade 6
Metcalf School, RI

Evan Schulte

Evan
small, picky, friendly
son of my mom and dad,
brother of my brother and sister and me
video games, skating, and Elvis
happiness, peacefulness, confusion
forest, darkness, and wild animals
all A's in school, 4th grade, 3rd 9 weeks
flying, driving, and baseball
Culpeper County, Virginia
Schulte
Aaron Schulte, Grade 6
Floyd T Binns Middle School, VA

Nature

I look out the window,
To see the beauty,
The magic,
The greenness of nature,
The tall homes of birds,
Towering above us,
The low homes of gophers,
Going lower and lower,
It seems as if,
There is nothing as beautiful,
As the planet we live on.
Dylan Finch, Grade 5
Clover Hill Elementary School, VA

Homer and Wilbur

Homer Simpson
lazy, yellow
boring, snoring, sleeping
fat, donuts, mud, trough
singing, reading, chanting
funny, pink
Wilbur
Ishmel Powell, Grade 4
Waller Mill Fine Arts Magnet School, VA

Digital Camera

I am a digital camera
All square and fantastic
And unlike Kodak
I am not cheap plastic.

Surrounding me
Are brothers and sisters
And lovely women
With their misters.

I am a digital camera
All square and fantastic
And unlike Kodak
I am not cheap plastic.
Kyra Watson, Grade 4
Crestwood Elementary School, VA

Limple

A limple is a dimple
Resting on my chin.
I'm sure that I can't get it off
Even if I grin.
A limple is a huge-o pain
It grows one hair each time it rains
I hope I can get my limple off at school
Because the hairs could fill a giant pool
It rained today, I lost one hair
Each day it's one less hair I wear
Finally, it's disappeared
Now what's that on top of my right ear?!
Emily Burdett, Grade 4
Waller Mill Fine Arts Magnet School, VA

Fires in the Woods

Crack, snap
the fire was going strong,
tents were set, banjo music,
burnt marshmallows all sticky,
and black, chocolate melting,
sparks flying, wood charring,
sleeping bags and pillows,
rolled out, ready to sleep on,
in the woods!!
Jared Keen, Grade 5
Oak View Elementary School, VA

Honey

There once was a wonderful land
That had a great brand
And that brand was very sunny
I tried their brand and it was honey!
Jake Rogers, Grade 4
Crestwood Elementary School, VA

A Lovely Mom

My mom is really pretty
Pretty as can be.
I like the way she smiles
When she looks at me.

She gets really mad
Because my things are not neat
Even though she yells at me
Deep inside I know she's sweet

When I make wrong choices
She always makes them right
I like when she helps me out
She is really bright

My mom is really friendly
She helps others out too
When I get good grades
She says I'm proud of you

My mom and I are close
She is like my best friend
No matter if she's mad with me
I'll love her to the end.
Alexis Spikes, Grade 5
Pine Tree Hill Elementary School, SC

The Tree Waved at Me

The tree waved at me.
It waved and said Hello,
hope you have a good day.
Jamie Peele, Grade 4
Edwards Elementary School, SC

White Personalities

White.
White is light, like snow.
White is fluffy, like a cloud.
White is flowing, like a wedding dress.
But sometimes White is as
Hard as ice,
And as cold on the heart as
Nothingness.
White has many personalities,
But which will you choose to
Show?
Maha Issa, Grade 5
Turner Creek Elementary School, NC

I Am

I am water
Flowing freely while writing
Bubbling with excitement
Always fishing for new ideas
Showered by love from friends and family
Can be a messy hurricane
Giving ice-cold stares when mad
Eyes like blue waves
Soaking friends with questions
Determined — hard as hail
Can be as wild as a dolphin

Sarah Thomas, Grade 6
Wakefield Forest Elementary School, VA

Summer

I see green grass and leaves
And children playing outside.

I hear the splashing and screaming
Of children in their pools.

I smell the barbecue chicken and burgers
In my backyard.

I taste the homemade ice cream
That came from the churn.

I feel the hot sun
Burning my skin.

Colby Little, Grade 5
Jonesville Elementary School, SC

Where I'm From

I am from Kenny and Yolanda
I am from a wonderful family
That loves you until the end
I am from a family that plays games
With you again and again
I am from a family that keeps you warm
A family that loves to sing
Happy dance songs
I am from a brilliant family that likes to eat
I am from a family that loves to sleep
I am from my grandma's mac n' cheese
She always makes you say please
A family that loves pizza and ice cream
I am from a family that plays football and basketball
I am from a family that can do it all
A family that loves to win
A family that talks in the den
I am from a place where the president is black
A place where we don't take any slack
That's my family
And that is where I am from

Kemani Jacques, Grade 4
Whittaker Elementary School, SC

The World Around Us

People coming here and there.
Some of us go everywhere.
And when we're all together,
The days get better and better.
We all join hands,
To keep us close inside.
You're all my friends.
Just keep that in mind.
Some try to leave me others stay up close.
But when we're all together nothing ever goes.

Nella Rouse, Grade 4
St Thomas More Catholic School, NC

Whipped Cream

Whipped cream oh whipped cream flying to my throat,
foamy and thin so light it can float.
Topped on ice cream, brownies and pies,
gives a little sparkle into my eyes.
The best part is sprinkles to add to the top,
I want to eat so much it would make my stomach POP!

Logan Baker, Grade 5
Cool Spring Elementary School, NC

Test Taking

"Test Taking" says the sign by the door,
My memory is making me dread this all the more.
Who can remember what implacable means?
For last night was filled with frightening dreams.
A Mesopotamian floated over with a frown,
While prime numbers danced all over town.
But what I remember,
Determines September.
Will I be held back?
Skip a grade, or be fine?
No time for deep thought; my grades are on the line!
Here come the answer sheets,
This is worse than eating beets!
Everyone tenses up, no time for play,
But still try so hard to get an "A."

Kamryn Leoncavallo, Grade 5
Oak View Elementary School, VA

I've Learned That…

I've learned that life is not easy.
I've learned that you have to earn respect to get respect.
I've learned that some friends will turn you down.
I've learned that everybody is different.
I've learned that all teachers have different rules.
I've learned that some things I like, and some things I don't.
I've learned that your family always loves you.
I've learned that your teachers are like your mom or dad.
I've learned that kids act out because they are having
        problems at home.
I've learned that people are people.

Khameelah Morris, Grade 5
Northside Elementary School, SC

I Miss

I miss your face, which always brought me joy.
I miss your voice, asking me about everything.
I miss how you would get mad if I said a boy you liked was cute.
But most of all I miss you, you were my friend, my companion, my cousin, mostly like a sister, Adrienne
But I know you're in a better place waiting on me, I just wish I would wait with you.
Every time I think of how it could have been me, I cry.
So when it is my time, will you wait for me by the golden gates, and welcome me with a massive hug?
Then we will be together again my friend, my companion, mostly my sister, Adrienne

Markilia Bivens, Grade 6
Berry Shoals Intermediate School, SC

A Clock

A clock is an item that can't speak but says so much. It has three hands all different sizes. It can be taken places or stay in one spot forever. It can be bigger than you or smaller that your wrist. A clock is a face. It could be analog or digital. It is what makes you tardy and keeps you on time. A clock is comfort and stress. A clock is a never ending circle, and it will never stop.

Eli Wilson, Grade 5
Rye Elementary School, NH

After Midnight

I am sorry I got you up so early to go to the show.
I am sorry I made you run two miles in the blazing hot sun.
You have to admit it was pretty fun.

I am sorry about working you so hard that you fell asleep every chance you got.
I am sorry about waking you to go into the ring and for jabbing my spurs right into your side.
I bet it did not feel too good, but you needed to move.

I do have to thank you for jumping so well!
I could hear your heart chime as we entered the ring.
You were so nervous.
You knew your job as we cantered around.
The judge just couldn't help but stare at your gorgeous white star.

I am sorry but it sure had its highs.
We soared through the sky.
It was just you and I.
We were proud of the ribbons but that wasn't what mattered.
What was really important was just between you and me!

Gillian Kelley, Grade 5
Rye Elementary School, NH

12 Months

January is my brother's birthday; we celebrate in a very special way.
February brings lots of love and joy: On Valentine's Day send a car to a very special boy.
In March my dad will be forty-three; when he was younger he could climb a tree.
April is when you say "April Fools:" I dumped on my mom some beautiful jewels.
In May, I have a birthday: I wake up and everyone shouts "Hooray!"
June's the month for splashing in the pool: When the bell rings, we all shout, "No more school!"
July brings beautiful fireworks: when we're at the store we don't see clerks.
August is a day for my mom: and on that day I say "Mom, you're the bomb!"
The day I hate is in September: it's a day my family always remembers.
October is when you get Halloween candy: it always tastes fine and dandy!
November is a day we eat beef jerky: in my dreams I imagine chasing a turkey!
In December I hear sleigh bells ring: we hear Christmas carolers sing, sing, sing!

Jordan Connell, Grade 5
C Hunter Ritchie Elementary School, VA

Ice Cream

Ice cream is good, tasty, and sweet
Ice cream is also great to eat
It is mouthwatering and delicious
And gives you brain freeze

Ice cream is a treat to eat
Instead of a yucky old beet
By the window I see all the flavors of ice cream
Which give me a big beam

Ice cream is cold
Which is really bold
Cause if you eat too much
You'll catch a cold

Ice cream is good
Ice cream is sweet
And ice cream is very delicious to eat!

Cody Simonson, Grade 5
South Smithfield Elementary School, NC

Winter

The snow fell gently on my leaves
and I squeezed my limbs close together to keep warm
and I danced with the flowing wind
and a smile spread across my happy face

Lena O'Connor, Grade 5
Central Elementary School, NC

Winter

Winter feels like hot chocolate on a cold day
Winter is like snow falling on the ground
Winter sings Christmas songs
Winter is children playing in the snow
Winter is like Santa Claus saying Ho! Ho! Ho!
Winter sounds like jingle bells
Winter is a warm scarf around you
Winter looks like a Christmas tree ready for decorating
Winter is like the wind blowing
Winter is a snowman waving at you

Samantha Sweet, Grade 4
Tabernacle Elementary School, NC

White

White is calm and very quiet
White is a cotton ball in the midday sky
White is your mind without thought
White is the baby brother of black
White makes colors great
White does never hate
White tastes like a marshmallow from the fire
White feels like snow in December
White looks like a sweater
White is me in the dark night

Jonathan Mroczkowski, Grade 4
Tabernacle Elementary School, NC

Change

Surprises in life can be innocent,
They can be unexpected.
But more importantly,
Depressing.
The day it began and the long frightful,
Overwhelming
Nights that I went through.
My mom's eyes as big as grapefruits,
In pools of sky blue.
My dad's eyes full of fire and anger.
The determination to do what he is doing.
I hear the piercing sound of what seems,
A life or death decision,
To feel the mountains of stress between two mortals.
I sit on my staircase with
Waterfalls of sadness in my eyes.
To see my parents almost in a brawl!
I sprint up the stairs and cry myself to sleep.
To see my life falling apart.
To know my heart's torn,
To know it's a horrifying change.

Eric Owens, Grade 6
Manchester Elementary/Middle School, VT

Gymnastics

Gymnastics is fun,
Although it may be dangerous.
My coach is fun,
Because he will laugh when you aren't hurt as bad.
He makes us work harder
Even though it's always hard.
You may even get what we call rips on your hands,
They may hurt if they're bad enough.
All my coach will do
Is pour peroxide on it and say go do something.
Gymnastics is easy if you get used to it.

Sean Casey, Grade 5
Queens Creek Elementary School, NC

Black Is...

Burnt toast on a rushed morning
The night sky on an empty night.
Black is a cat getting into trouble.
A blank TV screen
A power outage day.
A zooming car speeding to work.
An old TV show on an early Saturday.
Black is a black bird pecking black berries.
A panther in the jungle or a puppy at home.
Coal and ashes after a campfire.
Black is a rain cloud in a thunderstorm.
A speeding bullet in war or a black hole in space.
Black is an old photograph.
Black is...

William Smith, Grade 5
Olde Providence Elementary School, NC

A Day at Camp

Early morning light
glistening
on the water
waves,
waves,
waves,
people laughing
waves crashing
birds chirping
happiness,
happiness,
happiness.
Matt Estabrook, Grade 4
Maple Wood Elementary School, NH

Love

Love is a fuzzy couch.
It is warm and cozy.

Love is God.
God can be everywhere.

Love is a friend.
Friends always stick together.

Love is lightning.
Lightning can strike at any moment.
Gwendolyn Borer, Grade 5
Holy Cross Elementary School, DE

Golden World

Golden world,
Golden eyes,
Sneaky sneakers,
Peeky spies,

Golden memories,
Golden girls,
How I love…
This golden world.
Eerin Thomas, Grade 5
West Hartsville Elementary School, SC

Waterfall

Waterfalls foaming
Sending up the sheets of spray
Clashing through the night
Devin Lynch, Grade 4
Olde Providence Elementary School, NC

Trees

Flowing in the woods
Passing their leaves to the ground
Blooming in the spring
Daniel Clark, Grade 4
Trinity Christian School, VA

School's Out

School is out,
Time to shout,
Soda, candy, pool,
Being locked up in school,
Is so so very cruel.
Sinead O'Neill, Grade 4
Appomattox Elementary School, VA

Spring Will Be Here Soon

As the leaves fall on a breezy day
On the swing is where I lay.
I sing a nice little tune
Hoping spring will be here soon.

I walk over to the swing
Where my sister is mingling.
With a squirrel I have never seen
It was a nice little scene.

She never even noticed me
If only you could see.
I walked back to the swing
And did my own cool little thing.
Katelynn Deal, Grade 6
Monelison Middle School, VA

Football

F un and frustrating
O utside is where it's played
O n the field the teams play
T hey play to the end
B alls in the air
A ll people are in an uproar
L uck comes sometimes
L oving sweet victory!
John Harsh, Grade 5
Trinity Christian School, VA

Dragons

I like dragons
Big and strong
Fierce and wild
Is anything
Better than a dragon?
Allison Pine, Grade 5
St Mary School, RI

The Backyard

Large wooded field
Fresh morning air
Singing of a bird
Gentle breeze
Sweet honeysuckle
Beautiful day
Steven Erlenbach, Grade 5
Olde Providence Elementary School, NC

The Island

Crash! On the island
Across the sandy beach
Up the tree
Over the coconuts
Through the water
Onto the boat
Off into the sea.
Menley Hunt, Grade 5
Northside Elementary School, SC

Spring

Flowers blooming
Groomers grooming
Summer's near!
Spring's here!
It's fun to play.
Sky's not gray.
Snow is gone!
Green is the lawn.
Jillian Barnabe, Grade 5
Good Shepherd Catholic School, RI

Wind

Whirling and twirling
round and round it goes
Making leaves shiver and dance.
It could be as fierce as a tiger
or as mild as a baby.
It's a nice breeze at the beach
or a freezing chill in the winter
Hearing wind's whistle makes me smile
Helping birds fly, fly, fly.
Caroline Mitchell, Grade 4
Olde Providence Elementary School, NC

Brett Favre

Under center.
Above the roar.
Defense around him.
Up goes the ball.
In the end zone.
Touchdown.
Jacob Smith, Grade 5
Northside Elementary School, SC

Rain

Rain the clouds go gray
and the sun goes away.

The thunder plays in the rain
and the frogs sing a melody.

Children play in the rain
and then the rain goes away.
Rocio Navas, Grade 5
Woodlawn Elementary School, VA

My Military Mom

I have a soldier in my family
And that soldier is my mom.
She goes to battle to ensure our country's freedom,
she makes sure it gets done.
I'm concerned about her all the time
Because I know what the outcome could be
She needs to help the world be a better place
But the army never ends for her to have a little space
She loves me but has to go away
But mostly, I just want her to stay
To be with me and be all right
But I know she must go out there to fight.
I know the possibility
That she might not make it back to me
So I have to trust that when she leaves
She will be all right — I must believe.

Jasmine Murray, Grade 5
Manchester Elementary School, NC

Colors

Red is the color of a rose in the spring.
Blue is as pretty as the shining sky.
Green is as glistening as the fresh cut grass.
Gray is as gloomy as a wet rainy day.
Pink is as pretty as corn and wheat.
Yellow is as beautiful as the bright, happy sun.
How are colors wonderful to you?

Katarina Milic, Grade 5
C Hunter Ritchie Elementary School, VA

Rain

Rain is beating on the window
Whenever it rains
I think of all the sad times
running through my head
I start to cry
No one is home
No one is ever home
"Will someone come?"
"Please?"
The darkness is in my eye
"Will anyone ever foresee
what they have done to me?"
Nevermind, the darkness has now gotten me.

Zoe Mason, Grade 4
Waller Mill Fine Arts Magnet School, VA

My Uncle

My uncle's name was Travis — he was blind and could not see
The most amazing thing about him was how much he loved me
Now he lives in heaven where it is peaceful as can be
He walks among the angels and watches over me
I miss him more every day — can't you see
My heart still wishes he was here with me.

Chloe Bolen, Grade 4
Appomattox Elementary School, VA

Love Is…

Love is wonderful
Love is indescribable
Love is bigger than the biggest of feelings
Love is stronger than the strongest of feelings
Love is a gift which everyone deserves
Love is the most powerful thing when combined with hope
Love is the feeling I feel and…
Love is one thing I will never forget

Gavin J.M. Brown, Grade 5
Courthouse Road Elementary School, VA

Lake Bowen

This is my day on the lake.
The sun silently rising in the east.
Our boat gliding in the undisturbed water.
The bass jumping in the back water swamps.
My line flying through the air.
My bait making a splash on the glassy water.
The sandwich melting in my mouth.
The coffee burning my tongue.
My bobber going ploop! under the water.
Geese flying in a perfect "V" overhead.
I heard the water rushing over the dam.
I remember hooking up on a huge bass.
My day on the lake.

Jake Moore, Grade 6
Boiling Springs Intermediate School, SC

Oxygen

Like a rug and a floor I'm always there.
Like a heart in your body, I'm here.
You can't see me, but I can see you.
If you could see me like a ghost I'd be gone.
Stars in the sky at night, you can't miss me.
You need me, and I need you.
We go together like Peanut Butter and Jelly.

Shekia William, Grade 4
Crestwood Elementary School, VA

The Breeze

It's still outside, except for the breeze
And the breeze is pushing the birds and the bees
And the breeze is pushing the birds, bees, and trees
And me swinging…
Alone — not alone — but with the breeze

Adrienne Matuté, Grade 5
Courthouse Road Elementary School, VA

Fall

When I look around
I know that fall is here
All the trees are bare
Because leaves are falling everywhere
All reassuring fall is here

Noah Guttendorf, Grade 5
Wakefield Forest Elementary School, VA

Winter Night

W hite wonderland
I nvisible animals scurry
N ighttime breeze
T winkling stars
E xtreme colds
R ough trees, silhouetted
    Against the dark sky

N ever moving dream
I n peace
G usts of bitter wind
H igh, bright moon
T imeless…

Mary Elliott Porter, Grade 6
Main Street Middle School, VT

Bunnies

Adorable, sweet
Bunnies love to nibble fruit
Quiet and peaceful

Carrie Shabe, Grade 4
Trinity Christian School, VA

The Beach

Endless waves
Brushing on shore
So relaxing
Blistering hot rays of sun
Seagulls squawking
Variety of languages
Which one's which?
Sandcastles as tall as towers
I'm so relaxed.

Steven Hinchey, Grade 4
Maple Wood Elementary School, NH

Happy

Happy
Blissful, cheerful
Playing, laughing, celebrating
Cheerless, crummy, content, delighted
Crying, dying, moping
Glooming, blue
Sad

Bethany Smith, Grade 5
St Helena Elementary School, SC

summer

summer
sunny, hot
surfing, scuba diving, swimming
skiing, skating, sledding
wind, white
winter

Alejandra Cuytun, Grade 5
Pine Tree Hill Elementary School, SC

So Much Depends Upon

So much depends upon
The chocolate chip cookie,
Sitting on the plate
Gleaming in the sunlight,
Melting in the break of dawn.
Crunch it's gone!

Spencer Morphis, Grade 5
Cool Spring Elementary School, NC

I Am Fire…

I am fire…
I shine like the sun
I am a devil
I light up the world with excitement
I'm deadly and fierce
A volcano exploding with new ideas
As bright as neon colors
Everyone feels my warmth
I am fire, my light leads the way.

Katy Mastrota, Grade 5
Wakefield Forest Elementary School, VA

Dixie

I have a horse
of course
Her name is Dixie
She reminds me of a pixie

She loves treats
full of beets
Be careful she will buck
I told her about a book named Tuck

If she gets crazy
I get a little hazy
Sometimes she's a blur
I will always love her

Dylan Johnson, Grade 5
Forrest W Hunt Elementary School, NC

My Big Head

My head is big as a lemon head.
It is as hard as rocks.
Matter surely fills with a great amount.
Maybe it explodes when it gets bigger.
I can cover darkness on Earth.

Ralph Singleton, Grade 5
Pocalla Springs Elementary School, SC

Trees

Outside there are a bunch of trees
That are tall and lined up
The leaves fall from the tip top
And onto the ground they go

Dontel Farmer, Grade 6
Monelison Middle School, VA

War

War is like the tiger,
With mice at its feet
War is like the broken heart,
That skips twice a beat
War is like the raging sea,
Salt in her eyes
War is like the earthquake,
Ready to rise.

Megan Murphy, Grade 5
Oak View Elementary School, VA

Appetite

Hungry
Starving, panacea
Famished, ravenous, packed, ample
Stuffed, bulging, bloating
Jam-packed, overflowing
Full

Brandon Johnson, Grade 5
St Helena Elementary School, SC

Oh, That Bird

Oh, that busy little bird
going by without a single word
flying by in the big blue sky,
all he has time to say is hi.

Claire Martin, Grade 5
North Windy Ridge School, NC

Spring

Spring has come.
Winter has gone.
Flowers are blooming.
Tree leaves are growing.
Cold days are going away.
Warm days are coming to us.
Spring has come.
Oh, spring has come.

Morsal Mohamad, Grade 5
G W Carver Elementary School, VA

A Poem

To write a poem
Be clear of thought.
Except today.
I think not.
My mind is fuzzy.
My mind's a blur,
All tangled up
In my cat's fur!
Now, here an idea.
Un-fur the cat.
I could write a poem
All about that!

William Howells, Grade 4
St Christopher's School, VA

My Family

My Mom gives us treats
So she is so sweet.
She is the best Mom in the world.

For my sister's birthday
She gave her pearls.
My Dad gives us chains to wear on our necks.

A new pet he bought us makes everything a mess.
It got dirt on my sister's dress.
She went to the vet to get the dog checked.

Zarea Dean, Grade 4
Bensley Elementary School, VA

Pink

Pink makes me feel happy
When I'm eating cotton candy
Pink bubble gum and lip gloss are yummy tasting
Pink is my warm fuzzy blanket
It's my soft, comfortable, cuddly stuffed animal
The taste is out of this world
Pink lemonade on a hot summer day
Cool looking shoes
With a fancy, pink, girly-girl dress
A pink cell phone
Fantastic sweet crystal light
When I'm watching a movie
Stickers are fun to play with
While grading papers
Pink is also the color of note cards
Which are also my flash cards
Pink makes me want to smell
Wonderful pink poppies
In the summer
Pink is a true feeling

Danielle Mottram, Grade 4
Atkinson Academy Elementary School, NH

Attempt at Light

I trudge through the gloomy city,
The gunmetal buildings surround me
While I frantically look for sunshine.
My spirits are shrinking.
Suddenly I am blinded by something
As bright as headlights in a pitch-black night.

A delinquent in the night painted something bright.
Amid the grey gloom of the dark city,
A head-lamped stranger wrote to me.

Was it to me this graffiti I saw?
Was it my name illuminating the city?
Was it an attempt to brighten my day?
For I smile as I walk away.

Nick Whiteford, Grade 5
Manchester Elementary/Middle School, VT

My Delight Song

I am a manatee playfully splashing in the warm Florida water.
I am a giraffe sticking my blue tongue out as I eat.
I am a turtle gliding through the peaceful marsh water.
I am a wombat digging a burrow for my family.
I am a koala clinging with my strong claws to a tree.
I am a tree standing tall above the world.
I am a giant panda eating bamboo.
I am a monkey leaping from tree to tree.
I am a spider web glistening with the dew of the morning.
I am a maple tree with orange, yellow, and red leaves.
I am an elephant gracefully walking in the African plains.
I am Mount Everest watching from atop the world.
I am the rain forest providing shelter and food for the animals.
I am the wide fields of grain teeming with field mice.
I am a herd of buffalo grazing on the Great Plains.
I am an abundance of wildflowers growing along the road.
I am a weeping willow weeping my golden leaves.
I am alive, I am alive, I am alive

Betsy Cole, Grade 5
Rye Elementary School, NH

The Beddybye Worms

The Beddybye worms were dirty and sticky.
We love little feet on that comfortable bed.
We will defeat every clean thing in sight.
Don't get in our way.
Just be on your way.
You never know who is next.
Or where we will strike.
All I can say is leave your bed in a mess.
And you won't be next.
So if you wake up! CHECK!
If you don't you never know.
What you are sleeping on.
Next beddybye you go.

Timothy Sewell, Grade 5
Old Bridge Elementary School, VA

My Family House

My family house has toys
My family house has paper chains
My family house has kind boys
My mom has brown hair
My dad and boys have clown hair
I have down hair
My family house is the BEST of them all!

Taylor Lynn Breivik, Grade 4
Courthouse Road Elementary School, VA

Reading a Book

Flip, read, think
Review, restore, start over
Reading a book takes time to
understand.

Alec Catalano, Grade 6
Boiling Springs Intermediate School, SC

Bruno

My Chihuahua's name is Bruno
He thinks he's numero uno
He's really good at hide and seek
We couldn't find him for a week

He has a heart upon his head
He hardly ever goes to bed
Running up and down the halls
He likes to chase after balls

Being small in size
Except for his big gold eyes
By the sound of him you'd think he's a brute
But by his looks he's real cute

He's not too friendly with a fat old cat
For they mistake him for a rat
He likes to be tickled under his chin
Please don't stick him in a trash bin

Under the covers he might hide
Across the floor he will glide
He may not be big but he sure is funny
One time I found him in a cage with a bunny

Makayla Thurman, Grade 5
Forrest W Hunt Elementary School, NC

The Beach

My bare toes sinking in the sand.
The wind whipping my hair.
The waves crashing to shore,
escorting the sand on a never-ending journey, of life.
Dolphins splash in the surf
as a whale dives in the distance.
The sun beating down my back,
and toasting the sand.
The roar of the waves blend in
the sound of a seagull catching a fish.
The sparkling sea blinds anyone
who gazes out into the horizon.
The sun sets, as the tide rises,
adding on to the adventure the sea holds.
Nighttime comes and the moon reflects off the sea.
The sun rises, repeating the process again.

Barbie Sweet, Grade 6
Chapin Middle School, SC

The Car

One day as I crank the car vroom! vroom! went the car engine.
Tick! Tick! Tick! went the signals.
Beep! Beep! went the horn.
Swish! Swash! went the wipers.
Baam! Baam! Baam! Baam! went all four doors as they closed.
Then Boom! Boom! went the car as it hit the tree.

Tierra Pollard, Grade 5
Pine Tree Hill Elementary School, SC

Hope

Wind whistles through the trees.
Branches snap and earth goes black.
It is a dangerous night.
No one understands why we live
to see so many nights like this.
We don't understand it all all,
but we feel something strange.
We feel it. We cannot see it.
We cannot hear it.
We cannot quite put it to words.
We feel it waiting to be heard, seen, and said.
This feeling is hope.

Victoria Isenhour, Grade 5
Faith Elementary School, NC

Sand Dunes

Sand dunes dot the beach
A warm wind blows by, giving the dunes their rolling shape
Seagulls soar high above the dunes
Playfully flying in and out of kites

Sandra Webb, Grade 6
Wakefield Forest Elementary School, VA

Snow Day

Children love when it snows!
Their parents pick out their warmest clothes.
Some run outside to have a snowball fight
While others stay in, afraid of frostbite.
Some children like to sled;
They race each other head-to-head.
Their parents tell them to come in for a rest
While they make them hot chocolate, the kind they like best.
When the day is finally done,
They go to bed and so does the sun.
They look out and see the moon;
They know another snow day is coming soon.

Brooke Castleberry, Grade 6
Cape Henry Collegiate School, VA

My Flippered Friend

Graceful dolphin, strong and gray
Swimming both night and day
It jumps like a person on a trampoline
The coolest thing I've ever seen

Swiftly swimming, swish, swash, swish
Riding through the water on its back is my wish
Water swishing through my hair
People stop to look and stare

The sounds of dolphins are cries of a baby
Maybe I can swim with them again, just maybe
As I say goodbye to my flippered friend
My love for dolphins will never end

Madison Oliva, Grade 5
Manchester Elementary/Middle School, VT

Clothes

The feeling of getting new clothes is like
The cherry on top of an ice cream sundae
Feeling the slick material is like the long skin of a snake
Wearing the dress is as comfortable as sleeping on a cloud
The fabric is as beautiful as a million dollar art painting
The orange and pink blend together like an early morning sky
But what I love most about the dress is that it's just for me!

Emily Rocchio, Grade 5
Quidnessett Elementary School, RI

Disney World

Disney World is a place
Where all your dreams can come true.
There is so much to do,
Go swimming, ride rides
Or even go to gift shops.

The wind is a cool splash
Of water on my face.
The heat is tempting me
To go inside.
Walking and thinking
What to do next.

My freedom is an animal
Running free.
The intense heat is an oven
Baking us.

I wish the sun would come.
I walk around wondering
What is there to do?
What is there to buy?
Ah I see a ride,
It is as loopy as a bendy straw.

Grant Stevens, Grade 5
East Mooresville Intermediate School, NC

The Night I Was Alone

I remember being alone and staring in fright,
Staring at the pitch black night.
The night I was alone and no one could find me,
The night I was alone and no one could hear me.
Even when I loudly screamed,
No one tried to find me, it was not how I seemed
That night I was hoping to hear a sound.
I sat hoping to be found.

Christal Firmacion, Grade 5
Rosemont Forest Elementary School, VA

Competition

Competition is
As brown as a horse
Flinging mud across the racetrack.

Annika Vorsteveld, Grade 4
Vergennes Union Elementary School, VT

Lightning

Here comes a huge flash of light,
Throughout day and night.
Bright as could be,
Just hit a dark, brown tree.
That was swaying in the gentle breeze,
Waiting for the right moment to break free.

Chloe Butler, Grade 5
Clover Hill Elementary School, VA

Our World Is Beautiful

From the rise of the sun,
To the set of the moon,
To the wind in the air,
And the spray of the sea,
Our world is beautiful.

From the light coming in the window,
To the moonlit path outside,
To the animals that live and breathe,
And the radiant plants that thrive,
Our world is beautiful.

Mikhayla Powers, Grade 6
Hampton Christian Middle/High School, VA

Books

Meet Huckleberry Finn or even Moby Dick.
Meet the Swedish governor.
As you open a book you will find adventure
and magic like never before. You might
find yourself at sea or face to face
with a whale. Sometimes a leprechaun
will find its way under your bed or
a giant whale will find its way into
your pool. You never know what can
happen in a book, when you read.

Sierra Smith, Grade 6
Eagle's Nest Christian School, DE

Friends

These are my friends.
They are loyal and true.
They are always nice.
Getting along with them
      is an easy thing to do.

These are my friends.
They always make me smile.
I can always laugh around them.
My friends will go that extra mile.

These are my friends.
They like me for me.
They're there 'til the end.
My friends are great as you can see!

Megan Rosenberger, Grade 5
C Hunter Ritchie Elementary School, VA

Spring

Feel the sun beating down on your head
See the bright green leaves
Growing on friendly trees
Hear the beautiful birds
Tweeting rhythmic tunes
See and smell the flowers
With their festive colors
And fresh smell
Feel the splish splash of water guns,
Getting you soaked
With fresh grown tomatoes on your plate
And a perfect temperature of 88
All while relaxing on a hammock
In the wonderful season of spring
Hannah Thomas, Grade 5
Wakefield Forest Elementary School, VA

David

David, a funny guy
Who needs a friend
Who needs a cat
Who wants a pet snake
Who fears nothing
Who would like to make A's and B's
David Guffey, Grade 5
Blaney Elementary School, SC

Rain Fell

Rain fell to my window pane
Like a falling train
I like this kind of weather
People thought I was insane
Brian Johnson, Grade 4
Crestwood Elementary School, VA

Mia

You are my best friend,
My very best friend.
You make me happy
Every day.
You share your great snacks,
You share your best toys.
So please don't take
My best friend away.

When I cry you help me out,
When I'm happy you hear me shout,
When I frown you know I'm really mad
Because you are my best friend.

You're there through thick and thin,
You hear me out when I want to talk,
You help me out when I get mad,
You are the best friend I've ever had.
De'Andrea Crosby, Grade 6
CrossRoads Middle School, SC

Nightmare

I drift asleep and I am ready for dreaming,
Later, my mom ran in and I awoke screaming!

"What's the problem," my mom found me on the floor.
"Monsters," I cried, "monsters galore"!

I climbed back into bed shivering with fear,
My mom left the room, and I think I felt a tear.

"It's morning, it's morning!" I cheered with delight.
It's all fun and games until the next night.

So even if you are nice and cozy within your mom and dad's care,
Nightmares can scare you, you must be aware.
Walker Helms, Grade 6
St John Neumann Academy, VA

Valley

I live in the valley
Years pass like days
Dark turns to light over hill
The path I take is to a road to a new beginning
I was an unwanted guest,
Blown away like dirt to explore this vast land
The rainbows ahead is the only hope that I will find my pot of gold in America
For Ireland has only brought famine over my potatoes
I must walk on to a new world to find my pot of gold
I will miss you Ireland,
But I will miss the green rolling hills the most.
Lee Hayes, Grade 6
Wakefield Forest Elementary School, VA

Ha Long Bay

I remember the beaming sun at Vietnam, frying my back.
I remember the waves crashing on my feet.
I remember the cool breeze running through my hair,
and my family fishing on the edges of our tiny boat.
I remember my face, as cooked as a lobster.
I remember the delicious Vietnamese food we ate all day.
I remember the little crabs that tickled my feet on the white, dry sand.
Even though I'm across many seas, oceans, and continents,
I remember that amazing day at Ha Long Bay.
But my favorite memory is yet to come.
Vivian M. Tran, Grade 6
Boiling Springs Intermediate School, SC

Music

The way a butterfly's wings flutter to the beat of it;
sung by the beautiful voice of a blue bird perched high in a tree.
It's one of the most beautiful things on Earth.
How it dances on a page and even more, how it sounds
played by the sweet melody of a flute or violin.
You just fall in love with it when you listen to it.
Music is simply amazing.
Caroline Hall, Grade 6
Berry Shoals Intermediate School, SC

My Dog, Sara

She lies lazily, waiting for attention
eyes slightly open.
She hears the ball bounce, just once,
and jumps up, energetic and alive.
She runs down the stairs,
skipping some as she jumps near the bottom.
With the ball in her mouth,
she runs back up the stairs
dropping the ball, and licking my face.

Will Neese, Grade 6
East Mooresville Intermediate School, NC

Forest

Cut,
    Cut,
        Cut.
            Down,
                Down,
                    Down.
Each tree falls, like a baby bird trying to fly.
Before you know it…
paper,
    paper,
        paper,
No more trees.

John Alan Felton, Grade 5
Sanford Creek Elementary School, NC

Sleeping

It's the best time of the day
You brush your teeth
You put on your pj's
You're tucked in bed
You go snoring to sleep

Jordan Bibens, Grade 5
Courthouse Road Elementary School, VA

Grapefruit

Sugar coats it
like a new snow
yet it's ruby red hue
still shines through.

The instant the sour citrus
touches my tongue
I receive a blast
of sweet and sour flavor.

Sticky juices
glue themselves to my chin
what little can't hold on
drizzles like pink rain
to the awaiting plate below
dispersing on impact.

John Amigo, Grade 6
Manchester Elementary/Middle School, VT

How Many, How Much*

How many pictures on an old camera?
Depends on how many you take.
How many dishes in the trash can?
Depends on how many you break.
How many bees in a hive?
Depends on how many sting.
How many notes in a song?
Depends on how many you sing.
How much money in your purse?
Depends on how much you spend.
How many coats in your closet?
Depends on how many you lend.

Raven McCorkle, Grade 5
East Mooresville Intermediate School, NC
Inspired by Shel Silverstein

Cinderella Going to Graceland

Once I heard a bipatee bopatee boo…
Dressed from head to toe all covered in blue

On my way to big Memphis, Tennessee
Riding on the big trail with my horsey

I really want to see those blue suede shoes
Elvis always put them to such great use

In Memphis, Tennessee there is Graceland
Graceland is an estate that is so grand

I hope someday I'll meet Lisa Marie
Daughter of glorious Elvis Presley

Then I will be on my way to the ball
While I am there, I will see the great hall

So tata! I shall see you tomorrow!
Have to go so I won't be a no-show.

Kylie Truong, Grade 6
Beck Academy, SC

I Hate Soccer Balls

I hate you soccer ball
I play every day
I kick you so hard
I'm glad you go away

I hate you soccer ball
I'll kick you out the field
I hate you soccer ball
I'll pop you with a shield

I hate you soccer ball
Why won't you stay away
I will bury you in hay.

Tzion Lucas, Grade 4
Courthouse Road Elementary School, VA

The Stolen Cherry

On top of my ice-cream
There sat a cherry
I lost my poor cherry
Because of Jim Carrey

Jim Carrey stole it
and jumped to the floor
and then Jim Carrey
ran out the door

He dropped my poor cherry
then hit the door
and then Jim Carrey
flew through the floor

So there you have it
When you see Jim Carrey
Don't eat ice-cream
that has a cherry
Dakota Cheatham, Grade 6
Monelison Middle School, VA

Dylan Plays Football

Across the 50-yard line
Through the defensive line
Beside the halfback
After halftime
Behind the quarterback
Inside the stadium
On the touchdown line
I found Dylan.
Todd Carroll, Grade 5
Northside Elementary School, SC

I Am Fire

I am fire
I flicker happily
I dance excitedly
I explode creatively
Red, hot fun
Yummy as a marshmallow
Bringing warmth to others
Lighting the fireplace with embers
Emily Woodfield, Grade 5
Wakefield Forest Elementary School, VA

Winter

Winter is a warm white
The color of snow and marshmallows
Winter feels like a cold, cold breeze
It sounds like a big wind soaring by
It smells like hot cocoa
Winter tastes like candy canes
Winter is a cold long season
Elliane York, Grade 5
Vienna Elementary School, NC

I Am

I am
A young boy,
A smart kid,
Trying to be successful,
Learning to be someone,
I am unknown
Caleb Andresen, Grade 5
The Compass School, RI

The Book

The book
What could it be about
Do you dare to open it
It's taunting you
Like a bone taunts a hungry dog
You touch the book
Feeling its texture
Trying to read it with your fingers
Unsuccessfully
Ok
You open the book
And start to read
But
You never stop reading
You try to
But you can't
Until
You get to the very last word
On the very last page
Of
The book
Jessica Collins, Grade 6
Main Street Middle School, VT

Being Sick

Man, I hate being sick!
Like glue, it seems to stick,
Giving you the chills
And always eating pills.
The medicine you eat
Can make you feel BEAT!
All your school work is late.
Oh, man, it's just *great*.
Elliott Brooks, Grade 6
Wakefield Forest Elementary School, VA

Summer/Winter

Summer
Hot, sunny
Swimming, playing, visiting
Warm, loud, cold, quiet
Sledding, skiing, hiking
Frosty, snow
Winter
JaQuail Millidge, Grade 5
St Helena Elementary School, SC

I Love You

"I love you." that man told his wife.
She laid there as still as can be.
It was the last day of her life.
She looked up,
her eyes were shining so bright.
She put her hand out "I love you"
One more word "Forever" and
she was gone.

The grave was set up.
Olivia Crissman 1912-1994
the grave said.
He cried.
Teardrops fell.
He stood.
Then he left,
leaving flowers of all colors
and a note "I love you."
Blair Simpson, Grade 6
Beech Springs Intermediate School, SC

The Soldier

There was a soldier,
who had composure.
He missed his family.
With his guns, he was handy,
but when it comes to war, he was sober.

At first, he thought it would be fun.
When he heard a bullet, he dared to run.
He had his whole life to live.
He wanted to give,
give to his country as one.

He's aching,
he's even shaking.
He doesn't know why,
he doesn't even know if he'll die.
His vision is darkening.

This is the end of my story.
His friends called him Cory.
He gave his life for you and me.
I wish it didn't have to be.
And he did it all in the name of glory.
Jacob Matthews, Grade 6
Camperdown Academy, SC

Don't Touch

Don't touch the vase
It might shatter and/or break
Pretty and gorgeous
Until you knock it over
So do not touch the blue vase
Will Sherrill, Grade 5
St Christopher's School, VA

Window

The sun is shining
The snow on the ground is melting
Through the woods are the train tracks
Busy cars are making their way
Over the bridge
The evening is coming
The trees are getting ready
For a quiet night

Christopher White, Grade 4
Atkinson Academy Elementary School, NH

Winter

In winter
You see the sparkling white snow
Flying down from the ghostly gray clouds.

You feel the ice cold air
Rubbing against your soft, pale skin.

You taste the fiery hot chocolate
Flowing down your throat.

You hear the smart weather man
Calling for heavy snow and cold temperatures.

You smell the choking smoke
Diving through your nostrils
As it comes from the fireplace
While you stay in your warm and cozy bed.

Ethan Bailey, Grade 4
Lockhart Elementary School, SC

The Tick Tock Clock

A clock is the only thing keeping us from being free
It is a glass case holding a spider
And a moving schedule
A clock could be a maze for a tiny lady bug
A clock is the mimic of my heartbeat
Clocks are the planets with endless stars
A clock is wrong but right
All clocks have different times
But they all mean the same thing
A clock is a symbol of peace

Ivy Chace, Grade 5
Rye Elementary School, NH

My Mom

My mom is my role model.
I've learned so much about her over the years.
She's helped me get out of trouble and fear.
I can't help but notice, 10 years went by very fast.
I know She'd tell me anything. (If I asked.)
There is nothing else to say to you…
But I love my mom, and that's the truth.

Brianna Yoho, Grade 4
Queens Creek Elementary School, NC

January

January is the color of blue
The color is everything frozen
January feels cold to the bone
It sounds like the trees blowing cold air and ice
It smells like a fire is burning
January tastes like snow falling from the sky
January is here to come and go

Jordan Burkey, Grade 5
Vienna Elementary School, NC

Memories of a Loved One!

The house I used to go to every day,
But don't go to anymore
The place where most memories were made
The place where my grandpa had once lived
But doesn't live anymore!
The place where dreams were created,
Then ended that one day!
Memories of the days we spend together
I want to cry but the tears are gone
They have left with my dreams.
Now he lies in the ocean with the fish,
In the world below me.
He now lives with the angels of all gods,
And Jesus Himself!
I pray someday he will come back to me!
I think about him all day,
And dream about him all night
Even though he has left he is still with me
In my thoughts, my dreams, and my heart
I now have the memories,
Of a loved one!

Kaylie Benson, Grade 6
Manchester Elementary/Middle School, VT

My Cat, Poker

There once was a homeless cat
who was lonely and sad and all that.
He was looking for a good home,
so the streets he did roam.
Until one Sunday morning, a little boy, he did meet.
He was blonde, cute, and kind with a heart full of love.

Poker was all shiny and black
with a tail that swished back.
They both found each other.
A love that would last forever.

Over the years, he was loved.
Even for all the squirrels he got rid of.
A few months ago, we had to say goodbye.
We laid him down to rest under the morning sky.
We will never forget Poker.
He will always be in our hearts.

Nick D'Onofrio, Grade 6
Camperdown Academy, SC

12 Months

January is when I love to play in the snow. Let's go outside to sled...let's go!
February is the month of Valentine's Day a heart shaped box on your bed lay.
March is really a bore, let's have some fun, let's have some more.
In April my mom is turning thirty-four. I've had some cake and now I want some more.
May, the month of my birthday. This is when I go to the Chesapeake Bay.
June, the fireflies come out and make a bright glow, you should all know.
I love to watch the fireworks in July: I will always be close by.
August, it's the end of going to the pool: it's the start of school.
September, I always give an apple to the teacher. I drew a picture of a creature.
October is when I trick-or-treat: we trick-or-treat on Main Street.
November is the month of Thanksgiving Day, I know a turkey is on its way!
December, when you go outside it will be very cold, on Christmas Day you might find some gold.

Emily Yergin, Grade 5
C Hunter Ritchie Elementary School, VA

A Chain Message

Nigh and remote, neck and neck, eye to eye
All of our acquaintances are strolling by
Hello to you, sir; Hi, friend!; Cheerio, Madam; 'Bye, old pal
So many ways to salute them
Other people we do not know
We know naught of their lives, their plans, their ideas, their hopes, their dreams, their thoughts
But we can etch on them forever.
Politeness, a smile, a warm "Hello,"
Can make a small memory
But leave a large subliminal message
"Pass it on!" we encourage
With every positive gesture
Every smile, every demonstration
Of courtesy, recognition, encouragement, companionship
Engraves on our peers the message people go sometimes too far to convey
No protests, demonstrations, or violence is necessary to retain or reclaim peace
The irony of these situations is not fundamental
A simple gesture: a door held open, a minute clearing debris
Is all that is obligatory to make the world gyre and twirl rather than onerously rotate with its burdened load
Simple peace: pass it on.

Meredith Bain, Grade 6
Carmel Middle School, NC

12 Months

January is a winter wonderland, so I wear a warm band around my head.
February is full of chocolate hearts, cakes, candies, and lots of tarts.
March comes in like a lion and out like a lamb; no more warm head band.
April is when the rain comes down very hard; a good time to play lots of cards.
May is the time when all the flowers start to sprout, let's go get the water spout.
June is when school gets out; all the boys and girls like to shout!
July is when we look for seashells on the beach; they are very pretty, beautiful, and neat.
August is hot, hot, hot; I hope I don't get a sunspot!
September is when summer dies down;
Fall starts and leaves fall in mounds.
October is filled with big, round pumpkins.
For Halloween little kids dress up as munchkins.
November is when it starts to get cold; all the turkeys look very bold.
December is filled with holiday cheer, listen and you may hear a reindeer!

Carter Ware, Grade 5
C Hunter Ritchie Elementary School, VA

Noodles

Noodles is the best,
But he is a pest.

He's a huge joker
While he plays poker.

Noodles is completely yellow,
And he is shaped just like Jell-O.

He's always gettin' on my nerves.
He runs and jumps and slides and curves.

Sometimes I wish he'd just disappear,
But then he comes and sheds a small tear.

I despise that he's always doing this to me.
But I couldn't ask for a better friend. You see?

Morgan DiPippa, Grade 4
Trinity Christian School, VA

If I Were

If I were a soccer player I'd make goals.
If I were a hockey player I'd make shots.
If I were a football player I'd make touchdowns.
If I were a baseball player I'd make home runs.
If I were a basketball player I'd make free throws.
If I were a skier I'd win races.
If I were an athlete I'd be just like me!

Elizabeth Goodrum, Grade 5
Courthouse Road Elementary School, VA

Nature

The flowers are bright like the sun
The wind is strong like a hurricane
Honeysuckles taste like candy
The pine trees have pine straw
Robins are the birds that announce spring
I would let the universe be green
So I can be seen
By all the world
It's my home so don't lay down
Or else a snake will bite you!

Esmeralda Melchor, Grade 5
Manchester Elementary School, NC

Love

Love is a feeling you want and maybe need
Love is as fair and delicate like little dogs legs
Love is like a big secret no one should know
Love is as beautiful and caring as a new born baby
Love is like an amazing ride that never goes down
Love is just like a brother or sister but always loving
Love is like a whole century of kindness
Love is many things but it is not death

Jenna Morrin, Grade 5
Queen's Grant Community School, NC

Flying

Wind rushing
against skin
blowing back
thick brown hair
legs urging
to keep going
brain knowing
I have to slow
breathing is
becoming staggered
wanting
to keep going
wanting
so badly to stop
moving as fast
as a cheetah
maneuvering past
leisurely people
flying
on streets.

Hailey Brockett, Grade 6
Manchester Elementary/Middle School, VT

Swimming

Jumping into the wonderful wakening water,
Makes my worries fly far, far away,
Peaceful things jumping into my head,
While my hair is swaying left to right,
Feeling graceful approaches me,
My arms and legs
Moving in circles,
All sounds drain out of my ears,
My head is tucked under
The refreshing water,
Gliding like a ballerina
In the moonlight,
My mind transfers
To a happy mood,
While I'm swimming,
Carelessly.

Alexa Jervis, Grade 5
Olde Providence Elementary School, NC

Rain

It drips it drops it never seems to stop
It turns into a big puddle,
My dog jumps into it splashing
Me with muddy water

The birds fly down to peck the bread crumbs,
The people watching
Hastily the child runs to his mother's side,
I walk away
Leaving memories behind…

Ember Jetter, Grade 5
Cool Spring Elementary School, NC

Spring

Birds are chirping high
I smell the trees in the spring
You see lots of leaves

David Logan, Grade 5
Pocalla Springs Elementary School, SC

My Precious Box

I will put into my precious box,
The love of my puppy,
The fun of my four-wheeler,
The sound of The Jonas Brothers Band,
The sweet taste of chocolate,
The love of my family,
And all the warm special memories.

I will not put into my box
The sadness of unloved kids,
The sorrow of someone sad,
The sadness of my parents,
The sadness of my siblings
And the badness of bullies.

Maria Castaneda, Grade 5
Four Oaks Elementary School, NC

Sparkly Snow

Drip, Drip of snow
Melting off the trees
Falling on the sparkly snow.
No one will know
Until the next cool
Winter comes.
Come with me.

I have a mouth
Full of worry.
Tears drip down
From my eyes.
Nobody knows
I am here.
All I have left
Is faith and
Snow falling onto animals
Running around.

Maria Simard, Grade 4
Bethlehem Elementary School, NH

What Is Love

Love can make you happy
Love can make you cry
Love can make you ask why
Love can bring fears
Love can bring cheers
Love can make you smile
Love is worth waiting for a while

Tiesha Edwards, Grade 5
Four Oaks Elementary School, NC

Monsters

Monsters
Creatures of night.

Claws, fangs, horns, spikes.
Humanoid, plant-like, animal-like, and made up.

Earthly, unearthly, and from who-knows-where.
They slither, crawl, fly, and swim.

Gormiti, demons, and things that go bump in the night. Mwa-haaa-haa-ha!
But, if they all got together, the worst would be a little sister!

Matthew Desy, Grade 4
Queens Creek Elementary School, NC

A Book

Sounds like rustling, hushed up and quiet
Looks like a person, you wonder what's inside
Smells like a fresh spring flower, or a dark, crisp scent
Tastes like melted chocolate, you know that you want more
Feels like you're touching a blanket, maybe a soft one, maybe rough
Who knows? Open yours and you can decide.

Samantha Steeman, Grade 4
Waller Mill Fine Arts Magnet School, VA

Lena

Lena is as happy as getting an A on my test
She is like a pretty model wearing the finest dress ever
She is as warm as cuddling a new and clean blanket
She is as special as my heart and body
She is very loving as I am to my friends, family, and teachers
She is as smart as a dictionary and math book in one
Finally she is as kind as a little puppy kissing you a million times

Emma Melton, Grade 5
Queen's Grant Community School, NC

Where I'm From

I am from my mother as well as my father
I am from my grandmother, my brother and I
My family is awesome with many characteristics
As funny as a clown, as smart as a scientist
Even as devious as cupid on a Valentine's heart
I am from delicious and exotic foods
I am cool and smooth as an ice cream cone on a Sunday evening
I'm loved by others more than Grandfather's pizza
I can shake my thing better than Jell-o on a string
I enjoy hugs more than a slice of hamburger
Between two sesame buns
I am from the items I hold dear to my heart
My super fly clothes and my speedy moped scooter
My awesome PS2 and my fashion Nintendo DS
I am from the hobbies that are energetic and wild
You may think you are in a baseball crowd
That is my life and that is
Where I'm from

Tavora Brown, Grade 4
Whittaker Elementary School, SC

The Bubble

Gently floating in the air,
Going up without a care.
Went up higher than the old birch tree!
I can't imagine the things it might see!!

Gently floating into space,
Going up at a steady pace.
Floating up, way past the stars
Maybe it will get to see Mars!

Gently floating into the stars
Going up faster than 100 cars.
Here comes a star with a really sharp point
POP!!!

Emily Clancey, Grade 5
Olde Providence Elementary School, NC

My Little Golden Locket

Hanging on its golden chain,
worn every day,
gone everywhere,
been through everything.

Given to me
on my first birthday.

Its little bow,
an icon
of my best memories
and the people I love.

Once lost,
and many broken chains.
A little faded,
and not as shiny
but still perfect.

Resting on my skin,
like a hummingbird sitting on a flower.
My little golden locket.

Olivia Maeder, Grade 6
Manchester Elementary/Middle School, VT

Poetry

Poetry is a game that is a whirl of wonder
Opening new paths while I ponder
Words of wisdom thoughts of grief
Every day there is a new piece
Poems of nature and skies that are blue
While I think about words that describe you
There is always a place where I can sit and think
About times and places in only one blink
Some days I can think and some days I can not
Well that's too bad I'm on writer's block.

Sam Foer, Grade 6
The Compass School, RI

My Colors

Some days are white some days are blue,
for different days I'm in different moods

Now read my poem and you will see,
How different I can be

Tropical lime green is like a beautiful tree,
It is always pleasing for me to see

On days that are sad and brown,
Those days always make me frown

On days that are vivid yellow,
I always want to eat Jell-O

On the days that are the dreary blue
They always make me feel like the flu

As you can see I have different days,
On different days I have a different face.

Conner Springer, Grade 5
Clover Hill Elementary School, VA

Spring

God makes flowers in the spring.
I see the birds sing and I know who is my King.

Birds bring joy on their wings.
God has a thing for spring.

Oscar Amaya, Grade 4
Trinity Christian School, VA

Asia

Asia, the land of jade
Land of the sugar cane
It contains many common countries such as
China, Japan, the Philippines, etc.
From small villages, to vast cities,
Asia is a magnificent land.
From Israel to Bhutan, Asia is colossal.
Martian Arts were created in this land, also.

Sean Warren, Grade 5
Queens Creek Elementary School, NC

A Small Beauty

Her moonstone eyes gleamed
Like one-thousand mirrors under a moonlit sky,
Her red dress was as soft and sleek as royal silk,

There she sat, as motionless as glass,
Sitting there for all of eternity,
This was my prized possession,

A little China doll.

Ari Hayden August, Grade 4
Rehoboth Elementary School, DE

Magic Machine
M ight a magic machine,
A s a small child,
G o,
I nto the world and
C ause peace through the world.

M ight
A very small
C hild,
H ave enough confidence
I n themselves,
N ot to bail out, but to
E mpty the world of trouble.
Blade Lewis, Grade 6
Forestbrook Middle School, SC

Parents
Mother
Nice, neat
Loving, caring, knowing
Cooks, cleans, scolds, protects
Working, driving, fixing
Handsome, brave
Father
Jody Wilson, Grade 5
St Helena Elementary School, SC

New York Trip
I went to New York,
My family and me.
We had lots of fun on a shopping spree.
We ate cake,
And learned to bake.
We went on a walk to a fishing lake
And even met a snake.
Sabrina Patton, Grade 5
Trinity Christian School, VA

Aliens
I was
Doing my
Math…so
Patiently 'til an
Alien space craft
Abducted me. (They
Destroyed my math) they
Placed me down on a raft.
Chained me down so I couldn't
Squirm, and brought out a brain
Sucking worm. Sorry to say they
Absorbed my math half, but at least
I escaped (it was too great to explain) so
I can't do the problem on the board…
…Wait…a…one hundred page essay!
Andrew Rader, Grade 5
Sanford Creek Elementary School, NC

Mourning
Mourning people who have died
Is the hardest thing to do.
You have to accept the fact
That they are no longer with you.
You can be sad in bursts
I know that it hurts.
You have to let them go
Surely you will know,
That you go on with your life.
Emma Santee, Grade 4
The Compass School, RI

Running
Running
Energizing, exhilarating
Darting, racing, dashing
Lifting off the ground
Sprinting
Joanne Ensley, Grade 6
Midlothian Middle School, VA

Easter
Easter is a time for fun
Hiding eggs in the pretty flowers
Eating chocolate bunnies
Wearing new clothes
Playing with cousins at my grandma's
I love Easter!
Lane'sha Wilson, Grade 4
Lockhart Elementary School, SC

Fishy
Fishy
Small scaly thing
Jumping out, get him quick!
I love watching him swim all around
Silly swimmer
Rhett Deverich, Grade 4
Waller Mill Fine Arts Magnet School, VA

Messy Hair
When I wake up
I look up
All I see is messy hair
It looks like a bear
Everyone stares
This is my messy hair
Gabrielle Shodoan, Grade 5
Pocalla Springs Elementary School, SC

Flowers
Dressed in layered skirts,
At the begging of sweet spring.
Tucked inside their beds.
Margaret Gentry, Grade 4
Trinity Christian School, VA

Poems/Letters
Poems
Paper, imagination
Writing, describing, thinking
Poems are fun writing!
Letters
Ally Van Balen, Grade 6
Wakefield Forest Elementary School, VA

Sister
Sister
Kind, sweet
Forgiving, sharing, caring
I love my sister
Amanda
Sarah Kamen, Grade 5
Wakefield Forest Elementary School, VA

Squirrel
There was a squirrel in the house
We thought it was a mouse
We tried to get him out nice and quick
So I lured it with a tortilla chip
It ran out from under the chair
And gave me quite a scare
It climbed up the wall
And had a great fall
It fell to the floor
And ran out the door
Andrew Gardner, Grade 4
Mary Walter Elementary School, VA

Where Is My Topic?
Sing, cry.
Swim, fly.
Black, white
What to write?

Say 'em, sing 'em
Where is my rhythm?
I look here, there
Has it gone to a fair?

I look, search.
Hey look, there is a birch!
Lads and lasses,
Where are my glasses?

Rock, kite
What to write?
Rhinos, hippos
Nachos, tacos
Throw it, drop it
Where is my
topic?!!!
Lilly Adler, Grade 4
The Compass School, RI

Artemis Fowl

A n extremely remarkable teen he is.
R emember to put the cameras on a loop.
T o fail is to try again.
E verybody respects him, almost everybody.
M astermind of criminology,
I n Haven, he is,
S ometimes cowered at.

F airy's friend and enemy.
O utstanding plan-maker he is.
W ith Butler, they are almost unstoppable.
L oved by many young readers.

James Gilchrist, Grade 5
Trinity Christian School, VA

I Wonder…

I wonder why the sky is blue
Why reading is good for you
How the world changes from day to night
Why the sun is so light
How a day can be dark
How a butterfly can be a Monarch
I wonder about the world
How it started
Will it end?
Why are there so many wonders in the world?
Just from a single boy or girl

Shaylin Seddon, Grade 6
Dr Edward Ricci School, RI

If I Were the King of Money

If I were the king of money,
    Man it would be funny.
If I were the king of money,
    I would buy lots.
If I were the king of money,
    I could even get lessons on tying knots.
If I were the king of money,
    I would buy lots of food.
If I were the king of money,
    I would always be in a good mood.

Nick Lake, Grade 5
Courthouse Road Elementary School, VA

Everyday Boy

Everyday boy
sits in class, impatient
and awkwardly posed.
Stares desperately at the window,
as he fights the grueling pace of the clock.
Watching plants dangle and birds attempt to fly.
Everyday boy says to himself,
"I guess it's nice to play outside!"
And he falls gently asleep.

Connor Morgan, Grade 6
Chapin Middle School, SC

Seasons

The season wheel goes round,
It also makes no sound
Summer is so much fun
I always want to play in the sun
Fall is coming near
Now fall is already here
Leaves are falling off trees
Now Christmas is sure to please
Snowmen have started melting
And soon rain will start pelting
Spring is coming near
Now spring is already here
Flowers have started to bloom
Summer will be here soon
School just got out, it's summer
When summer ends it will be a bummer
Then the wheel of seasons will start again
And it will go round all over again

Will Hays, Grade 5
Waccamaw Intermediate School, SC

The Two Sides of Pink

Pink is love
Bright and bold
Soft and sweet
Everyone's friend

Pink can be hot
Bright and excited
Jumping and spinning
Dashing on tulips and raining on flamingos

Pink is soft
Like hearts on a card
A soothing love song
Sweet like candy
She's a friend to all

Daring, sweet, lovey edgy
They're all part of my friend pink

Cady Bailey, Grade 4
Youngsville Elementary School, NC

Star

Super-
star
inside
yourself you shine like the brightest
star in the sky you believe
in yourself
and give 100%
all the time and never
give up   THEN
you   succeed

Skyler Cahill, Grade 5
East Mooresville Intermediate School, NC

I Love the Outdoors

I really love the outdoors.
I never stand at the door.
When the rain comes down
I make a big frown.
When it stops and goes away
I go out and play.
And when the rain comes back
I feel like it's going to attack.

Kaitlin Vannatter, Grade 4
Grace Miller Elementary School, VA

Chantel Williamson

Sweet, nice, kind,
Wishes to go to Hollywood,
Dreams of saving the world,
Wants to be a singer,
Who fears wolves,
Who is afraid of clowns,
Who likes boys that are funny,
Who believes in the boogyman,
Who loves when you get free ice cream,
Who loves to play volleyball,
Who loves soft tacos only,
Who plans to finish school,
Who plans to be a dancer and a singer,
Who plans to learn how to fly.

Chantel Williamson, Grade 5
Manchester Elementary School, NC

My Mom

My mom is really cool
she treats me really well.
She helps me when I need her
her love is like a ringing bell.

Whenever I need something
she gets the best kind.
She always gets them for me
I love the things she finds.

When I am uncomfortable
she's there beside me.
I love the way she does it
she tells me I'm her sweet pea.

When I cough and sneeze
she grabs me a tissue.
Takes me to the doctor
and says I have an issue.

My Mom does a lot for me
she really makes me smile.
She tells that she loves me
and ALWAYS goes the extra mile!

Heather Wennersten, Grade 5
Pine Tree Hill Elementary School, SC

Creepy Woodland

Unseen deep woodland
Yet mysterious silent
Miracle wilder

Dan Lin, Grade 5
North Windy Ridge School, NC

Angel-May

Angel May
Is a baby
She is sweet and loving
Very pretty and cute
She is small and chubby but cute
Baby

Rachel Hudson, Grade 5
East Albemarle Elementary School, NC

Seasons

July
Hot, bright
Swimming, surfing, tanning
Sunny, humid, snow, frost
Skiing, snowing, snowflakes
Frigid, cold
January

Brian Williams, Grade 5
St Helena Elementary School, SC

Refraction

Night of darkness
Slays the sunlit sky
Turning all to black

Day of light
Undoes the spell of darkness
And suddenly everything is clear

Moon that glows
Brings a hint of daylight to the night
And spotlights the earth

Sun that shines
Keeps my spirits high
And warms creatures of every sort

Jack Readman, Grade 4
Memorial School, NH

New York City

New York City
dirty, loud
fast, busy, crowded
people, food, actors, taxis
pollution, art, rivers
concrete, bright
New York City

Nolan Dunagan, Grade 5
Queen's Grant Community School, NC

Riverview Panthers

Riverview Panthers are blue.
That is a wonderful hue.
Riverview Panthers are black.
They've always got your back.
Riverview Panthers are white.
What a beautiful sight.
Riverview Panthers are cool.
They rule our SCHOOL!

Hailey Phelps, Grade 4
Riverview Elementary School, VA

Love

Love
Nice, good
Tender loving kiss
I really Love Love
Care

Elizabeth Mondloch, Grade 4
Trinity Christian School, VA

Beautiful River

Beautiful river
The fast, swift, deep blue water
Runs through the forest

Olivia Gentry, Grade 5
North Windy Ridge School, NC

I Walk Alone

I walk alone
Through the bear's territory
He's eating his berries
Snap goes a twig —
I could be next.

Ryan Rossum, Grade 6
Wakefield Forest Elementary School, VA

Summer

In my mind,
I know today's the day.
Summer, summer,
is finally here.

School's finally over,
it's time for fun and play.
Clouds disappear,
sun show your face.

Let's go to the beach,
feel the sand between your toes,
the wind in your hair,
on this summer day.

Summer, summer,
is finally here.

Zach Pendergrace, Grade 6
Chapin Middle School, SC

May

May is calm yellow
The color of zesty lemons and roses
May feels like chocolate melting in your mouth
It sounds like country music
It smells like fresh flowers
May tastes like strawberries
May is warm and wonderful

Clare Richardson, Grade 5
Vienna Elementary School, NC

My Pajamas

In the morning I feel bare.
I get out of bed with a scare.
I run downstairs and I see my pajamas on the run.
I grab a pair of pants this wakes me up it's fun.
I think I will do it more you should do it to.
When you go shopping if you buy them we'll have a clue.

Jacob Goble, Grade 5
Old Bridge Elementary School, VA

Armadillo

armadillo in a ball
some think he is ugly
he doesn't look like a doll
sleeping in his burrow snugly

he has a hard shell
it is just like metal
if he were human he would not be pale
he loves to eat flower petals

when he rolls in a ball
he is as hard as can be
sometimes he rolls over cacti and might fall
but his armor is his safety

he scurries across roads
and moves really fast
he dodges snakes and toads
home is where he goes at last

he goes over to the burrow
to visit his family
he loves to watch his children grow
hoping they are not shy and clammy.

Ben Childers, Grade 5
Forrest W Hunt Elementary School, NC

Winter's Late Day

A blue sky,
Sun is setting,
Trees darken,
Snow on the ground,
The world is silent.

Thomas Doyle, Grade 4
Atkinson Academy Elementary School, NH

No One

No one for you
No one for me
No one for the eyes to see
No one to scream and cry to
No one except me
From me to you and you to me
Then we'll finally have it together
Our love will be won
And the battle will be no longer
The battle between my heart and yours
My ideas turn into nightmares when I think of you
Does this happen to you too?
Your life is on its last strand
But my life is still in my hands

Kelsey Clemons, Grade 5
Myrtle Beach Intermediate School, SC

Grizzly Bear

Ode to Grizzly Bear
Oh grizzly bear, oh grizzly bear, you're so soft.
You're the guard of my life.
I protect you with all my heart.
You're very nice to me and family.
When intruders come you always let me know.
If there's a problem I can't handle, you do it.
I couldn't ask for a better bear than you.
I'm so glad to have a friend to play with.
You're the best.
I don't regret having you as a pet.

Kasey Dixon, Grade 5
Vienna Elementary School, NC

Penalty Kick

With sixty seconds running down on the clock —
   The anxious boy waits to lock in the game
   Spotting his target
   He observed the goalie,
   Knowing he carried the team.

He charged toward the ball —
   Slapping it with all of his strength
   And then...
   They had won a game of skill,
   A game known as soccer.

Ronald "Trey" Berry III, Grade 6
Northwood School, NH

My Grandfather

Sounds like classical music playing in his head.
Smells of a pipe with tobacco.
Tastes like a warm melted mint.
Looks like a man with gray hair.
Feels like the nice sun.
My grandfather is warm.

Katelyn Jenkins, Grade 4
Waller Mill Fine Arts Magnet School, VA

Lightning to Thunder
Lightning
Strange, powerful
Flashing, shining, glimmering
Bright, brilliant, clapping, killing
Shocking, frightening, crashing
Loud, magnificent
Thunder
Xavier Lewis, Grade 5
Northside Elementary School, SC

Christmas
The family went to buy a Christmas tree
Except for my sister and me.
We went to buy some Christmas lights
Because they were colored so bright.
We went to get the Christmas star
Because we left it in our blue car.
We rode to the big mall
to get some shiny bright Christmas balls.
Maria Cabrera Gonzalez, Grade 4
Bensley Elementary School, VA

My Headache
I have a terrible headache
And my mom told me what to take.

It hurts really bad
And I am feeling sort of sad.

I went in my room to lie down
And then my face developed a frown.

After a while, the pain went away
I told my mom and she said, "Okay."
Alisha Brown, Grade 4
St Helena Elementary School, SC

Alaska
One warm wolverine
Two towering tourists
Three thick polar bears
Four fighting grizzlies
Five frightened falcons
Six sailing eagles
Seven snowy towns.
Kylie Muir, Grade 5
Blacksburg New School, VA

Sword
I dreamed
I was a sword
In the civil war
Looking at all the dead people
Sadly.
Donovan Pace, Grade 5
Cooper Elementary School, VA

Summer
Boating along the shimmering sea,
lots of lakeside fun,
Mosquitoes biting and sandy feet,
and sizzling tar upon the street.
Sun-warmed grass across my yard
hot dogs and hamburgers too.
Sun burned red. Ouch that hurts,
and no more school for you,
Summer is lots more too!
Krystyna Keller, Grade 4
Memorial School, NH

My Mother
My mother
Can clean
My mother
Can cook
My mother
Can be mean
But she is the
Queen

My mom can read
My mother
Is cute
Like I
Said she's
The Queen
Goldie Jones, Grade 4
Appomattox Elementary School, VA

The Rain Dropped
The rain went drip, drop, plop, plop,
All over the pond beyond the woods.

The rain went drip, drop, plop, plop
And never stopped.

The rain went drip, drop, plop, plop
All over the shed ahead of the woods.

The rain went drip, drop, plop, plop
And never stopped.
Breanna Brown, Grade 4
Edwards Elementary School, SC

Ever
From here to there,
And back again.
Never knowing where to go.
Always missing something,
Leaving behind forever.
Never coming back.
Not now, not ever.
Michael Lieb, Grade 5
Oak View Elementary School, VA

Wind
The wind blows, the wind dies.
Up and down in the sky.
Having fun blowing leaves,
And trees.

Can be gentle,
Can be rough.
Can be soft,
Can be loud,
But the wind is not proud.
The wind is kind, to me.
Faith Dudley, Grade 5
Four Oaks Elementary School, NC

iPods
iPods, oh iPods, they are so cool
but you can't have them here in school
an iPod holds my favorite songs
when the ride is really long
I can listen to them on headphones
I can change the volume and tones
Kept safe from damage by a clear cover
Music makes me happy
I'm a music lover
Cheyenne Sebold, Grade 6
Main Street Middle School, VT

A Snowy Day
When I trudged outside
My friends and I built a snowman.
It was tall and round
We dressed it with hat, scarf and buttons.

After we finished
We went into the house.
I took off my wet clothes.
We played video games.

It was a fun time
Being in the snow.
I hope my friends come over
Next time it snows.
Marquis Evans, Grade 4
Bensley Elementary School, VA

Nature
The vicious thunder crashes
While the rain quietly splashes.

The snow comes twinkling down
With hardly any sound.

The wind wildly whistles
Making tremble the thistles.
Glenn Canfield, Grade 5
St John Neumann Academy, VA

Little Irish Girl
Little Irish girl her Irish
Accent, and her blond hair, and
Her freckles, and her big
Smile.

Little Irish girl her little
Home and her big excitement,
And the warmth of her
Home, means she doesn't
Need to be warm.

Little Irish girl, her big
Smile means that her
Home is very fun and very
Irish.

The little Irish girl's
Background has the school
That is as big as a mountain,
And the tree that is stickier
Than maple syrup
Jordan Heingartner, Grade 5
Manchester Elementary/Middle School, VT

Laughter
Laughter is a smiley face on a Walmart receipt.
It makes everything even better.

Laughter is a feeling like you just won a Super Bowl.
It is the best thing ever.

Laughter is a vibrating phone on your ear.
It always calms you down.

Laughter is a huge wave for skim boarding on a boring day.
It turns the day around.

Patrick Matsko, Grade 5
Holy Cross Elementary School, DE

Mine
This is my house,
So cozy and warm,
The doors and windows shut tight,
To keep me safe from the storm.

This is my house,
The TV is on in the room where we dine.
I don't watch it much,
Which suits me just fine.

This is my house,
It sits at the top of a hill.
I sit on the porch,
In evening when all is still.

Michelle Rosenberger, Grade 5
C Hunter Ritchie Elementary School, VA

Song of Myself
I sing of colorful sneakers
And Garfield.
Basketball games
And big tennis rackets.
Hats from Pac-Sun
And short cartoon movies.
All a part of my life.

A life that is alive within
Soft pillows with smiley faces
Colorful flowers in gardens
The sweet smell of cinnamon buns
Books with cliffhangers
Rainbows that arch the sky
My mom's homemade home fries
And snow globes that sit upon my shelf

A life with sounds that live within
Dogs barking at invisible objects
High heels hitting a marble floor
The quiet tapping of raindrops hitting the roof
And my fingers banging on the piano keys

All, yes, all living sounds within my song.
Caroline Cunningham, Grade 6
Main Street Middle School, VT

The Wind
Bam!
Mother nature was mad, oh so sad, taking house by
house there they go, when there's wind here comes
snow, then soon hail will show, when this comes you
better flee cause they're after thee, the wind will come just
like a tornado not standing down for any tomato, the sky
Will turn into a black cat,

Mother nature will flap her
Arms to adjust the wind speed, the speed will lead the
wind to victory, the wind goes faster as it destroys the
Pasture, the wind is fierce and will pierce anything at all,

So you better flee, cause they're after thee,
When the wind comes they're after you not stopping for
any cause, so you better watch out when the wind
comes out.

Dylan Parker, Grade 5
Manchester Elementary/Middle School, VT

Star
I see you as a star
A star that is shining bright
'Cause you are the shining light in my life.
So if you leave me, my life will be dark
So please don't leave, I want my life to be lit up by you.
Shamarr Graham, Grade 5
Manchester Elementary School, NC

Cats

I love a cat's meow.
I wish I could hear one now.
I also love a cat's purr.
It's better than a dog's grr.

I have a cat that's fat.
Oops, she's on my hat.
I just don't get how,
She eats like a cow.

My fat cat is black.
I love my fat cat.

Kimberly Sak, Grade 4
Grace Miller Elementary School, VA

Summer

Summer is fun
Come play in the sun.
Take a break
Or swim in a lake.
Come outside
And have some fun.

Darrius Harris, Grade 4
Bensley Elementary School, VA

Spring

I creep after the winter,
And appear when it dies away;
The sun shines brighter,
As I beat the winter out of the way.

My April brings the showers,
During a warm summer day;
My May blossoms flowers,
And petals get into a fray.

I bring out the sun,
Which the kids cherish;
Even though snow was fun,
It must perish.

I am the season,
When the bees come out to sting;
To bring warmth is my reason,
My name is spring.

Imran Alam, Grade 6
Midlothian Middle School, VA

The Battle

The sky is gray.
I smell the gun and cannon smoke.
I can hear gunfire everywhere.
I can feel the raindrops on my face.
I taste the rain now.

Henry Comber, Grade 4
Waller Mill Fine Arts Magnet School, VA

Brutal Trail

I dream like a bird soaring in the sky it doesn't matter, if it's day or night
The water is just like ice but it has the color of dice
I would love to go to the moon but it shapes like a loop
As I walk along the trail, with black clouds on top
For a little minute, down came some hail
As the wind blew upon my face
I didn't admire, for a little jump I go a little bit higher
A deer from the woods, scampered along
With its shiny color like golden yellow
As I walked along, I saw a figure of a snake
The figure is like a large rope but as I look closer, it's a large vine
The wind danced around me as I walked
It was 12:00 p.m. and there was a full moon
I wish I was home, near the fireplace
I walked like a lonely soul from nowhere
I walked from here and there
Soon I felt something stretching inside me,
Like I'm going to be something else
But then I feel a little bit ill I can feel my bones stretching
Very soon, I look at myself, I look like a large wolf
Then at last I gave a long howl

Anthony Vang, Grade 5
East Mooresville Intermediate School, NC

Pencil

Life stinks whenever you make new friends
They always have these little evil creatures biting their bodies.
I have no eraser anymore it is horrible one of those creatures bit it off!
You never know what is going to happen when you get picked up.
You could get snapped or bit. It stinks.
Noooo I am being picked up don't do that ow snap crunch!!!

Dan Fritz, Grade 5
Rye Elementary School, NH

Matthew's Life Lessons

I have learned that if it's sour, most fifth graders will eat it.
I have learned that there is always another book to read.
I have learned that you don't always have to like your friends.
I have learned that you should always know where your wallet is.
I have learned that eventually every pet dies.
I have learned that it's okay to not like every book.
I have learned that your family is always growing.
I have learned that your brother isn't always your friend.
I have learned that you're not always going to be the best in the class.
I have learned that watching TV isn't always bad.
I have learned that teachers aren't always your friends.

Matthew Suffern, Grade 5
Northside Elementary School, SC

Blue

Blue is the color of the ocean that so many lives were lost on.
Blue is the color of the sky that the north and south fought under.
Blue is part of the United States flag.
Blue is a helpful color.

Zac Cowden, Grade 4
Waller Mill Fine Arts Magnet School, VA

Weeping Willow

An old willow
Just sittin' all lonely like
Many times climbed
Jumped
Or swung from.

Now it's winter,
And poor old tree
Looks like a hungry dog
Just hankrin' for some friends

Little kids,
Playin' n' laughin'
Lyin' back against its trunk,
After a hard day's play.

Now tree's sad and lonely
Like a hungry dog
Just hankrin' for some friends.

Cubby Arvin-DiBlasio, Grade 6
Manchester Elementary/Middle School, VT

Sweet Sounds

I wake up in the morning
hearing sweet sounds.
Beautiful sounds of parades.

As the wind gently blows,
I hear a soft voice.
It said "follow the sound,
follow the sound."

William Medellin, Grade 5
Courthouse Road Elementary School, VA

As…

As loud as a trumpet
As mean as a dinosaur
As scary as a witch
This is how my sister is

Elizabeth Sydnor, Grade 5
Courthouse Road Elementary School, VA

I Wonder…

I wonder why the grass isn't yellow,
I bet it would distract a very young fellow.
I wonder why crocodiles don't even fly,
That would surely catch someone's eye.
I wonder who had the time to make words,
That would really give me a nerve.
I wonder why the time doesn't go to 5:545,
Then time would really have to fly.
I wonder who thought of musical notes,
I mean who has the time,
I would just lose my mind.

Olivia Capraro, Grade 6
Dr Edward Ricci School, RI

Nightfall

I look outside and see…
A dazzling sunset…
A swing set and porch,
And plants.
Silent as night begins to fall,
Growing darker,
Darker still,
Fading off behind a hill,
Until night falls,
And the stars begin to shine.

Emily Hammond, Grade 4
Atkinson Academy Elementary School, NH

Park

Long lines
Roller coaster zooming around the tracks
White lights
Dark blue sky
Screaming people
Yelling on the rides
Very fun and exciting
Thrilling experiences
Thrilling
Thrilling
Thrilling

Jack Caron, Grade 4
Maple Wood Elementary School, NH

Me

FAST
Quick, speedy, light, gravity
I chewed gum so fast it got a cavity.

MOVIE
Flick, film, tape, DVD
I watched the movie and then I had tea.

SLEEP
Slumber, relaxing, nap, doze
Sometimes my mom wakes me up with a hose.

JUMP
Bounce, reap, spring, hop
If you jump you feel a little pop.

Patrick Farney, Grade 5
Olde Providence Elementary School, NC

Flower

F is for fantastic look.
L is for lovable.
O is for outrageous color.
W is for wonderful smell.
E is for enormous petals.
R is for a rose that shines in bright sunlight

Andrea Mejia, Grade 5
Woodlawn Elementary School, VA

The American Flag

The stars and stripes stand on our flag. The red stands for blood, war, and courage. Blue stands for justice and freedom. White stands for purity. The stripes stand for the original 13 colonies that our ancestors found. The stars mean the 50 states of our country. Stars symbolize heaven and the men who gave their lives for our freedom. We get the colors from the soldiers bravery, courage, and respect. The lives soldiers gave show they want freedom and liberty for our country. When a soldier stands on the battlefield they know that what they're doing is right and I respect their bravery and courage. Without them we would not know what terror our country would be under. The soldiers stand for our country.

Owen Gould, Grade 5
Queens Creek Elementary School, NC

The Weather's Way

When the skies are gray, I say "its time to play!" I put on my raincoat, my hat, and my boots
I go outside. Then the weather changed. It was hot like a summer's day.
I went inside, put on my bathing suit, and got the water hose.
I went outside again, and I yelled to the sky, "Whatever you do now, it better not make me cry!
Cause you keep changing, and it's making me mad!
So, stop changing or I'll just stay inside for the rest of the day."
The clouds made a sound like evil laughter, and the thunder roared.
I stomped back in the house with nothing to say.
Then I squatted down on the couch to look outside for the rest of the day.

Katey Martin, Grade 4
Edwards Elementary School, SC

Float

So much potential and capability, only restrained by my own immaturity.
I would try to break free but I was defeated again and again,
it as as if I was drowning in the ocean as soon as I got my head above water
another wave would come crashing down on top of me.
I live like a prisoner constantly in trouble with no privileges.
All because I pushed the rules to see how far their boundaries would move.
I have finally realized fighting the water is pointless
to stay out of trouble I must learn to float.

Logan McAbee, Grade 6
Berry Shoals Intermediate School, SC

Pink

Pink looks like strawberry yogurt that I eat every morning. Pink sounds like popping popcorn fresh from the popper. Pink smells like damp clothes immediately being put into the dryer. Pink tastes like a chewy cherry taffy as it dissolves in my mouth. Pink feels like a dewy flower on a summer morning.

Katie Kozel, Grade 5
Holy Cross Elementary School, DE

Emmalee's Life Lessons

I have learned gum doesn't go well with shoes.
I have learned that you can't mail a letter without a stamp.
I have learned that brothers are not always annoying.
I have learned not to change the subject when I'm in trouble.
I have learned that you cannot grow a lizard like a plant.
I have learned to make sure my cat is out from under my house, before I close the latch.
I have learned that my mom is a superhero.
I have learned that jumping out of a tree doesn't mean you'll always land right-side up.
I have learned never to ask my dad for the weather.
I have learned not to wrestle with a chunky boy.
I have learned that being a daredevil is not for me.
I have learned that family is EVERYTHING.

Emmalee Rawlings, Grade 5
Northside Elementary School, SC

Oh Homework Oh Homework

Oh homework oh homework
I wish you could fly high in the sky

Oh homework oh homework
I wish I could flush you down the toilet

Oh homework oh homework
I would rather have my hair like a mullet

Oh homework oh homework
I would rather walk down the street with a clown suit on

Bailey Lankford, Grade 5
Cool Spring Elementary School, NC

The Shiny Shiny Star

The shiny shiny star
So little, so far
In the dark sky
But it's still bright.

It gives us hope
And becomes a rope
For us to climb
Up the right path.

The star is light
In the dark night
To help us find
Our way home right.

It makes us happy
By lighting so shiny
In which we smile
From now and forever.

Thanh Nguyen, Grade 6
School of International Studies at Meadowbrook, VA

Hockey

H itting it's a contact sport.
O utstanding there is lots of action.
C lobbering people with ease.
K nowing there's still penalties.
E veryone still hits as they please.
Y ou'll always know you still have fun.

Alex Lehman, Grade 5
C Hunter Ritchie Elementary School, VA

Tornado

A gentle breeze goes over,
the plain of Arizona.
Everything wet; soaked.
Animals come back out in the moody sun,
lighting thunders in the distance.
Hard to believe a tornado was just here.

Paul Brown, Grade 5
Oak View Elementary School, VA

The Game

My mind races
as the clock on the wall yells
that there is nine seconds
in the game that had
accelerating moments
where you just wanted to scream to the world,
"Hey clap for my team,
clap for the spirit,
clap for this game!"
As the seconds on the clock tick away
my energy pushes out from within me
to steal the ball when the game means the most
I dribble as fast as I can
and I make the winning basket
just as the buzzer yells,
"Hey the game is over! You won!"
Score: 51-49.

Lily Sexton, Grade 6
East Mooresville Intermediate School, NC

Snug with Family

Lying in bed watching a movie
With my sisters, parents and dogs,
We have ice cream, popcorn and smoothies.
All of us are eating like hogs.

Our teardrops are like rainfall to the dogs.
Buttercup and Muffin were laughing and crying too.
Then here comes a scary part
We all yell "AHHH OHHH!"

Safe and sound in the bed,
Loved and adored like little princesses.
I have a fluffy pillow under my head
With my teddy bear Ted.

Sleeping like a bear in hibernation
Our snoring was like thunder storms and earthquakes
Dreams of soccer and band and all of the above
The next day we do it all over again.

Madison Jay Ronnow, Grade 5
East Mooresville Intermediate School, NC

I Wish

I wish I could be a pilot.
I would be flying to Hawaii on a long flight.
I'd start my loud engine,
And the doors and hatches would close.
I'd push on my smooth thrusters,
And my copilot would check the system,
And away we'd go!
We are in the air!
I look all around. All I can see is puffy white clouds.
Hawaii awaits on a sunset horizon.

Michael Marinosci, Grade 6
Wyman Elementary School, RI

Colors

Many colors have meanings to me
Some are scary, so you may want to flee!
So read along and discover
The colors that you'll uncover

Evergreen green reminds me of the lush grass
That blooms together in a large mass
Flamingo pink makes me think of happy, exciting days
When I like to go outside and gaze

Cadet blue reminds me of times when I was sad
When I see those images, it really makes me mad!
Hearty red is love to me
Since it fills me with glee!

Sandy white wants me to have a normal life
And that includes having a wife
Trenchy black makes me think of scary times
Especially when I dream of those really bad mimes!

So as you can see, colors can be any shape or size
Each having its own little prize
I hope you enjoyed reading this poem
And next time, I'll write one about a little gnome!

Andrew Garcia, Grade 5
Clover Hill Elementary School, VA

Love

Love is an oven because it keeps getting warmer.
Love is a rock because it never breaks.
Love is an ocean because it keeps on going.
Love is a tree because it keeps on growing every day.

Lauren DeRocili, Grade 5
Holy Cross Elementary School, DE

Home

Home is where I eat and play
Home is where I "hit the hay."

Home is where I eat a snack.
Home is where I pack my backpack.

Home is where I run around.
Home is where I settle down.

Graham Walker, Grade 5
C Hunter Ritchie Elementary School, VA

Too Fast

When I was afraid you comforted me.
When I was bad you taught me.
And all of those years when I was helping you,
And smile and stay for a while.
But now you are gone and I am alone.
It just happened too fast.

Thomas Kenneally, Grade 6
Berry Shoals Intermediate School, SC

Haterz

Haterz are
unappreciaters not celebraters
when they see you
filled with joy
they try to make you
unemployed and when
you stumble and
sometimes fall
they'll be there
to see it all
when you make
mistakes they'll
be there to point it out
and laugh at it they want
to make you feel so small
that you'll be a tiny crumb
to them so kick them to the curb or
ignore them even though they might be in your face

Ary'Anna Johnson, Grade 4
William T Brown Elementary School, NC

Appleicious

Succulent apple
exploding with flavor.
Pungent flavor of sweet and sour.
The smell — enticing
I just wanted to savor it
never finish.
Intricate bumps and grooves
natures beauty
in one small package.
The skin a mixture of darks and lights
Citrusy aroma with a strawberry sweetness
Take a bite — ahh!

Josh Monesmith, Grade 4
Maple Wood Elementary School, NH

Lost

I can't find my iPod
I can't find my bed
I can't find my TV
I think I have lost my head.

I can't find my candy
I can't find the food
I can't even tell who's who!

Now I am having a bad day
That is, until I found my glasses,
Now I can see everything oh so clear
My face is full of joy, can't you tell my dear?

There are my things, right there on the ground,
I thought I was lost but now I'm found.

Malik Baptiste, Grade 6
Benjamin Syms Middle School, VA

Chocolate

I am rich.
I am dark.

I am luscious.
I am tart.

I am chocolate.
My bold taste.

I hid dark.

Some ask why should I be.
Chocolate.

All know I am.
Chocolate.
Chocolate.
I am.

I am rich.

I am white.
I am savory.

I am sweet.
I am chocolate.
My bold look.
I shine white.

Some ask how can I be.

Chocolate.
Most say am not.
I know I am.

Chocolate.

Chocolate.
I'll be.

Chris Harwood, Grade 5
North Windy Ridge School, NC

Basketball

Basketball is cool
Basketball is fun
It's not like football not at all
You don't carry it
You bounce it, that is all
You shoot it and hear the crowd roar
Saying, "Go, go!" like a pro
That is what I like about basketball
So come on and have a ball!

Chasity Thurmond, Grade 5
Courthouse Road Elementary School, VA

Colors

The shimmering sky holds them in wisps,
the oceans wash them in and out with the tide,
the deserts keep the blinding color within,
Beautiful blues of all shades dance in the skies,
Aquas and greens swirl in the oceans,
Oranges and pure golds shine within the deserts,
Spring holds all colors far and wide in the woods,
Winter's icy white and silver covers the ground like magic,
Summer brings the cool lime greens and hot pinks,
Spring's miraculous colors in the sunsets are amazing,
Winters have miracles too,
Summer's luxurious stillness brings peace in many colors,
The color purple brings luck,
all of the colors of the rainbow make up the world,
looking down to earth from outer space you can tell,
the earth is full of many colors.

Stephanie Brougher, Grade 6
Chapin Middle School, SC

Love

Love is a squishy chair,
That warms you with its hugs,
And sits all day long with you,
Making you happy and snug.
It just sits there, never changing,
All its life and forever,
It is always very strong,
Even as its life goes one,
And is slowly aging.
Love stands up tall,
And makes you happy when you're down,
If this old chair belonged to you, you'd never wear a frown.
It's for anyone who passes by to take a sit right there,
For so many have been made happy,
By this squishy chair.

Holly MacAlpine, Grade 5
Rye Elementary School, NH

Sad Day

I'm sad when people talk about me.
I'm sad when I don't get my way.
I'm sad when people say I'm ugly.
People say I don't need any friends.
I feel like I am cute whenever anyone says I'm ugly.
It's not going to hurt me.
I was sad when I was put back in the third grade.
I am sad because I am frustrated.

Chantal Wyatt, Grade 5
Cooper Elementary School, VA

The Creek

The creek is a place for me
I am Karana in the sand
Like a shell on the beach.
On my feet.

The creek is a place for me
Where I can look for things
Happily with my friends
I am as happy as a bee buzzing

The water so silky
The trees so green
My friends laugh, and play.
We try to catch tadpoles every day.

We search and search
But we find nothing
Except the friendships
That we have now.

The creek is a place for me
My friends and also family
The creek is a place for me.

Maria LoVullo, Grade 5
East Mooresville Intermediate School, NC

Holly

Holly is a Twizzler.
The color of bright red to show
A happy personality.
Bendy and flexible;
A gymnast up for any challenge.
Ends untwisting to reach out
And wrap her arms around you,
Just to comfort and protect you
From everything else
Going on in the world.
A straw to suck up your problems
Or a chewy delight just to comfort you.
A Twizzler that anybody
Would love to have a piece of.

Caroline Peay, Grade 6
CrossRoads Middle School, SC

March

March comes in surprise.
March "comes in like a lion.
It leaves like a lamb."
The flowers start blooming,
and the birds are coming back.

Katie Meeks, Grade 5
Wakefield Forest Elementary School, VA

Clean/Dirty

Clean
Beautiful, spotless
Mopping, scrubbing, washing
Mops, buckets, soap, water
Littering, ignoring, disgusting
Icky, nasty
Dirty

Mac Ukrop, Grade 5
St Christopher's School, VA

In the Summer Light

The flowers bloomed
In the summer light
The sky was blue
The animals played
In the summer light
The butterflies danced
The animals played
The world was alive
The butterflies danced
The fairies sang
The world was alive
The night would never come
The fairies sang
The sky was blue
The night would never come
The flowers bloomed

Katie Cole, Grade 5
Rye Elementary School, NH

Pumpkins

Do pumpkins want to be carved in a day?
Do they want to sit on a stack of hay?
Do they want to be empty inside?
Do they want a face or an eye?

Caila McHugh, Grade 5
Trinity Christian School, VA

Love

Love is a kitten,
It is soft.

Love is a gold necklace,
It is valuable.

Love is a fire on a cold day,
It is warm.

Love is a poem,
It is comforting and peaceful.

Kelsi McBarron, Grade 5
Holy Cross Elementary School, DE

Swim

S peed
W ater
I gnition
M aster

Mason Belawske, Grade 4
Chesterfield School, NH

Branches

Branches are twisty
As they reach
Like a pair of arms
Who want a hug.

A cold wind blows
As a bird flies by
When it flew into a birch tree
Its fluffy tail brushed my skin.

A bird chirps in the distance
A deer snaps a twig
With all these things around me
I feel at home.

Bethany Pelotte, Grade 4
Bethlehem Elementary School, NH

Jesus

Jesus
Lord's son
Forgave our sins
Christ is my Savior
Emmanuel

Daniel Seitz, Grade 4
Trinity Christian School, VA

Snowmen

Snowmen teach you how to have fun.
Snowmen melt in the sun.
Snowmen are so weird.
Mine has a black beard.
When it is hot snowmen are done.

Drece Cabrera, Grade 4
Battlefield Elementary School, VA

My Dream

My dream is to stop world hunger
Everyone should have food
Now and then I may wonder
What are the things I can do?

I can donate to a food drive
For people in need
And if I was to try
Then I can succeed.

People will have food
And water to drink
It will be great to stop hunger
At least that's what I think.

Kikkio Alvarado, Grade 6
Hand Middle School, SC

Birds

If I could fly like a bird
I would try to say one word

I would say, "Hello, Hello"
I would say it wherever I go.

People would just smile at me
As they pass me up in a tree.

And when I see a bird fly by
I would say the word, "Bye-bye."

Savionna Glover, Grade 4
St Helena Elementary School, SC

Artemis Fowl

A mazing with computers
R ascal
T ime traveler
E lves are his allies
M illionaire and mastermind
I ntelligent
S neaky

F olly
O bsessed with computers
W ell known
L oves to be a criminal

Mitchell Brazier, Grade 5
Trinity Christian School, VA

Where I'm From

I am from a family that loves me so well
Wherever I go, it's like a hotel

There is so much excitement
And so much to eat
After 11, I still can't sleep

Friends are always pranking
Shamira is always dancing
I sure wouldn't be surprised to see
A dog laughing

With Falana, Angela, Janasa, and Jackie
You can always turn around with someone smiling

I'm close to pigtails, barettes, and dresses
Going to school, everything is interesting

I'm usually home, not really traveling
I am from the great city that goes by,

Manning, SC

Keshauna Goines, Grade 4
Whittaker Elementary School, SC

My Little Sister

My little sister is very, very sweet,
   but she's not very neat.
      She usually gets in trouble,
         she's not humble.

      My little sister loves her things.
         She likes her rings.
            I didn't tell you yet,
               she also likes her tea set.

         When she has a fit,
            she will hit.
               She will jump for joy,
            when she gets a new toy.

Hannah Grimmett, Grade 4
Queens Creek Elementary School, NC

Green

Green is a soft crunchy leaf
Green is soft music playing on the radio
Green is the feeling of your heart swelling with joy
Green is the sight of an angel sleeping
Green is the smell of good 'n juicy Smarties
Green made it rain M&M's
Green is the moon on a peaceful night
Green is a book with a fresh new cover
Green is a human diving in the water WHOOSH
Green is footsteps pitter patter pitter patter

Raekwon Seibles, Grade 4
Tabernacle Elementary School, NC

Video Games

I play video games every day.
I play video games my way.
I play video games half of the time.
I play video games that are mine.
Day in and day out thumbs on the controllers.
I would lose my mind if somebody stole 'em.

Gabe Spruill, Grade 5
Cooper Elementary School, VA

The Bear with No Hair

Once there was a bear who had no hair
He thought I must be rare,
He thought and sat
Maybe I could wear a hat,
You must be thinking of hair on your head
No it was mustache hair instead,
His hair wouldn't show
Because his lips wouldn't grow,
There was a rat who made fun of him,
He did not get mad
All he said was bad, bad, bad.

Alonso Carter, Grade 4
Courthouse Road Elementary School, VA

1929

It's 1929
My family's not doing fine

We have no money
so we go to the land of "Milk and Honey"

We're running out of food
and every moment I'm in a sad mood

My parent found a job
now I don't sob

Hoover is to blame
but FDR won't do the same.

The New Deal is here
Thank God as the U.S. cheers.

TJ Ford, Grade 5
West Hartsville Elementary School, SC

Spaghetti and Meatballs

Spaghetti without meatballs
is like a house without the roof and walls,
or the sky without the stars
or the little green men on Mars.
There would be no taste,
it would only be like paste.
So next time the waiter calls,
make sure you order SPAGHETTI AND MEATBALLS!!!

Jordan Crocker, Grade 5
Micro Pine Level Elementary School, NC

Green

Ireland is green
With shamrocks all over the scene
Broccoli looks like a tree
But tastes disgusting to me
While the Celtic fans cheer
The Irish drink their beer

Daniel Langella, Grade 5
St Mary School, RI

War

With fake action figures —
The boys
Played and laughed
When the fake action figure
Fell off the table.
War
With real people —
Losing their lives
Everyone crying
When the real person
Fell off the cliff.

Frost Wood, Grade 4
St Christopher's School, VA

Can You Imagine...

School with no sheets
baseball with no cleats.

Soccer with no goal
the Panthers winning a Super Bowl.

Bees without honey
movie stars without a dime of money.

Earth with no water
Lunch without even one tater-totter.

Cafes without meat
a house lacking heat.

A book with no words
a sky with no birds.

No I cannot, I might say
Not here, not today.

Daniel Zimmermann, Grade 5
Olde Providence Elementary School, NC

Alone*

So much depends upon
The massive prickly pine
Scent of crushed needles
Alone by the brook

Jay Sherrill, Grade 5
Cool Spring Elementary School, NC
*Inspired by William Carlos Williams

My Grandpa

My grandpa, you are my hero, my leader,
But I just call you grandpa.
You and me love to walk on the beach,
Or just be stuck in a car together.
Whatever it is that we do you make it a fun thing to do.
You are my grandpa you and me together forever whatever the weather.

Gabriella Alves, Grade 6
St Rocco School, RI

Green Is Lucky

Green is like grass streaming through the wind.
Green is like clovers happy and lucky
Green is like lime jelly beans sweet and yummy
She is one of the most important things in the world because she flies on tree.
She makes everything happy.
You can welcome her anywhere.
Green is like glitter, pretty and proud.
You can see her at a soccer game because that is her favorite sport.
She tries everything and does her best in everything
Her favorite food is kiwi and she makes a good team with anybody
I'm just like her.

Emily Walker, Grade 4
Youngsville Elementary School, NC

Sunset Beach

Pitter-patter of crabs going to a
Bright blue ocean. Cold, wet ocean
Blaring in my ears. Roaring waves crashing on the
Shore. Water lapping my toes, in and
Out, with the tide. Soft,
Gritty sand tickling my feet, hard and
Wonderful.
Fingers of the sun stretch out to meet the
Ocean, colored like a parade. Red, orange, blue,
Purple — all the colors a canvas of beauty. Glamorous rays,
Begging for attention, reach and touch the many shells, like glass
In a church. Sand gray-white, a plain but marvelous
Background of a portrait of peace. Palms
Adding to the peace, making the view an amazing
Photograph. Sunset beach, the canvas
Of beauty.

Christy Coghlan, Grade 6
Chapin Middle School, SC

My Brother

I was waiting in the sitting room at the hospital.
I fell asleep and dreamed of me and my brother playing in the woods.
My aunt woke me and pulled me into a hospital room.
My mom was half asleep on the bed.
Mallory was sitting on my grandma's lap.
Dr. Nick walked into the room, and handed a bundle of cloth to my dad.
My dad looked inside and grinned.
He handed it to me, and I saw my brother for the first time.
I knew from that moment on that we would be best friends since, and we are.

Clay Blackwood, Grade 6
Berry Shoals Intermediate School, SC

Family

I was walking through the woods one day,
And I came across a small brown dog on my way.
The dog was sad, frightened, and alone,
It looked like this dog did not have a home.
I took the dog to my mom and said,
"Can we keep him and name him Fred?"
The little dog that was once frightened and sad,
Now had a loving home which made me glad.

Thomas Peterson, Grade 5
Courthouse Road Elementary School, VA

Rain

I was at the beach
And I was swimming like a dolphin,
Swimming in a big pool
And the big pool
Was the ocean.

And it started to rain,
It rained all over me.
Instead of a sunny day,
It was a rainy day.

Rain dances as it falls.
It has parties in puddles.
Rain can be good or bad.
In this case it was bad.

The bad thing about rain
Is that it can ruin good days.
The good thing about rain
Is it can cool you off and end droughts.
This is rain
And you should respect it.

Chase Popple, Grade 5
East Mooresville Intermediate School, NC

Share the Love

Love is something you have,
No matter how you feel, it's still there
Even if you're filled with sorrow or frustration
There is always love to give.

Shelby Holmes, Grade 5
Queen's Grant Community School, NC

A Day with a Duck

Little ducklings swimming here and there,
Swimming down a river everywhere,
Quacking very loudly when they see someone,
But then they are quiet when the day is done,
Sleeping quietly in their nest,
That is when they are quiet best,
But when the sun comes on over the hill,
You can see every little duckling's bill.

Elizabeth "Burke" Kelleher, Grade 6
Linkhorne Middle School, VA

Friendship the Meaning of a True Friend

Friends forever!!
Friends for life!!
They keep your secrets locked up tight.
They like you for who you are
and never betray you at all.
They make you happy when you're sad
and always calm you when you're mad
Friends forever!!
Friends for life!!
They keep your secrets locked up tight.

Michaela Vivian, Grade 6
Metcalf School, RI

Seasons

Summer, spring, winter and fall
   And fall
   How do you love them all?
Don't you love them all?
   No
The one I love most is fall
   Mine is when the rain will fall
That's not the one I love most of all
Mine is when the snow will fall
   Really?
Yes, I do like that one
   Yes, I do like that one
They fall small as dots though many different shapes and sizes
That's how we know
   That's how we know
We love it most when
   We love it most when
The rain and snow will fall   The snow and rain will fall

Meghan Holdredge, Grade 5
North Windy Ridge School, NC

Trees

Somehow trees are the glory of the Earth,
The glowing red maple, the sharp smelling pine,
They protect hidden places:
Crystal water and sweet smelling groves.
The forest is filled with secrets,
And the trees are its guardians,
Tall and fierce,
Small and strong,
Together they make an unstoppable army,
An impenetrable fortress.
And in them lie many things,
Nests of bird, and sparkling streams,
Green moss and dappled sunlight.
But the biggest secret of all,
Is that outside them is turmoil,
But inside is peace,
Which few know about,
But even less find.

Mary Connor, Grade 4
Riverview Elementary School, VA

The Bright Night

Bright star in the night.
Pitter patter of the rain.
Watch the clouds drift by.
Sara Young, Grade 5
North Windy Ridge School, NC

The Last Lap

The last lap.
It pushes me forward.
The last lap.
My goggles fog up.
The last lap.
The cool water
rushes against my face.
The last lap.
My hands
meet the
welcoming concrete.
The last lap.
It is complete.
I take a breath and
congratulate myself
Winston Harvey, Grade 5
Oak View Elementary School, VA

Where I'm From

I am from a fabulous family
That helps me when I am in trouble

I am from fantastic foods
Like fish, chicken to sweet peas,
Rice and collard greens

I am from gatherings like cookouts
Sleepovers and church

I am from unbelievable places
Like D.C., Las Vegas
And a small town called Orangeburg

I am from hobbies
Playing games, watching football,
Even playing basketball

That is where I'm from
D'Andrá Thompson, Grade 4
Whittaker Elementary School, SC

David

D avid
E ats
F or
G ood
H ealth
Charles Eugene, Grade 4
St Helena Elementary School, SC

Friendless

"No one?" said Mom,
"No friends at all?

No one named
  Paul or
    Jerry or
      Larry or
        Mary?

No one to hear you in the hall?
No one to catch you if you fall?

No one?
No one at all?

Wait, you do have a friend:
You have me!
We will be friends until the end!"
Hannah Foster, Grade 6
Cape Henry Collegiate School, VA

Books

A book unread is sad,
hoping to be opened and read
yet it's unopened, untouched.
Andy McLinden, Grade 5
The Compass School, RI

Birds

Chirping away
They didn't know where to lay.
Not one, but two
One red, one blue.

Trying to make a nest
So they could rest.
You want to hum
Then winter comes.

Fly away, fly away
Look at the birds chirping away.
Fly away, fly away
They will be back another day.
Tyler Willis, Grade 4
Appomattox Elementary School, VA

Love Hurts

Being lied to it hurts.
Not being loved it hurts.
I wish to be loved
every day and every time.
Loving can be so easy.
Getting loved is hard.
I can give love, can you?
Antonique Boone, Grade 5
Cooper Elementary School, VA

Celebrations

Holidays
Special treat
Making holiday wishes
Has a joyful touch
Celebrations
Lexie Miller, Grade 4
Trinity Christian School, VA

My Friend

You are my laughter
When I am sad
You are my joy
When I am mad
You are the song
Lifted in the air
You are the answers
To my prayer
You are the crazy
You are the weird
And with you
I shall never fear
Among the dark
You are the star
You stick out
Wherever you are
You make me happy
When I am down
You are the funny, crazy class clown
You know I don't want to pretend
That you aren't my very best friend
Megan Anderson, Grade 6
Prince of Peace Catholic School, SC

New Flower

The Hana Kimi looks up to the sun
While her sprite has so much fun!
Never was there such a dance,
Everywhere there was a prance.
Rachel Conrad-Burton, Grade 4
Waller Mill Fine Arts Magnet School, VA

The Night

The night is so soft and sweet.
You see things differently there.
It's like the lead on this pencil
Sometimes there, but then it breaks.
The sun, that's what breaks the night
Night…
Night…
Night…
What started the Earth
And will end it
Like the end of this poem
…Night.
Rob Mitchell, Grade 5
Buffalo Elementary School, SC

My Friend

I hear the kind, encouraging, and unselfish
Words that come out of her mouth.

I feel her gentle, caring touch
When she hugs me to make me feel better
When I am depressed.

I smell the wonderful fragrance
That always follows her
Wherever she goes.

I taste the warm English tea
She makes to cheer me up
And show her love for me.

I see my honest, kind
Best friend.

Baylie Myers, Grade 4
Lockhart Elementary School, SC

Blind Memory

The stars shine in my eyes
It reminds me of my life
Little snowflakes dance across the sky
Though the absence of my childhood is still a wonder

Cynthia Wang, Grade 6
Wakefield Forest Elementary School, VA

Friends

Friends are glass.
You have to be careful not to break them.

Friends are trees.
They grow up and become different.

Friends are pets.
They keep you company when you need it.

Friends are diamonds.
They are very fragile.

Kaitlin Bergold, Grade 5
Holy Cross Elementary School, DE

Nature's Delight Song

I am a wise old star.
I am a cloud bringing rain to the deserts.
I am a tree waving my leaves in the wind.
I am a cactus sprouting fruit.
I am a bird circling an island.
I am a bat looking down on the world.
I am a beautiful flower.
I am a squirrel eating nuts in my favorite tree.
I am a galaxy with all the little animals.
I am alive, I am alive, I am alive.

Kevin Szmyd, Grade 5
Rye Elementary School, NH

Sorrow

Life is full of sorrow
Life is full of pain
I see a mother who for once wants to gain
Children's clothes all wore and tore
Don't have enough money to go to the store
Can't stay in one place
Have to migrate
Pretty soon sorrow will pass
Peace at last
Life without tears and pain
And the mother with seven children
will finally gain.

Payla LaFountaine, Grade 6
Dr Edward Ricci School, RI

The Middle Toe

I'm the middle toe
All squished in the middle
I feel stinky and sweaty
This sock is blocking my view
I can't see and I'm not blind!
I'm afraid of the dark please someone help me
I feel broke inside
I'm never free help me
Let me breathe
I'm claustrophobic inside this shoe!
I'm hot as a flaming fire —
Ouch!
That ball hurt me
Yeah, I see light
Sometimes, it is worth it
Getting hurt!

Phoebe Parker, Grade 5
Rye Elementary School, NH

Random Poem

In an open field, we stand.
His hands on my arms, mine on his.
We draw close.
I look longingly into his eyes,
He looks longingly into mine,
As if he knows.
His hair, it blows so perfectly in the wind, so perfect.
He pulls me to him, takes his hand,
Pulls my head toward his.
This Is It.
His breath on my neck, sends a shiver down my spine.
I close my eyes, he closes his.
So close…
THUD!!!
I'm on the ground, in my room, about to kiss my pillow.
Disgusted, I push it away, and get back in bed.
"Dream On" is all that I can say.

Harley Bourgeois, Grade 6
Holbrook Middle School, NC

A Bird

I dreamed
I was a bird
Among the colorful sky
Watching the clouds go by
Peacefully.
Kioshi Lettsome, Grade 5
Cooper Elementary School, VA

Us

Madison and Lilly
we are so silly
we're great
we rule
we're really cool
we're up
we're down
we're all around
we're here
we're there
we're everywhere
Hey, where you going?
I don't care, I'm outta here!
Madison White, Grade 4
The Compass School, RI

Exploring

I love going to the creek
Seeing the huge logs fallen across it
Balancing on them,
Trying not to fall
I am prince of all
That is exploring
Robert Lamb, Grade 6
Wakefield Forest Elementary School, VA

Nutty Walnut

Your color is so bland
As I hold you in my hand
I crunch you with ease
With a nutcracker squeeze

Your taste is quite rare
Yet I would easily share
So when I swallow you down
I don't have a frown
Allen Jacot, Grade 5
Manchester Elementary School, NC

Rob

R ob
S tudies
T echnology
U sing
V enn diagrams
De-quarious Major, Grade 4
St Helena Elementary School, SC

Psalm of Jessica

Oh, Highest gracious Lord
For all you have done
For all you have given
I love you and thank you
The food on the table
The clothes on my skin
The house I dwell in
I thank You forever
The Earth I dwell on
I thank you forever
The Earth you have made
The animals
Are no bigger than my love,
Jessica Park, Grade 4
Trinity Christian School, VA

Spring Is Here

Birds chirp all day long
Birds fly in a formation
Birds fly everywhere
Richard Lee, Grade 5
Pocalla Springs Elementary School, SC

A Psalm

O Lord, You are so strong,
O Lord, You are so great,
Lord, You are as merciful
As a forgiving father,
I thank You for Your blessings,
I thank You for all Your grace.
Alexis Huggins, Grade 5
Trinity Christian School, VA

I Am…

I am special and serious.
I wonder when she'll come.
I hear her laughs in my mind.
I see her as a flower in the middle.
I want to be with her.
I am special and serious.

I pretend she's with me when I'm alone.
I feel her heart beat.
I touch her hand with joy.
I worry that she won't come back.
I cry when I think of her.
I am special and serious.

I understand she's gone.
I say that I love her.
I dream…we're together.
I try to stop and think about her.
I hope that's her in the sky.
I am special and serious.
Franco Guevara, Grade 6
Beech Springs Intermediate School, SC

Write

My mind
Is sparkling
My ideas
Are flowing
The afternoon is quiet
I listen
And write
Shira Steinberg, Grade 6
Wakefield Forest Elementary School, VA

Daycare

While at daycare many sounds are heard
Wahh!
of the infants and the toddlers yelling
STOP!
or when they are fighting over toys
Ahh!
that's when you hear the teachers yell
TIMEOUT!
and the
BANG!
of their feet kicking and the
BOOM!
of the teachers running to stop them.
Darian Layne, Grade 6
Salem Church Middle School, VA

Sleeping

Sleeping
lazily
hourly
aggressively
willfully
meaningfully
Sleeping
in the shower
on the couch
under the bed
on the floor
in the tree
Sleeping
because he hasn't slept for weeks
when he got home
although he had a soccer game
because it was late
although he was hungry
Sleeping
John Haller, Grade 6
St Mary's School, SC

Ocean

Very big and vast
Sometimes can be dangerous
But is very fun.
Vincent Sharikas, Grade 4
Grace Miller Elementary School, VA

Home

When I get home I get on the phone.
Everything is the same, I play my game.
I go to bed I have dreams in my head.
I read a book about a man with a hook.
I ate some spam with some ham.
There was a girl named Pam and she had to scram.
Sam likes ham in a box with a fox.
An ox chases a fox into a box.

Michael Fox, Grade 4
Riverview Elementary School, VA

Grass

When I look at the grass
I think it looks like glass.

The grass is green
and very clean.

I took a ride on my bike
because I wanted to feel what it would be like.

While the grass was moving
it was like watching a movie.

When my day came to an end,
I was dreaming about going back to bed.

Jocelin Gonzalez, Grade 4
Bensley Elementary School, VA

What Bugs Me?

What bugs me is my dog.
He just stares at fog,
He loves to eat frogs
He drinks out of mugs,
He hates the taste of bugs.
He loves to tear up things in the house,
He also chases this one mouse.
He also tore up my mom's blouse,
Just to get back at us for not buying him a doghouse.

Juwan Saunders, Grade 5
Courthouse Road Elementary School, VA

Friends

A friend is someone you can trust.
Someone you can talk to and is fair and just.
They help you discover new things,
Like how to read a book, or to sing.
From preschool to college,
Through years of knowledge,
A friend will make you smile,
And always go the extra mile.
So remember who your friends are,
Either near or far.

Amanda Reid, Grade 6
St Rocco School, RI

A Side You'll Never See

The side you'll never see is an aggressive girl
who has fire in her eyes and a face of fury when she gets mad.
I try to ease my pain and anger by writing this poem.
It helps, but my heart will always be broken.
He left — didn't have a choice, but I will miss him always.
He was my father, the light of my life.
He saw the light. I must listen to my heart and ease it.

Ashley Barcellos, Grade 5
Quidnessett Elementary School, RI

Ode to a Friend

Oh Sarah, oh Sarah
What a great friend to have all the time
You are always there when I get hurt outside
You always ask questions
But I guess that is a good thing
You are good at dodge ball
And when somebody gets mad,
You are always there to fix it.

Cameron Edwards, Grade 5
Vienna Elementary School, NC

No Loveliness

This planet will never be lovely again,
With flowers and birds,
No trash on the ground,
But no, we live in disaster,
With dull colors, no money
And no joy.

Dead birds on the ground,
More killings, less food,
Less rich, more poor,
Can't we live in a world of peace?
Where everyone is living in harmony.

But if we try,
Maybe this world won't be so bad,
We can bring sunshine,
And rainbows and maybe even flowers,
So it may seem like all hope is lost,
But we can bring this world to life somehow!

Mary Reis, Grade 6
Metcalf School, RI

Violin

I'm learning to play a song called "Prelude and Dance."
When I start to play, the notes begin to prance.

I am learning my part,
And trying to memorize it by heart.

I love the music and I love to play.
In fact, I could play all day!

Katherine Flynn, Grade 4
St John Neumann Academy, VA

Granddaddy and Me

I remember that morning, the sun on our backs, the worm on our lines.
The cool summer breeze blowing through our hair.
Granddaddy and me fishing on the pier.
I see the water, still and calm, reflecting the light like a sleek, shining mirror.
I see the fish swimming gracefully in the water like a ballet dancer performing.
We cast out our lines, hoping for the fish to bite.
I felt a tug on my line, a snap of my wrist, and the next thing I knew I had caught my very first fish!
Granddaddy and me fishing on the pier.
After we reeled in that fish; it flopped around on the pier.
It was scaly and slippery, shiny and slimy.
It was a dull sad color of green, like it didn't have any sunlight in life.
My fish.
I was so exited catching my first fish.
That night when we got home, we cooked that fish, my fish, my very own fish.
The one that we had caught, the one that me and my granddaddy had caught.
Granddaddy and me.

Eric Merten, Grade 5
Hunters Woods Elementary School, VA

You Know That Feeling?

You know that feeling? When you're really sad,
Really messed with, really misunderstood, and nobody knows how hard it is for you?
Nobody really knows what you're going through?
And when someone tries to relate they still don't get it?
Don't you just hate it when you're at that age,
Where you're not young enough to be with the kids anymore,
But yet you're still not old enough to hang with the teenagers?
You're at that time where you're all alone and there's nothing you can really do about it…
Nobody can be there for you because you're the only one and you take it out differently than others
You don't talk about it, you keep silent and that makes things worse…
Don't you know that feeling, where you feel like you're the only person on earth that's going through this?
I do, don't worry you're not.
Someone in the world is doing the same thing,
Making the same actions, going through the same phase,
And boy I hope this blows over, I can't take it.
Soon I'll be old enough to hang out with the teens,
I'll have a major growth spurt, and I won't look like an eight year old.
I'll be free to be with whoever I want to be, and nobody can tell me what to do, nobody.
You know that feeling where you think there's hope?
That feeling where things aren't so great,
But you have a good feeling they are going to turn out just awesome?

Skyler Trice, Grade 5
Bell's Crossing Elementary School, SC

Flying High

Birds are the things above all.
They each have a role in life.
A peacock shows off its feathers for beauty in the world.
An eagle sends peace around the world.
A turkey brings fall and soon to be full bellies.
A cardinal brings love to everyone.
A morning dove awakens people and gets them ready for a beautiful day.
A yellow chickadee brings sunshine to the Earth.
And isn't it neat that above all is God, and He is the one who gives thing roles and purposes to all life.

Charlie Kendall, Grade 5
Rye Elementary School, NH

January

January looks like a fresh snow fall
January tastes like hot chocolate on a snowy day
January feels like a brand new year
January smells like snow cream
January sounds like the crunching as you step out into the snow
January is like the smoke rising from a chimney
January is like staring into a winter wonderland
January is a snowflake falling from the sky
January is cold like ice cream
January is the feeling you get when the cold wind blows

Adam Bryant, Grade 4
Tabernacle Elementary School, NC

Shattered Heart

There you stand with nowhere to go.
Trapped by your own lies.
You turned your back against the world,
and look what you have done.

You are unfaithful to yourself and everyone around you.
With a shattered heart,
you walk away from the cold,
lonely world you once knew.
Trapped by your lies,

Unfaithful and Unloved.

Alexandra Sauro, Grade 6
St Rocco School, RI

The Panda Bear

The panda bear, with its black and white hair —
they eat bamboo, so they aren't a scare.

With their bamboo, just like Winnie the Pooh,
my favorite bears are so cute, it's true.

Pandas are furry, never in a hurry,
if they were too fast, they would become blurry.

Though Pooh bear loves honey, pandas may think it's too runny.
They mostly live in China where it's very sunny.

I really like pandas.
I think I might mention, this poem is ending,
it's my own invention.
For me to write more about this lovable bear
this small poem would need an extension!

Madison Bonavita, Grade 6
Our Lady of Lourdes Catholic School, NC

Fire-Crackers

I love the sounds of fire crackers popping in the air,
The BOOMS AND POPS high in the sky
make me laugh and cheer.

Brandi Melton, Grade 4
Edwards Elementary School, SC

Nature with Birds

She sits in class, watching the birds fly by the window.
She urges herself up in her chair, her back straight.
She closes her vacant, sapphire eyes and ponders.

She ignores the friend trying for her attention.

As she daydreams, she thinks about herself.
Herself, flying with the birds.
Her large wings expand into a beautiful assortment of feathers.
She starts to sing as if a bird herself.
Soon, her body transforms into a snowy owl apparition.
She lifts off, deep into the sky.

Then, she awakens,
motionless in front of the class, posing like a bird.

Lydia August, Grade 6
Beacon Middle School, DE

Creeks

C reeks flowing with pure water as clean as can be.
R ounding the bends with a gentle motion.
E very leaf floating and turning in a graceful pattern.
E very stone so smooth and round.
K eeping a slow rhythm with its peaceful sound
S lowly making its way across pastures, forests, and valleys.

Shannon Baird, Grade 5
C Hunter Ritchie Elementary School, VA

Spring

Spring stops the cold of winter,
Like a policeman would stop a speeding car.
Spring is full of creativity and colors
Like an artist with a brush.
Spring is time for new life,
For flowers to grow and buds to blossom
Spring is like a musician
Singing a new and beautiful tune.
Spring is everything
Beautiful, joyful, and full of new opportunities.

Morgan Collins, Grade 5
Wakefield Forest Elementary School, VA

Red

Red smells like smoke when something's on fire
Red feels like roses setting in the sun
Red looks like a fresh apple off the tree
Red is like blood when it is pouring down your skin
Red is my brother getting mad
Red is the color of her glasses
Red is the color of her lips
Red is on the bed
Red is bad it makes me sad
Red is the color of our flag

Brandon Nealey, Grade 4
Tabernacle Elementary School, NC

Rose
Red as dripping blood
Thorns as sharp as knives
Petals in the wind.
Jaqueline Jimenez, Grade 4
Grace Miller Elementary School, VA

Farm/City
Farm
busy, quiet
growing, raising, selling
animals, crops, cars, buildings
rushing, driving, yelling
loud, fast-paced
City
Sam Oien, Grade 6
Floyd T Binns Middle School, VA

Spring Day
Listening quietly
At the banging in the woods
Sitting on a log
Stretched out across
The wide lake.
Feeling the cool water
Brush the feet.
Looking at the clouds,
Picking out animals.
Tasting the cool September air,
Sharp and strong.
Sitting quietly
Listening
Looking
Feeling
Tasting
Smelling
Doing.
Jackie Le, Grade 5
Oak View Elementary School, VA

The Fawn
Fawn covered in spots
Her deep almond eyes staring
So frightened, yet brave
Hannah Baghdadi, Grade 4
Waller Mill Fine Arts Magnet School, VA

Fall and Spring
Fall
Colors, wind,
Raking, baking, shivering
Cold, humid, leaves, bees
Blooming, watering, raining
Flowers, showers
Spring
Tamaira Holmes, Grade 5
St Helena Elementary School, SC

Life
You are born by the Lord to enjoy the essentials in life.
To experience family and love.
To make friends forever.
But be happy when you die because you are letting somebody be born.
Nathan Singleton, Grade 5
Courthouse Road Elementary School, VA

Lizards Oh Lizards
Lizards, oh lizards, you're the coolest pets around
I wish I could see you on a tree upside down.
Lizards are cool, active, and fun.
Noles are fast. Chameleons are slow.
They live in cages, houses, tree, and more.
Lizards, oh lizards, your main foods are
Wax worms, crickets, grasshoppers, and lots more.
Lizards, oh lizards, you like to play, run, jump, and have lots of fun.
I wish I had you. We would be best buds for life and have lots of fun.
Damien Douglas, Grade 4
Courthouse Road Elementary School, VA

Spring
Spring is a beautiful time of year
Use your senses to bring you cheer
Smell the flowers freshly blooming
Smell the pie in the oven
See the depressing gray turn to glowing green
See the beautiful Martins returning from South America
Hear the dog barking at the cat in the tree
Hear the bat cracking as it meets the ball
Taste the water slithering down my throat after working in the yard
Taste the dinner that my grandma made after church
While eating on the porch
Spring is a beautiful time of year
I wish it could be spring all the time
Ryan Vaughan, Grade 4
Lockhart Elementary School, SC

Dreams
Dreams are something that aren't seen,
they show your desires to an extreme.
They can be big or start out small,
but they are the best overall.
Dreams show determination and goals for you,
they analyze what you do.
Dreams can make you happy, angry, or sad,
dreams bring the good out of the bad
They can bring down your confidence or put a smile on your face
yet dreams are only something one can chase.
So never mind the tears and sadness they bring,
only think that dreams can bring happy things.
A dream is an inspiration for all to obtain,
they can keep us calm or drive us insane.
We all experience this feeling that we have within,
our dreams tell us where our journeys begin.
Kristen Colucci, Grade 6
St Rocco School, RI

If I Was Queen of the World

If I was queen of the world,
I'd dye my hair blue and green,
I'd pierce whatever I wanted,
Everyone would live happily,
I'd get so much money just being me!
I'd get all the pets that are awesomely cute.
During the spring, chocolate cake would sprout from trees,
In the winter it would be ice cream cake, without a doubt.
Everything would be free!
It would be raining cats and dogs
While snowing horses and ponies!
I'd be queen of candy throughout the land.
I'd call peace throughout the Earth
If I was queen of the world…
Good night, Orlando! I mean, New York!
Wait! We're in China?

Grace Hattler, Grade 4
Vergennes Union Elementary School, VT

Request

Take me home where the honeysuckle and yellow jasmine
grow wild, where their gold blares out through
the pine, the smell overpowering.

Take me home, to the lakes, and the creeks,
and the rivers scatter. Their songs will sing of themselves.

Take me home, maybe I'll rest
under the orange pollen and green needles.

Where the cedar is seen wherever you turn,
their faded blue berries all over the leaves.

Take me home, where mountains are to my north and west,
the beaches to the east, swampy marshes to the south.

Take me where the birds sing.

Katherine Zobel, Grade 6
Chapin Middle School, SC

Ode to a Ripstik

Ripstik oh ripstik you are so twisty
I found you in Target near the skateboards
You make it look so hard but you are too easy
When you take me down a hill you go so fast
I adore your twistiness and how you carb
You're a wonderful thing and I am glad I bought you
I fell off at first but now you are fun
Every time I twist you
From my mailbox to the end of the street
But my legs hurt so much after I ride you too much
Without a twist there is nothing to enjoy about you
If you get dirty I will wash you so you will shine

Drew Johnson, Grade 5
Vienna Elementary School, NC

Home

The creaky door swings open,
and the cluttered stairway greets me.
Mom's clear voice rings
through the hallway
as the aroma of dinner
fills my nostrils.
My dog's growling
quickly quiets
once he recognizes me.
My siblings yelling
playing with their toys
like wild animals.
I feel safe.
Even with Matthew's piercing scream
ringing in my ears.
'Cause I know
I am
home.

Megan Grabher, Grade 6
Manchester Elementary/Middle School, VT

Monkeys

Monkeys are brown
they swing from trees
looking for bananas
so they can eat and leave
they peel bananas
throw the peel down
then bears and seagulls come
and eat them down.

Chelsea Sisco, Grade 5
Courthouse Road Elementary School, VA

Dark

D ead people
A rising from the ground
R eaping horror and
K eeping the balance of scariness in the world.

Jakobi Tharpe, Grade 5
Cooper Elementary School, VA

Life

Life is a circle
because life has no end.

Life is music
because there are many rhythmic feelings.

Life is a flower
because the flower has beauty like life.

Life is a book
because in a book you never know
what's going to happen like in life.

Joanna Petrosky, Grade 5
Holy Cross Elementary School, DE

I'd Like to Be

A dog that runs fast,
A snake that slithers around,
A tiger that can roar,
A bear that can climb a tree,
A bird that whistles,
A beaver that can chop wood,
A horse thundering on the ground.

Ethan Thao, Grade 4
Cool Spring Elementary School, NC

Horses! Horses! Horses!

Horses! Horses! Horses!
Galloping everywhere!
Some were in the hay pile,
others in the tack room,
the ring, the bathroom,
they were even running out the door!
In the stalls, in the office,
even on the dance floor!

Horses! Horses! Horses!
Running, cantering, galloping
across the street to the fields
to the trails, to the trailers.

Friesians, shires, Clydesdales,
paints, appys, pintos, buckskins,
Arabians and all! All breeds and sizes,
colors and shapes, even a mule!
Horses! Horses! Horses!

Tabitha Pion, Grade 6
Metcalf School, RI

Death

I am harmful and intangible,
I wonder why I am unforgivable,
I hear the screams,
I see the suffering,
I want to be set free,
I am harmful and intangible,

I pretend to be tolerable,
I feel the vigor fade away,
I touch the condemned,
I worry that I will be overcome by wrath,
I cry when I erupt turmoil,
I am harmful and intangible,

I understand that I am a part of life,
I say that everyone will feel me,
I dream for incessant serenity,
I try to bring solace,
I hope that poise will come to be,
I am Death.

Austin Rich, Grade 6
Beech Springs Intermediate School, SC

The Beggar

That Man,
He was there,
Shaking his Dunkin' Doughnuts cup,
The coins jingling,
The bills fluttering,
He must be so cold,
So lonely,
I gave him 30 cents,
I walked away,
Painful guilt in my stomach,
So snobby,
So ungrateful,
I was,
Why do I have heat?
Why do I have a house?
There he was,
Then he was gone,
Standing,
Shaking,
His Dunkin' Doughnuts cup.

Owen Koucky, Grade 6
Main Street Middle School, VT

The Earth

Man has almost cured cancer,
but why can't man figure out
when the world
is going to come
to an end?

I hope I die
the way
I'm supposed to die.
Everyone
is cutting down trees,
and everyone
is dying because of it.
I hope I have kids.
Hopefully they die
the way
they're supposed to die.

I know I'm not as smart
as Albert Einstein,
but I'm going to make a difference.

Cole Williams, Grade 5
Daniel J Bakie School, NH

Chase

Chase
Fun, friendly
Wave-Boarding, biking, golfing
Fun to play with
Caulder

Aaron Murphy, Grade 5
Pine Tree Hill Elementary School, SC

Blades

While gazing at the Frisbee
Panting outside
Waiting for me to flick my wrists
I toss it

While running through snow
Jumping over rocks
He spots his prize

His toy is lying in
A snow bank
He's barreling towards it
And CRASH!!
He's stuck in the snow

When he walked out
He looked like a
Giant powdered doughnut

He learned his lesson
Jumping into a snow bank
Can give you a mega brain freeze

Patrick Fields, Grade 6
Metcalf School, RI

The Water Cycle

The water cycle happens every day
Sometimes you can go out and play
First evaporation
Then precipitation
And then it's sunny hurray!

Hannah Shaw, Grade 5
Vienna Elementary School, NC

Uganda

I used to live in Uganda,
There are many tribes like the Buganda.
The place is very green,
All the banana leaves have a sheen.
I slept under a mosquito net,
I kept a rooster as a pet.
I went to Rwanda,
I went in a Honda.
I wish I could go back sometime,
And this is the end of my rhyme.

Ellis Caiola, Grade 4
St Thomas More Catholic School, NC

The Lady and Cow

There's a lady that rode a cow
The lady was wandering now
They saw a big bee
They ran into a tree
She got hit by him POW!

Shailyn Tucker, Grade 5
North Windy Ridge School, NC

cake

cake
good, great
eating, celebrating, partying,
pie, ding dongs, ho-hoes, oreo cakesters,
tasting, buying, chewing,
delicious, spongy,
twinky

Matthias Kotek, Grade 6
Floyd T Binns Middle School, VA

Father Up Above

Father your hand is as vast as the universe,
It holds me, me and all my curious thoughts.

When I look in the sky,
I see your face shining down at me.

When I sniff the fresh, crisp air, and hear the birds chirping,
I think to myself, you've created another day.

Another day for me to love,
My father up above.

Cailyn Lee, Grade 6
Beech Springs Intermediate School, SC

Colors

Green is the greenish, darkness in the rain forest.
Teal is the storming sea.
Light blue is the shining tropics.
Black is the final frontier.
Blue is a glass tear.
Red is a fiery flame.
White is the shining snow.

Zander Ackerman, Grade 5
C Hunter Ritchie Elementary School, VA

Colors

This poem is about me,
and all my colors you'll see.

Some days are ocean blue,
when I am not selfish and I think about you.

Other days are neon green
when I feel grumpy, and want to scream.

The best day is flamingo pink,
so I feel laid back and do not think.

Jet black days are very sad
On these days I feel so bad.

That was my colored poem about me,
and all my colors, did you see?

Kayla Garcia, Grade 5
Clover Hill Elementary School, VA

June

June is bright yellow
The color of the Wake Forest colors
June feels like me smashing my face into the water
It sounds like my family singing happy birthday to me
It smells like sweat
June tastes like cake
June makes me feel older every year.

Tanner Parrish, Grade 5
Vienna Elementary School, NC

Rain

As the cold rain
falls to the ground
I shiver in the cold wind
like standing in the snow.
I pull out my umbrella
and hear the "pitter patter"
of rain

Johanna Evans, Grade 5
South Smithfield Elementary School, NC

I Wonder if I'll Be in the Air Force Reserve

Flying a jet
Protecting my country
Putting on shows while afterburners are glowing
Dodging bullets, rockets, and missiles
Taking off and landing
Heart-stopping dogfights
United States fighters
My copilot and I
Radioing our tower
Am I ordinary?
Yes
Am I doing something extraordinary?
Yes
Loving the skies

John DiMarzio, Grade 6
Dr Edward Ricci School, RI

My Best Friend

My mom…
Cleans my room for me
Cooks for my brother and me
Does my hair for me
Cleans the house
Reads to me at night
Helps me with my homework
Gives me snacks when I'm hungry
Helps me find something to wear
Buys things for me
Gives me big hugs and kisses to make me happy,
But the best part about my mom is that she's my
#1 mom and my best friend.

Christella Bejarano, Grade 5
Manchester Elementary School, NC

Candy

I love sweet candy
It's yummy to my tummy
Dreaming of candy
Sugary sweet I eat yum
Until I feel almost sick
Chelsey Spencer, Grade 5
Cool Spring Elementary School, NC

Sand Castle

Yesterday I built a great sand castle
in the sand
with many rooms, tunnels, and a moat
But today
I think my castle is floating
on the wavy sea
Alexandria Rodi, Grade 5
St Mary School, RI

My Dog, Louie

I have a dog named Louie,
but he likes to be called Lou.
He's a friendly dog
he meets me at two.
He really likes to run and play,
almost every day.
When he is sweet,
I like to give him a doggie treat.
In his spare time
he is funny
he likes to chase bunnies.
When he is sad he acts really bad,
then he makes me extremely MAD!!!
I always say hey
this dog is okay.
My dog Louie is the best that he can be.
I can't wait 'til he greets me.
Andrew Karo, Grade 5
St Christopher's School, VA

Emotions

Mad
Frustrated, confused
Hitting, kicking, complicating
Hateful, stressful, all right, good
Contented, delighted, elated
Calm, cheerful
Happy
Dashon Floyd, Grade 5
St Helena Elementary School, SC

Summer Time

Warm weather is here
Summer time is very fun
Warm and beautiful
Anthony Butler, Grade 4
St John Neumann Academy, VA

Country I Love

In the country that I love
Mornings wake to roosters
Crowing.
Dogs barking.
In the country that I love
In the afternoon you hear birds and
Kids playing
In the country that I love.
At night it is quiet and it's
Solid black except for the
Moonlight sky.
Ryan Bass, Grade 4
Barnardsville Elementary School, NC

A Walk in the Woods

Crunch! Crunch!
A glimmering sun
Fallen leaves
A crisp breeze
A magnificent autumn day
A squirrel scurries
Gathering nuts for hibernation
A brown, orange, and yellow blanket
Covers the ground
Shelby Holmes, Grade 5
North Windy Ridge School, NC

Me Chandler

I am strong
I am funny
My pinky is two inches long
and my friend is a bunny

I love to play
I love to run
I will eat some hay then after that
we can go have some fun

I have brown hair
and it is long
I love the fair
will you let me sing you a song

Never mind
because if I sing
you won't be able to hear
and plus you might shed a tear
Chandler Anderson, Grade 5
Pocalla Springs Elementary School, SC

Bed

Going to bed now
I pull the covers on me
Dozing off to dream
Hailey Adkins, Grade 5
North Windy Ridge School, NC

Little Paige

Little, little Paige,
a cousin to me.
You squint and you squint,
But you still cannot see.
Where do you sleep, where will we meet?

Pushing to crawl,
I hate to see you squall —
between the blankets and the crib wall.

Gooing and gaaing… please stop crying.
Little, little Paige
Alyssa Houston, Grade 5
Cool Spring Elementary School, NC

Winter

I like winter the best
You can build a snowman
And have snowball fights too
And drink hot chocolate
And best of all
You can have fun on
Christmas day
Michael Fremeau, Grade 5
Rye Elementary School, NH

What if I Could Fly?

What if I could fly?
I might touch the sky!

What if I was a spy?
I could do flips.

What if I was rich?
I would buy an island.

What do you wish you could do?
Nicole Waters, Grade 5
Blaney Elementary School, SC

Good Friends

A long time ago,
I had good friends.
We would laugh together,
We would sing together,
We would eat together and,
We would be together.
Yes I remember those days.
Wonderful feelings,
Happy thoughts,
Love was in the air.
I was so young,
But that was then and this is now…
A long time ago.
Francesca Falvo, Grade 6
Wakefield Forest Elementary School, VA

Knights and Dragons

My dear friend don't complain
That horrid dragon must be slain
So all the knights of that table all had to say
All those horrid dragons must definitely pay

So many years later
Their technology was greater
The dragons must be vanquished
Like a fly, they must be squished

All the knights went to battle
That was with some cattle
The dragons lay in ambush
Then all the knights were mush.

Braden Hildebrandt, Grade 5
Sanford Creek Elementary School, NC

What Is an Heir?

Is it not the air we breathe?
Or is it a Da Vinci, the past and present?
There is only one true heir for the present.
He is the air we breathe, but we drive him
    away like air in summer wind.
And this word, rich with truth, instead of
accepting it, we break it in two like toasted bread.
Yet some of us concur with his words,
and as his time draws nearer, we swell like
warm yeast. Finally humanity is beginning
to see a bold horizon with a new celestial
heaven and earth. But until then, we shall
say "nay" to any hypocrites and evil.
And I also say that he's the air we
breathe, for without him we would not exist.

Hayden Lawrence, Grade 5
Queen's Grant Community School, NC

Mini-Me

The polka-dotted mini-me
Chewed, enormous, neon-purple
Plaid, slippery, splattering
Flying, swinging, spinning, zipping,
Tall, giant, striped,
Mountains.

Orion Chabot, Grade 4
Vergennes Union Elementary School, VT

Love Is…

Love is a tear falling from a face standing in the rain.
Love is the beginning of a new relationship.
Love is watching a teenager grow up and leave for college.
Love is the faith that keeps a family together.
Love is the friendship of the Lord and a young child.
Love is the strength that keeps us together.

Loren Wales, Grade 5
Northside Elementary School, SC

Lonely Puppy

In the rain at night
I see a puppy walking
Back and forth into trash cans

He disappears
There he is again, walking

I feel the crackers in my pocket
Yet, I'm so hungry
I slowly take it out of my pocket

The lonely puppy sees me
I set the crackers on the ground and head home

When I turn back, there he is again
Right behind me I see him, his tail wagging
Half a cracker in his mouth, I pick him up and
Carry him home

Connor Walpole, Grade 6
Chapin Middle School, SC

Good Bye Forever

Amari was a 1 week old baby.
She passed away,
it took my breath away.
I had a lot of buddies but she was my favorite.
Everyone loves her and hopes the best,
this is her time to rest.
She was so adorable and everyone adores her.
When she cried, it was a really big surprise.
Her eyes glimmer like the night sky.
She was sad,
and sometimes mad.
She was very brave,
but they could not save.
We lost her earlier.
I miss you
and I will never forget you.

Kadijah Eura, Grade 5
Courthouse Road Elementary School, VA

Heaven

The sand is cold on my feet.
The sun shines above as if an angel has been born.
My life flashed in front of me.
I am a feather.

Now I am walking above the clouds in a world of peace.
I am speaking to people that
I always wanted to know. Everything is golden as the sun.

This is a weird feeling, I feel invincible.
Before this I was a soldier.
I am here because I died believing in God.

Nathan Gourd, Grade 5
Manchester Elementary/Middle School, VT

Jordan

J ust a person
O rdinary…not
R eally real with people
D aring and exciting
A n interesting person
N eat and tidy

Jordan Hawkins, Grade 5
Queen's Grant Community School, NC

Pink Is Lucky

It makes me very lovable,
Pink is love
It is very bright.

Pink is very friendly,
It is everybody's friend
Both boys and girls
You can find pink almost anywhere.

Everyone wears pink,
It swirls on your skirt.

Pink is happy
Her friends are green and blue,
Her enemies are red and black.

Arianna Fuller-Bell, Grade 4
Youngsville Elementary School, NC

Baby/Kid

Baby
Small, cute
crawling, laughing, hugging
giggling, teething — talking, texting
school, walking, dating
short, funny
kid

Taylor Lutz, Grade 6
Floyd T Binns Middle School, VA

Love

love spoken in words
happy with itself and sad
life spoken in phrase

Dedra Oliver, Grade 6
Piedmont Middle School, NC

Wolf Pup

Wolf pup
small, cute
nipping, crawling, whining
helpless, weakling — biting, killing
hunting, large, fighting
clawing, eating
Wolf

Terri Badger, Grade 6
Floyd T Binns Middle School, VA

Larry and Lulu

Larry is a cow, who went to Moscow.
He met a horse named Lulu, and they had a big luau.

But Larry was blue. This made Lulu sad, too.
Lulu made a joke, but Larry didn't laugh on cue.

She found he was broke. She said, "HOLY SMOKE!"
This made Larry feel bad, so he only drank Diet Coke.

So Lulu met a goat named Chad. Larry moved in with his mom and dad.
He also rented a pogo stick. To Chad, Lulu said, "Too bad."

Lulu vacationed in Lerwick. Larry tried to learn a new trick.
Lulu took two boats and a ferry. She realized she had to return quick.

Lulu had to find Larry. She thought Chad was scary.
They really liked each other, so then they got to marry.

Maggie Dever, Grade 6
Our Lady of Lourdes Catholic School, NC

My Cat

My cat's fur looks like bark, charcoal, and snow
My cat is as cute as a newborn puppy's face
My cat runs as fast as a cheetah
My cat sleeps a lot like a person who works the night shift
My cat purrs as quietly as a sewing needle dropping on the ground

Michaela Bergwall, Grade 5
Quidnessett Elementary School, RI

Here I Sit

Here I sit
Wondering where you've gone.
Staring out the window watching as cars go by,
Hoping a car will hold the one I love.
Still no sound of arrival, silence is all that is heard.

Here I sit
Waiting for a sign of return. Hope is slowly depleting,
Knowing that the possibility of him never returning is high.

Here I sit
The phone is ringing.
I pick it up with hope that it is him,
The only voice I want to hear.
It's not. I get the news.
The arrival I've been waiting for will never come.

Here I sit,
All meaning of life is destroyed.
The sun in my life is gone, gone forever
But I can still remember the beauty.
It is all I can cling to.
Now I wait for the one thing that will bring us back together, death.
It's now all I want and need.

Mary Sell, Grade 6
Dixon-Smith Middle School, VA

Blackbeard

Blackbeard's ship *Queen Anne's Revenge*
Lie waiting for battle.
Blackbeard got ready.
Thinking the navy as cattle.

English lieutenant came speeding,
No fear in his eyes.
Sent by the king,
After saying good-byes.

The ships drew near,
Blackbeard sent a blast.
English took cover,
Holding on fast.

Englishmen boarded,
Whooping away.
Blackbeard fought fiercely,
But the pirates gave way.

Blackbeard died,
Five shots in his chest.
Many sword stabs,
Ended his conquest.

Ross Grigsby, Grade 5
Trinity Christian School, VA

Puppies

The puppies
Sit quietly
Every day
In the kennel
Waiting to have a home

Cameron Murphy, Grade 4
Atkinson Academy Elementary School, NH

Freedom

Life is short
But life is sweet
I sometimes hate my life
But others hate theirs too
Freedom is different to many
But to me it is water
I could swim and swim all day
Just trying to work my sorrows away
In my freedom there is nothing I can't do
And I'm not looking for anyone
Not even you
Some may call me weird, sad, angry, upset
But as long as I know my freedom is still there
My body isn't going anywhere
So as long as I have my freedom
I'm not leaving this place
I call home

Zachary Sheehan, Grade 6
Dr Edward Ricci School, RI

Laundress

A black woman in a dress,
Stirring her laundry,
Outside someone's house,
Working for some money,
Stirring her laundry,
Using a stick,
Working for some money.
She has been working for a while,
Using a stick,
Wearing a hat.
She has been working a while.
A black woman in a dress.

Taylor Bresnick, Grade 4
Vergennes Union Elementary School, VT

The River of Emotion

The picture represents
where you go when you're sad.
It's the freeing place of your emotions.
It's the river that holds your dreams.

It's as blue as sapphires.
It's as clear as glass.
It's the mirror of your wishes.
It's the river of your past.

The sun drifts to the water
and glistens like diamonds.
Water rushes down like a tear
on your face.

Hannah Parker, Grade 5
Manchester Elementary/Middle School, VT

Hunger

The chair faced in the other direction,
separating me from any other friends.
The dark metal frame was cold and mocking.
I really wanted it to end.

The girl in the chair sat with her back from me —
a calculated move on purpose, I am sure.
So intent from keeping me out of the circle —
how much of this can I endure?

Isolated, I sit, my sandwich is tasteless.
I feel so alone, watching the clock.
Each lunch is the same, with time moving slowly.
TICK TOCK TICK TOCK TICK TOCK

She laughs with the others, then looks over her shoulder,
with a snicker and sneer, she fills me with sorrow.
Thankfully the bell rings, and lunchtime is over,
but 23 hours till lunchtime tomorrow…

Helena Boldizar, Grade 6
Myrtle Grove Middle School, NC

Kelsea

She is a bubble full of laughs.
She is the sister I never had.
She is the multi-music to my ears.
Her personality fills her blonde hair.
She is the sun that protects me from the storm.
She is the love that belongs in the heart.
She is the safe that holds my money.
She is the palm tree that belongs in South Carolina.
She is the stick in the middle of the yard.
She is the rose when I am the thorns.
She is my best friend.

Madison Wilson, Grade 6
Boiling Springs Intermediate School, SC

Dad

Dad, you are everything — earth, air, fire, water
You are earth, powerful and amazing,
You are air, free, fresh, and alive
You are fire, blazing and invincible
You are water, so peaceful and flowing

Myranda Stawowczyk, Grade 5
Wakefield Forest Elementary School, VA

She Sits There

She sits there and thinks
Wondering what to do.
She sits there
She laughs
She sits there
And starts to rock.
She sits there
And looks at me and says, "I've been saved."

Jasmine Westfield, Grade 6
Beech Springs Intermediate School, SC

The Plump Plum

I bit into a plum yesterday,
the juice splashed into my mouth,
like a wave,
breaking on shore.
It's maroon on the outside,
and reddish purple on the in.
It bursts with flavor
like an Icebreaker,
popping in your mouth.
I slurp the juice after each bite.
It drips on my blouse
forming a stain.
I savored each bite,
until it was gone.
And still I can remember
that soft vibrant plum
that was juicy and plump.

Hannah Goepel, Grade 6
Manchester Elementary/Middle School, VT

Fall

Fall is the sound of leaves rustling
Fall is the sight of blood red leaves
Fall is the smell of turkey in the oven
Fall is a cold spring
Fall is the taste of pumpkin pie
Crunch crunch is the sound of fall
Fall is the feel of the wood handle of a rake
Fall is dressed with color
Fall is a crunchy golden leaf
Fall is a starry night sky

Will Crews, Grade 4
Tabernacle Elementary School, NC

The Apple

Apples are red, some are green
and they all have their own flavors both sour
and sweet but two things you can't change is
their greatness and nutrition.

Dalton Bartlett, Grade 4
Barnardsville Elementary School, NC

I Bought My First Car!

I bought my first car.
When I turn it on the engine roared like a lion
and the wheels were fast as a cheetah.
And every time I could race I would always win.
I love that car and one day I could race it some day.
I wish I had lots of cars in the world.

Sabe Hodge, Grade 4
Courthouse Road Elementary School, VA

The Goggles

Petu riding with me
On the horizon of the sunset
Future waiting for me to fall in
My whole life ahead of me

Petu pulling down the goggles
The way he rides it feels like he is a god
When I look through the tinted glass

On the horizon of the sunset
Future waiting for me to fall in
My whole life ahead of me

I'm waiting for him to pull his big move
Then I see me pulling down the goggles
Helping a kid I don't know
Pulling my big move

On the horizon of the sunset
Future waiting for me to fall in
My whole life ahead of me
Through the tinted glass of the goggles

Nicholas Warns, Grade 6
Manchester Elementary/Middle School, VT

June

June is light blue
The color of the pools
June feels like the coolness of the pool water hitting your body
June sounds like people singing Happy Birthday to me
It smells like fresh cut grass
It tastes like birthday cake
June begins our long summer break!

Sarah Scrattish, Grade 5
Vienna Elementary School, NC

Black

Black looks like the night sky
on a humid summer evening.

Black sounds like bat's wings
frantically flapping through the darkness.

Black smells like the smoke of a blazing campfire
warming 5 cold and wet scouts after a long day of hiking.

Black tastes like the dark juices of black licorice
swishing through my teeth.

Black feels like the cold asphalt
as I fall to the ground after a blow to the face.

Billy Hart, Grade 5
Holy Cross Elementary School, DE

Anger Is…

Anger is not being able to sleep late on rainy days.
Anger is someone starting rumors about you.
Anger is getting a whippin' and being on probation.
Anger is someone drawing bad pictures about you.
Anger is this school year.
Anger is not getting what you want.
Anger is people talking behind your back.
Anger is not liking someone at all.
Anger is people saying you can't sing well.
Anger is not being able to buy something.
That is what anger is.

Daniel Rogers, Grade 5
Northside Elementary School, SC

Summertime

Summertime, summertime, so so fun,
Out of all the seasons, I'd rather have this one,
Hot outside, cold in there,
You'd want to be outside than anywhere.

Once I get tired I sit in the shade,
It is so nice drinking lemonade,
When I am done go out and play,
I think I might even go in a parade.

Caleb Veldkamp, Grade 5
Courthouse Road Elementary School, VA

My Life

Just waking up in the morning
Have to thank God
For my life always seems kind of odd.

I don't know what I would do without my mom
It'll be the end of my world
Teachers staying on my back
Trying to get my grades up
I don't know, I'm not trying hard enough
I'm going to prove to my teachers
That I AM SMART ENOUGH.

Tyler Fleming, Grade 6
Benjamin Syms Middle School, VA

Trickle of the River

As I stand there
listening to the slow and steady trickle of the river,
I think to myself
This river is one of the millions of rivers in the world.

This is an interesting concept.
As the river flows,
I think to myself,
About all of the things in the world
Such as animal abuse, and world hunger.
The river is as peaceful as a night on the beach.

As I stand there,
Listening to the river,
I see fish jumping around,
And tiny tadpoles playing tag.

The world is a large place,
And when you take things like
Rivers, mountains, and trees,
You make up Earth.
And Earth is a wonderful place.

Grace Provost, Grade 5
Manchester Elementary/Middle School, VT

Chelsie Woodall

Chelsie
Loyal, friend, dependable, honest, friendly
Daughter of Mary and Keith,
Lover of good grades, chocolate, and pizza
Who feels bubbles in my tummy when I see my sister,
When Mom wins stuff, happiness when I'm with my family.
Who needs a kitten, a mom and dad, and a happy family.
Who gives hugs, love, happiness.
Who fears spiders, slavery, and the world ending
Who would like to see the Grand Canyon,
The biggest pizza, and a really long snake
Resident of Four Oaks
Woodall

Chelsie Woodall, Grade 5
Four Oaks Elementary School, NC

My Mother

My mother was more than a mother to me; she was a proud black woman that was glad to be my mother who took care of me.
My mother was there for me through thick and thin. My mother always told me to be strong because you don't always win.
My mother the love of my life taught me how to be strong and fight.
My mother knew how to play. I wish my mother had been on Earth to stay.
Since August 15, 2007, my mother has been *resting* in heaven.

Lanasia Wardlaw, Grade 5
Macedonia Elementary School, SC

Christmas Day When All the Sky Was Blue

Christmas day when all the sky was blue, Alex ate all of her breakfast and then went to play with Sue.
Dad went on the roof as they started to play, to see Santa's boot print on that Christmas Day.
Surprised that the boot print was still there, Dad turned his head and started to stare.
"What is it," they asked him, "what have you found," Dad turned and looked at them and climbed down to the ground.
After playing with snow and thinking about the boot print, they all went inside to have hot chocolate, marshmallows and celebrate present time.
Mother got jewelry, Father got new shoes, Alex got a Bratz doll and so did Sue.
They all gave hugs for the presents they got, it's the best Christmas ever, Alex did think.
We've been in an old house, now this one is new, but we are all grateful all the year through.

Savannah Boisvert, Grade 4
E O Young Jr Elementary School, NC

My Step Dad

T.J
Hilarious, short, caring, loving
Dad of Salem, Austyn, and Bree
Lover of, golf, martial arts, and music
Who feels, amused when sleeping, mad when house is not clean, and disturbed when you interrupt him
Who needs, a rest sometimes, a nice warm shower, and a shoulder to cry on
Who gives, advice, help, and cheers you up if you're down
Who fears, spiders, and his kids getting hurt, and death
Who would like to see, my sister never cry, the opera, and my mom sing a Christmas carol in the middle of October
Resident of Pfafftown NC
Styers

Bree Davis, Grade 5
Vienna Elementary School, NC

Where I'm From

I am from Burlington, Vermont
I am from the rolling valleys, and shallow plains
I am from the peaking mountains, and drowning snow
I am from the short, sweet, savoring summers and dark, cold, endless winters
From creation and light, sorrow and destruction
I am from the life I live at night, where I discover and learn from my dreams
I am from that road, down that street, across that high school, and beside that river
I am from that other road, up that other street, surrounded by those trees, and beside that barn
I am from Swiss, Scottish, Welsh, Irish Lithuanian, and native American ancestors
I am from the Rackas's and the Burton's
I am from the memories shared between
I am from me
From my personality, my choices, my thoughts, my goals, my life
I am from the small town of Montpelier
From the new life it brought me
From the new friends, new homes, new life
Where I'm from, never stops

Nathan Burton, Grade 6
Main Street Middle School, VT

Mary

Mary
active, funny, playful
daughter of Kenneth and Jeanne, sister of Mo and Kenny
loves playing softball and loves freedom
who loves her family, lost grandma, and cares for her dog
fear of losing family, dog, and friend
who got published at eleven in a book
who would want to be a pro athlete or many things
who lives in Culpeper, VA
Kirk

Mary Kirk, Grade 6
Floyd T Binns Middle School, VA

My Laptop

This is my laptop.
It's little and small.
Has a good battery,
And takes up no space at all!

This is my laptop.
It may be small.
But let me tell you.
It has 150 gigabytes in all.

This is my laptop.
It has a small mouse.
Get it angry
And it's ready to pounce!

Kody Preil, Grade 5
C Hunter Ritchie Elementary School, VA

Summer

Summer tastes like ice cold chilly lemonade
Summer feels like pool water splashing against my soft skin
Summer feels like another world
It sounds like a hippo splashing in the muddy water
Summer looks like leaping dolphins in the cool ocean
Summer is a beach ball being hit back and forth
Boom
It sounds like rock and roll music
It is someone swimming in the ocean
Summer is a party thrown by your best friend
It is a sprinkler spraying water everywhere

Crista Wyrocki, Grade 4
Tabernacle Elementary School, NC

Orange

Orange is the color of the sunset.
Orange is the color of cool in the summer.
Orange, orange, orange
The color and drink have the same name.
How funny is that?
Orange is the color of the sun,
And it's the son of red and yellow.

Kevin Iglhaut, Grade 4
Waller Mill Fine Arts Magnet School, VA

Born an Orphan

Still under a roof but unwanted
With towels wrapped up
Against Russian cold snow
Not knowing the truth until being adopted
Soldiers every block
Machine guns lined up
All buildings black and white
Quiet as a fish
No home until I get love
Still, not knowing if I was abandoned, maybe not
Why was I put up for adoption, though
Finally, Bev and Ralph, mom with grandpa
Off the plane to danger land
Stealers and thieves
Scared but determined
Bringing toys for me and my pals
Even though I was 10 months old
Hours in the air, above cumulus clouds
Safety next stop
It's over
Home!

Teren Donovan, Grade 6
Northview Middle School, NC

Green

Green is the color of the environment
With grass and leaves
Clovers and weeds
St. Patrick's Day is full of green with
Celtics and leprechauns
Turtles and anoles
Are green all over
Green jolly ranchers and gummy bears are great
Mint green is a popular color
Green is an exciting color
Green pencil boxes, pencils and water bottles
Sit on school desks
The fourth color of the rainbow is green
Recycling is green
For the environment
Green is the thick cozy comforter
On my bed
Green is the scent of growing grass
In the spring
What would happen if we didn't have green?

Carolyn Johnston, Grade 4
Atkinson Academy Elementary School, NH

Sun

Does the sun get tired of sitting in the sky?
Does the sun want to fly?
Does the sun like to bring light?
Does the sun like to be bright?

Hailey Fulk, Grade 5
Pine Tree Hill Elementary School, SC

Mom
Mom
Helpful, dear
Caring, pretty, loving,
Nice, leader, teacher here
Love
Michelle Totty, Grade 4
Appomattox Elementary School, VA

mist
cloudy grayness
enshrouds
everything
but walking
just walking
not knowing
where feet will step
just walking
not wandering
just slow
steady
footfalls
as though
they know
where
they are going
slowly disappearing
into the shroud
mist…
Caleb Smith, Grade 6
Prince of Peace Catholic School, SC

Football
Football players play
Running in fall every year
Tackling people
Connor Hogan, Grade 6
E Taylor Hatton School, VT

Friendship
Friendship is a seed
because your friendship
keeps growing every day.

Friendship is a crowd
because you are never alone.

Friendship is a rollercoaster
because sometimes
your friendship
has ups and downs

Friendship is a cupcake
because friends make
your life sweet.
Caroline Waple, Grade 5
Holy Cross Elementary School, DE

Seasons
Winter
Wintry, breezy
Ice skating, eating, sleeping
Vacation, presents, beach, television
Sweating, playing, cooking
Sunny, flowers
Summer
Vernese Best, Grade 5
St Helena Elementary School, SC

Wedding Book
So pretty,
Yet so sad
Sitting in its dusty, white cover.
It shows pictures
Of memories
That should be happy
But now,
Are just
Sad.
A past life,
Something
That shouldn't have
happened…
Laura S. Cassetty, Grade 6
Main Street Middle School, VT

Sweet and Sour
Sweet
Delightful, friendly
Loving, caring, outstanding
Enjoyable, likable, brutal, mean
Wicked, unfeeling, upsetting
Tart, bitter
Sour
Kaie Heyward-Saunders, Grade 5
St Helena Elementary School, SC

Pool Party
Summer
sunny, hot
sweating, swimming, playing
happy, tired, thirsty, shade
July
Jeanette Johnson, Grade 6
Floyd T Binns Middle School, VA

Cat
A cat prowls through the woods
He spots a mouse eating a seed
Crawling slowly and low
He shakes his haunches
Then he pounces, taking his catch
All is peaceful as the cat walks away.
Keara McAnelly, Grade 6
Monelison Middle School, VA

Maddie
I once had a dog named Maddie,
That was a very big fatty,
My mom goes crazy,
When she is lazy,
But we all loved good old Maddie.
Tyler Goldsmith, Grade 5
North Windy Ridge School, NC

Lyrics
Song
Rhythm, notes
Singing, composing, revising
Exciting, entertaining, peaceful, enjoyed
Compared, relaxing, creating
Recite, spoken
Poem
Jamin Johnson, Grade 5
St Helena Elementary School, SC

If I Could Make a Rainbow
If I could make a rainbow,
It would be mighty fine,
If I could make a rainbow,
It would be divine.
If I could make a rainbow,
It would be so special,
If I could make a rainbow,
It would be all mine.
I could toss it in the sky,
It would go very high,
Way up in the sky,
Very, very high.
My rainbow would be the best,
Above all the rest.
Zoe Minor, Grade 5
Clover Hill Elementary School, VA

Friendship
Trent
Cool, fun
Drawing, reading, biking
Does not tell lies
T-rent
Brandon Dow, Grade 5
Pine Tree Hill Elementary School, SC

Too Much TV
Channel 7, channel 9, channel 63.
Too many people are watching TV.
Turn off the set and go play!
It is beautiful out today.
Go out and play says me!
You'll be healthier
Just wait and see!
Ray VanDevender, Grade 4
Queens Creek Elementary School, NC

The Beach

I see the shimmering sand
Sparkling before my eyes.

I feel the warmth of the setting sun
Beaming on my face.

I taste the salty, bitter water
As the waves crash down on me.

I smell the bitter seaweed and the scent of fish
Flowing through my nostrils.

I hear the waves crashing against the shore
As the seagulls sing their night song
To go to sleep.

Logan Berry, Grade 4
Buffalo Elementary School, SC

My Life as a Maze

My life is a maze.
I may never know what turns I could make,
nor how many incorrect directions I had chose.

Some days I might be trapped in a dead zone.
As years pass, I find my door out of the maze
and moving on.

But sadly, I didn't read the signs on my path to victory.
I'm in a maze once more, in that same dead zone.
Other days I shall escape but then brought back.
There is always a maze,
always a maze.

Nathalie Espina, Grade 6
Berry Shoals Intermediate School, SC

If Your Sock Could Talk

If your sock could talk what would it say?

Would it say "eww give me a bath"
or say "ahh your feet smell good?"
Mine would say "fix my hole would ya."

What would your sock do if it could walk?
Would it go to the zoo or walk to the park?
Mine would go to the kitchen for a snack.

What would your sock do if it could shop?
Would it go to the mall or buy a chimpanzee?
Mine would buy a flat screen TV.

What would your sock do if it had a brain?
Would it get a degree or build a laboratory?
Mine would build a concession stand.

Isabel Contreras, Grade 5
Courthouse Road Elementary School, VA

The Bee

Once I caught a bee,
the size of flea.

And I said to that bug
that I would name him Tug.

And his stinger that was super sharp
seemed it could go through a tarp!

When I found that bee,
I shouted out with glee.

And his tiny antennae that was super small
Seemed to be less than one inch tall!

Now it's not just me,
It's me and the bee.

Carly Brennan, Grade 4
Trinity Christian School, VA

Sea Water

When you wake up you smell
Sea water. Sea water is nasty
Sea water is like swimming in your own filth
When you get up you don't want to smell filth
You want to smell beautiful things like flowers

Or refreshing water or that yummy smell of
the restaurant serving food on the beach just thinking
about it makes me hungry
Or maybe you don't like the Ocean maybe you like the tub?

Or maybe a pool but everyone likes different things
But I myself prefer the sapphire blue sea
So please just keep our crystal blue sea clean or people
Will not be able to swim there

Hannah Phillips, Grade 5
Manchester Elementary/Middle School, VT

King and Queen

She and he will be married at the shining sea,
Because the king asked the queen
Someday will you marry me?

Sarah Jo Williams, Grade 4
Spring Run Elementary School, VA

Ocean

The blue water.
The sharks with bellies so white.
The sandy tan beaches.
Many people are here.
Kids parents and babies too.
The hermit crabs small.
The sharks big, but we are all the same inside.

Nicholas Browne, Grade 4
St Thomas More Catholic School, NC

Our Environment
Environment
Save whales
Give, animals, home
Never litter God's creation
Earth
Anna Bordell, Grade 4
Trinity Christian School, VA

Easter Is Coming
Easter is coming and I just
can't wait.
Cause me and my family
will have an Easter hunt date
and me and my cousins
will have laughs and cheers.
Cause Easter is coming and it's
already here.
Kyleigh Day, Grade 4
Angelus Academy, VA

I Love Dogs
I love dogs yes it's true,
when I don't have them I turn blue.
When my dogs come home
I have no time for the telephone.
Katlin Marie Girnis, Grade 5
North Windy Ridge School, NC

Sorrow and Fear
Sorrow
I feel like a part of me is missing,
a gaping hole in my soul.
My head filled with sorrow,
grief for you.

Fear
As I put my head down
I feel dread, fright, terror, panic, horror.
Abigail Holbrook, Grade 5
The Compass School, RI

Disney Magic
Day one starts at Magic Kingdom,
I want to make the line go faster.
smiling kids
awesome rides
my turn
screaming people
laughter
Where dreams come true!
Where dreams come true!
Where dreams come true!
Never ending happiness
Where the sky is never dark.
Liam Longmire, Grade 4
Maple Wood Elementary School, NH

Rainbows
I think I will cry,
When I look in the sky,
And see a rainbow,
Just waiting to fly.

When I say no,
He doesn't hear me,
I will just continue to plea.
Deanna Hamilton, Grade 5
Clover Hill Elementary School, VA

School
At school we learn
Math and reading
Do you think it's fun?
It can be fun
You can't wait for recess
I hear the bell
I have to go
GOOD BYE
Emily Klem, Grade 4
Queens Creek Elementary School, NC

Sweet Pea
S weet as can be
W ild and crazy
E xciting and jumpy
E ats like a flea
T errific!

P aige is her last name
E ager and yet cocky
A mazing and a little bit sleepy.
Daile Paige, Grade 4
Angelus Academy, VA

Chevy
Stopped at the light,
Trash rattling in the bed
Lights on waiting
Waiting patiently.
John Holt, Grade 6
Floyd T Binns Middle School, VA

Trees
Some are large
Some are small
Some allow you to sit on them
Others want you to sit beneath them

Some provide fruit
Some provide shelter
You think you can do without
But we cannot
Stephanie Vetter, Grade 5
Cooper Elementary School, VA

Full of Love
I am a baby, I keep going up
I am a leopard, I growl
I am a book, full of words
I am a camera, I get the picture
I am a hummingbird, I love to sing
I am a bank, full of money
I am a light, shining in the night
I am a heart, full of love
Alisha Williams, Grade 5
Four Oaks Elementary School, NC

Love Is...
Love is two people together.
Love is marriage.
Love is roses and violets.
Love is between father and son.
Love is between mother and daughter.
Love is in a family.
Love is a passion for someone.
Love is great, maybe.
Love is all over the world.
Kendrick Greene, Grade 5
Northside Elementary School, SC

Sore Roar
There once was a lion so sore,
It even affected his roar.
His roar was so boring,
That he just quit roaring.
Now this lion's not king anymore.
Zachary Mercer, Grade 5
North Windy Ridge School, NC

Bad Food
Bad food is filled with mold.
It's very old and very cold.
I looked at the food and saw a worm.
My stomach churned and squirmed.
Out went my lunch,
All up in a bunch.
I can't explain how bad it looks.
This is what my mom cooks.
David Kraus, Grade 4
Grace Miller Elementary School, VA

I Like to Spread My Wings
I am a horse, I like to stay with the herd.
I am a web, I am everywhere.
I am a phone, people can talk to me.
I am grass, I sway with the wind.
I am the water, I go with the flow.
I am honeysuckle, I smell sweet.
I am a photographer, I take the shots.
I am a bird, I like to spread my wings.
Heather Heath, Grade 5
Four Oaks Elementary School, NC

America

I am America
Setting people free
Helping lots of immigrants
Be who they want to be
I am America
Next to the Atlantic Ocean
Fueling people's desires for a new chance
Like a magic potion

Sam Turner, Grade 5
St Christopher's School, VA

Our Earth

Sometimes I think that the world is numb,
It seems we don't know what war has done,
The world is starting to waste away,
It's up to us to save the day!
The world is ours,
It's up to us,
Take care of it,
Don't make a fuss,
Don't have a fit,
We should understand,
This is our land,
Reach out a helping hand.

Eve Coleman, Grade 4
Waller Mill Fine Arts Magnet School, VA

Oh School!

Oh school how boring are you!
We always have to go to you.
You make me so sick with just one flick!
You can put me in a jar and send me so far.
Oh, I just hate the work it is such a jerk.
Oh, school you are a fool.

Vanessa Campos, Grade 4
Courthouse Road Elementary School, VA

Whispers

Whispers are lonely,
Like one branch fighting against the wind.
They're frightening,
Like a cat's hiss when it's afraid.
They're hilarious,
Like a little sister learning to talk.
They're worrying,
Like mothers waiting for their children to come home.
They're warm,
Like a fire at its highest, crackling away.
They are like a cloud missing its sky,
A dream missing its sleep.
If you're going to say something —
Everyone deserves to know.
Whispers,
They're almost as bad as secrets.

Paige Brigham, Grade 6
Main Street Middle School, VT

Day at the Pond

I decide to spend the day at the pond.
I see dragonflies flying over the water.
I have my fishing pole to catch some fish.
I watch in awe as they jump from the dark blue water.

Matt Dennis, Grade 6
Wakefield Forest Elementary School, VA

My Mom

Mom you are so dear to me
You are kind and sweet as can be
You never think of yourself
Your needs are always put on a shelf
You say your children come first
Yet there are things for which you thirst
When questioned why your needs are not met
You always say, "My child don't fret,
God will provide for me and thee.
So leave it alone and let it be."
Mom you're so precious to me.

Ashanti Peters, Grade 6
Benjamin Syms Middle School, VA

Puppies

Puppies are cute,
Puppies are sweet,
Puppies jump all over me,
They play with your feet,
They love to eat,
Oh how puppies are so sweet!

Danielle Fletcher, Grade 5
South Smithfield Elementary School, NC

History

Sounds like history is interesting
Looks like it will help me become smarter
Tastes like paper
Feels like I am becoming smarter
Smells like an oak tree that I am allergic to.

Marcos Piggott, Grade 4
Waller Mill Fine Arts Magnet School, VA

I Am Thankful For…

I am thankful for my family
Because they give me love and warmth.
My house, musical beyond imagination,
Keeps me warm on those cold winter nights
And gives me protection from the bitter cold.

I am thankful for being healthy.
I am thankful for my friends
And their playful company.
I am thankful for having the things I have
That some people don't.

Ethan Crocker, Grade 6
Wyman Elementary School, RI

Clocks

clock
numbers hands
second minute hour
time digital watch analog
clock

Anthony Messina, Grade 5
Queen's Grant Community School, NC

Coming Home

I come home
from a friend's
birthday party.

"Hello!" I say.
"How's Grandma?"

My parents force a
smile and say:
"She passed away."

"No!" I shout, crying.

I run into their arms,
tears streaming
down my cheeks.

"She's gone." I whisper.
"She's gone."

Kirstin Reed, Grade 5
Oak View Elementary School, VA

His Eyes

His eyes sparkle
At me every day.

His eyes are what
Keep me going.

His eyes are as patient and calm
As the ocean.

His eyes are two perfect diamonds
On his beautiful face.

His eyes look so innocent
In the sunlight.

His eyes, at night
Shine under the moon and stars.

His eyes are looking straight at me
And then he plants a kiss on my cheek.

My baby brother's eyes!
Cara Phillips, Grade 5
Buffalo Elementary School, SC

Blue Is

Blue is like blueberries just plucked
Blue is the color of the sky after waking up
Blue is the color of Carolina blue
Blue is like the blue ocean
Blue feels like you're jumping into the ocean
The blue raindrops flood the earth as the sky cries
Blue looks like the sky during the day
Blue is the color of my jeans
The sky shakes as it starts shooting down raindrops
The raging blue river tumbles and rolls under the sleepy dark sky

Julian Zimmerman, Grade 4
Tabernacle Elementary School, NC

Parents

Parents are teachers who teach you the things you need to know.
They tell you what to do and what not to do.
Parents are servants who do what you ask them to do.
Parents are a seatbelt holding you in place in case of danger.
Parents are a book full of information.

Emmalee Dellert, Grade 5
Holy Cross Elementary School, DE

The Broken Fence in the Desert

The broken fence stands alone,
crippled in the desert.

The wire is torn, trailing on the ground
you hear the whisper of the wind, the only sound.

The round sun rises, shining down on the desert sand,
looking down upon the broken fence that used to guard the land.

But now the fence's power is broken, damaged by someone or something unknown.
Something broke it, tore it down, and now the fence is standing alone.

The once proud protector, poised to stop
anyone who tried to pass, took a fall,
And who knows? Maybe in a thousand years the poles will crumble,
the wire will snap, and the fence will be nothing at all.

Gil Osofsky, Grade 5
Hunters Woods Elementary School, VA

Being a Swing

If I were a swing
I'd fly
I would swing kids back and forth when they are sad.

If I were a swing
I'd flip
I would make kids happy and try not to hurt them, while flipping upside down.

If I were a swing
I'd twist
When kids are flying high in the sky, I would twist like a roller coaster.

Kayla Goodnow, Grade 5
Symonds Elementary School, NH

I Saw a Pig That Can Fly

Mom, Mom,
I saw a pig that can fly,
Mom, Mom,
Look! Look!,
Look high in the sky,
Right before my eyes,
I saw another pig that can fly,
Mom, Mom,
You got to believe me,
Come on Mom,
I saw a pig that can fly!

Alicia Jacobs, Grade 4
Courthouse Road Elementary School, VA

Centuries

The 19th century was just like a gun,
But not as bad as the next one.
WWI and WWII,
There might be a bullet under your shoe.
There was Nagasaki, too,
North Korea, south Korea, which one are you?
Hitler dies in WWII.
Axis or Allied, which inspires you?
This century is not good either,
9-11 performed by AL-QAEDA.
And this war in Afghanistan,
Rose up the Taliban.
WWI and WWII
All war, no peace is what we do.

Sam Lensenmayer, Grade 4
Waller Mill Fine Arts Magnet School, VA

Ms. Sims Is So Cool

Ms. Sims is so cool
She is better than the rest,
She barely gives us homework
So that we can rest,
That's why she is the best.
I'm glad to be in her class
Because it is a blast,
She is really the best
Better than the rest.

Jeremy Hokenson, Grade 4
Courthouse Road Elementary School, VA

If I Was 18

If I was 18, I would stay with my parents
So I wouldn't have to pay for rent.
I would get a job I desire
And just hope I didn't set anything on fire.
If they fired me for any reason I would just say, "I QUIT!"
Then I would go to the pet store to get a cat to calm me down.
So I could be ready when my parents kick me out of town.

Rockling Afariwaa, Grade 5
Courthouse Road Elementary School, VA

Flags

Flags are different colors.
Some flags have two or three colors.
Some flags have green like the grass,
Blue like the sea,
Red like inside a watermelon,
And yellow like the sun.

Flags have symbols.
Some symbols represent their cultures.
Flags' symbols are stars like in the sky,
Circle like my dime,
And a few have a sun like in the morning in the sky.

Flags have rectangles,
And others have a little square and stripes.
The stripes represent colonies.

Jorge Alvarez, Grade 5
Woodlawn Elementary School, VA

School's Out

School's out let's run and play
School's out let's shout hooray
School's out let's play hopscotch
School's out I'll go get the chalk
School's out let's put on some shorts
School's out let's sweat a lot
School's out summer's finally here
School's out let's go swim
School's out let's ride bikes
School's out let's wear flip flops
School's out let's put on t-shirts
School's out let's shoot some hoops
School's out let's make some goals
School's out but only for a bit
But we can't throw a fit

Cassidy Holt, Grade 4
Courthouse Road Elementary School, VA

The Dancer

Turn and leap with power and grace,
Three piqué turns and one tour jeté.

The eyes of those watching think it is an ease,
But all dancers know you need expertise.

Do triple pirouettes and slide into splits,
Arms moving with grace — fingers apart not in fists.

Who knew there would be such an art,
Combining strength, power, grace, and your heart?

So express who you are through how you dance,
For life is a dance that is waiting for you,
The dancer.

Susan Donaldson, Grade 6
Cape Henry Collegiate School, VA

Love Is...

Love is like the deepest ocean;
Love is like the tallest mountain;
Love is like a shining star;
Love is being who you are;
Love is like the rising sun;
Love is like the sparkling dew;
Love is like being born anew;
Love is as endless as space;
Love is a wonderful place.

Julie Duetsch, Grade 6
St John Neumann Academy, VA

Ancient Athens

Breezes blowing,
Democracy growing,

People learning in the Agora,
Strengths being built,

Oh, quiet city...shhh,
Oh, full of grace,

Parthenon shining bright,
All throughout the night,
Representing learning and beauty.

Elizabeth Kane, Grade 6
Warwick Neck School, RI

The Meaning of the Panther

P urrfect to all of us.
A wesome to our school.
N ice to us.
T eaching us new stuff.
H appy all the time.
E xcited all the time.
R espected at our school.

Samantha Randall, Grade 4
Riverview Elementary School, VA

Glass

When I peer out my window
I can see through it.
It resembles a door to the outside
World that only I can see.

When I peer out my window
I can see the grass.
It resembles a piece of glass that
Is smooth and green.

When I peer out my window
I can see plastic that is new and clean.
It resembles a piece of glass that
Is not transparent and has color.

MyKel Gates, Grade 4
Bensley Elementary School, VA

Mountaintops

I see mountaintops
They are very beautiful.
They are really big
They go up and down and all around.
How beautiful they seem.
I see mountaintops.

Destine Berkley, Grade 4
Appomattox Elementary School, VA

Spring

Spring is here,
Flowers are near,
Children play in the meadow,
You can hear their joyful cheer,
"Spring is here!"
Rejoicing of clear blue skies,
Winter says good-bye,
Flowers dance in the new fresh air,
Trees singing praise from above,
Wild animals celebrate,
We are well pleased of this new season.

Nicole Bowman, Grade 6
St Rocco School, RI

Family

A family is an honorable,
peaceful kin
They're kind, smart,
and always lovable.

Alex Westbrook, Grade 4
Crestwood Elementary School, VA

Basketball

Shoot the basketball
In the basket watch it fall
Swoosh, swoosh net is all

Autumn Kletsch, Grade 5
Cool Spring Elementary School, NC

The Ocean

I dreamed
I was the ocean
Peacefully swaying
On the beach front
Gracefully.

Kayla Gatling, Grade 5
Cooper Elementary School, VA

Kinetic Energy

I dreamed
I was a rock
On a hill
Rolling down the hill
Quickly.

Demetrius Strickland, Grade 5
Cooper Elementary School, VA

Valentine's Day

My mama has pretty black hair
She treats me right she treats me fair
My mama is so smart
And has the biggest heart

My mama is very funny
And as cuddly as a bunny
I love my mama very much
I buy her chocolate, a bunch

My mama is small
but not very tall
On Valentine's Day
I have a lot to say

My mama's so cool
She picks me up from school
She takes me to play
Every single day

I love my mom
She is the bomb

Kelsey Hollifield, Grade 5
Forrest W Hunt Elementary School, NC

Miles to Go

Miles to go almost there,
What it is I don't know
So close but yet too far to distinguish.
Miles to go almost there,
I see a figure moving through the fog.
I'm sweating,
My heart is racing.
A man?
Who is he?
Creeping through the night,
Moving swiftly like a ghost.
Who's there?

Ian Smith, Grade 6
Metcalf School, RI

Fishy Wishy

There once was a fish
He wanted to make a wish
He was blue with the flu
All he wanted was to be cool
But in the end he was in a dish.

Haili Roberts, Grade 5
Vienna Elementary School, NC

Oceans, Oceans

Crashing and foaming
Smashing unexpectedly
Rocking back and forth

Jason Goodrick, Grade 4
Trinity Christian School, VA

Black

I like black
It's the color of a dog or a cat
It reminds me of my bed that I sleep in during a storm.
Black are the owls in the trees going "Woo, Woo"
Hungry bats that echo in the dark
the sound of my dog when she barks
It's fire when there's lots of smoke that makes me choke
Black is burnt black rubber in the tree from a car crash
It's black olives that I love to eat and "pop" off my fingers
It's chocolate cake with lots of sugar
this is why black is the best!

Nathan Moore, Grade 5
St Mary School, RI

Friendship

Friendship is something someone should always have
A friend is someone you can trust
Tell a secret and say "don't tell" they know they must
Friends will come and friends will go
With one true friend you know it is so
Friends will fade and some friends will stay
Remember the times when you were little and used to play
Some friends are great and some are fine
Some you will wish you will be friends 'til the end of time

Gillian Murphy, Grade 6
St Rocco School, RI

Balloon

If a child lets go of it they might think it went to heaven.
Though it has always been a lifeless thing.
It is like a soul floating out of their hand.

Virginia Williams, Grade 4
Crestwood Elementary School, VA

Fall

The leaves crunched as
The squirrels munched.
The bears told me to
Sing them a lullaby.
As we kiss the leaves goodbye.
The birds flew west.
Kids think fall is the best
They rake the leaves up and the
Kids leaped
Before winter creeped
Upon us.
As we headed to
The bus.
The air was so cold,
That the leaves were frozen under our toes.
Winter waited wonderfully
As fall was wonderful
Fall is like a
Beautiful sunset.

Kylie Johnson, Grade 6
School of International Studies at Meadowbrook, VA

I Wish

Oh, I wish
to be a professional dancer
even though the sweat is
dripping down my face
with the bloody cuts hurting my feet
because I love it!

Oh, I wish
to be a star twinkling
way up high in the sky
to be free —
as free as a bird flying carefree.

Oh, I wish
to have world peace
for everyone to be happy
and for a final end to war.

Oh, I wish
the bad would turn
into the good
for the poor unfortunate souls in the world
and for people to do good deeds.

Sara Baribault, Grade 6
Wyman Elementary School, RI

Rosa Parks

How would you feel if you were Rosa Parks,
Fighting for your seat?
Would you sit in the back, or would you
Get up on your feet?
Would you fight for what's right?
Would you fight for what's fair?
Even if you knew the police were out there?
Rosa is an example for us.
She wouldn't sit on the back of the bus.

Caroline Toole, Grade 6
Forestbrook Middle School, SC

I Have a Dream

I have a dream that everyone will have a home,
A shelter to stay under,
During long rains and thunder.

I have a dream that everyone will love,
Just like two beautiful doves,
And there will soon be no hate,
Because all the people have closed that gate.

I have a dream that everyone will have money,
Most being spent to put food in their tummy,
So don't think I'm a dummy,
I have a dream!

Alia Hampton, Grade 6
Hand Middle School, SC

Feelings

When I am at home
I feel all alone.
I don't feel really bad.
I really feel sad.

I don't have brothers.
I don't have sisters.
It is just me.
My parents make three.

Carlos Scruggs, Grade 4
Bensley Elementary School, VA

The Beach

When I go to the beach
It is as fresh as a peach.
I sit on the sand
And mold with my hand.

The castles I make
Are as big as a cake.
It washes away
Swiftly dissolving into the bay.

I love the beach
It is within my reach.
I go all day
By using the highway.

Anthony Barron, Grade 4
Bensley Elementary School, VA

Summer/Winter

Summer
Hot, water
Swimming, playing, sports
Beaches, boats, surf boards, swimsuits
Cold, shivering, snow
Ice, coats
Winter

Emmett Hatcher, Grade 5
St Christopher's School, VA

Flowers

Stand bold and perfect
Beautiful as any color
Roses and lilies

Madison Manuel, Grade 4
Trinity Christian School, VA

Boys

They are very rough.
They really like to play sports.
They like to get hurt.
They really like to wrestle.
They really like to have fun.

Jeffrey S. Bartolucci, Grade 4
Battlefield Elementary School, VA

Change

Change is the word I fear
My worst enemy
I hate it
But I don't know why
Change and I are
So alike
We are sisters and
Like sisters we
Fight
We cry but it makes
Me who I am

Elizabeth Hernandez, Grade 6
Prince of Peace Catholic School, SC

Vampire

V icious beasts with fangs
A ah is the sound you will fear
M onsters that transform into bats
P eople fear his name
I gnoring may cause you a bite
R un while you still can
E nter his doom!

Ali Girard, Grade 5
Good Shepherd Catholic School, RI

Reba

My dog, Reba, is so fun
When we run in the sun.
She has a lot of fur,
But she can run like a blur.
I will throw a small ball.
I just hope she will not fall.
I will give her something raw
I hope she will come when I call.
If she will only come
I just hope she will be done.

Chris Harmon, Grade 4
Grace Miller Elementary School, VA

Signs of Spring

blowing pink petals
misty mornings in April
these are signs of spring

Lauren Riley, Grade 6
Salem Church Middle School, VA

I Love May

May is the color blue
The color of mayflowers
The feeling of sitting under a shade tree
It sounds like splashing water
May smells like flowers
It taste like pink lemonade
I think May is the best month of the year

Avery Feith, Grade 5
Vienna Elementary School, NC

My Family Is a Forest

My mom is the water
she gurgles to give advice.

My dad is the tree
he reaches out for us.

My sister is the bridge
she is the good path.

I am the rope swing
I swing out to help people.

Alexis Jordan, Grade 4
Hemby Bridge Elementary School, NC

Day and Night

Day
Light, bright
Shining, waking, rising
Plants, bike riding, ice cream, outside
Sleeping, laying, dreaming
Dark, cold
Night

David Glover, Grade 5
St Helena Elementary School, SC

My Silly Hair

Oh! my silly hair
It just sits on top my head
It makes people scream, scream, scream
I pick up a brush after I got out of bed
My hair is just so mean
Whatever will I do with this
Hair on top my head.

Lacey Browder, Grade 5
Pocalla Springs Elementary School, SC

I Have Big Ears

I have big ears
That I've had for ten years
I have big ears
That will make you shed a tear.

Ryan Orr, Grade 5
Pocalla Springs Elementary School, SC

Me? Who Am I?

T errific character
Y oung child
S ensational personality
H ilarious joke teller
I ncredible talent
E nergetic person
K ind to my family and friends
A bility to do anything,
I put my mind and heart to.

Tyshieka White, Grade 6
Benjamin Syms Middle School, VA

Bumper Cars
Bumper cars are turning
while you are crashing, bashing, thumping,
bumping and steering while passing family and friends
who are waving and laughing.
Josh Tamminen, Grade 4
Blacksburg New School, VA

A Life with God's Blessings
As I was sitting on the grass,
I thought of many things,
Things That I had never thought of before,
Like freedom and God's blessings.

I noticed that freedom to some is a privilege,
Freedom is an eagle soaring in the breeze to me,
It is like a long trail in life.
But when you have it, you don't ever notice it,
Like a snake slithering away.

Freedom is one of God's many blessings,
But there are more than you think.
A lake is like a glass of water in Jesus' hand for the poor.
The sun is like a star,
A heavenly light of angels,
Pointing at us with a caring glare.

The wind feels like God's holy breath blowing at me,
As the sand feels like teardrops of the many Saints.
These are gifts from God
But truly, your family's love is the best of all,
So appreciate these gifts and don't let them go
For these gifts are the most prized of all.
Aranxa Fernandez, Grade 5
East Mooresville Intermediate School, NC

Pink
Pink makes me feel spoiled
When I look at all of my accessories
Which are my favorite things
Pink is the color of watermelon,
Which is…juicy, juicy, juicy
Bubble gum is also…
Chewy, chewy, chewy
I LOVE PINK when I snuggle
With my blankie and teddy at night
Every day I wear my pink lip-gloss and eye shadow
When it's summer
I love to drink ice cold pink lemonade
And eat cotton candy
You can call people on your fancy, girly-girl
Pink razor cell phone
When it's Halloween I love to wear pink fake nails
And that's what pink is to me
Jessica Pilcher, Grade 4
Atkinson Academy Elementary School, NH

Family and Friends
F un to have around
A nd when I hear you laugh, it's a beautiful sound
M erry and happy when I'm with you
I have fun and I'm not blue
L oving in every way
Y ou love me every day

A day in the park is so much fun
N o way am I going to be done
D on't you love your friends and family too

F riends are always there for you
R un and play in the sun
I will play until there's none
E very one of them is very nice
N ot cold as ice
D o they see you every day
S upportive in every way
Justine Brunt, Grade 5
Queen's Grant Community School, NC

Through the Eyes of the Beholder
Staring through the looking glass,
Watching the unknown souls,
Lurking through the shadows of the Nether Regions,
Not knowing which way to turn,
Through the eyes of the beholder,
See how they float,
As if they were feathers,
Into the tunnel,
And through the darkness,
An unfinished poem.
Patrick Yeboah, Grade 6
St Rocco School, RI

Cake
The cake is so bright
It blinded me
So now I cannot see
It did the same to my cuzin Lee
Now nor can he see.

The cake is so good and bright.
I could eat it all day and night.
But that would give me a fright.
Because I can't eat cake all day and night!
Ariana McFadden, Grade 4
Edwards Elementary School, SC

My Cat Matt
I have a noisy black cat
It turns out his name is Matt
He enjoys to sleep on the rug
When I turn my head he licks my coffee mug
Josh Crowley, Grade 5
North Windy Ridge School, NC

Time for School!

In the morning around six o'clock the alarm goes tic toc, tic toc then… RRRIIINNNGGG!!!
Then I yell, "Time for school!" I think the day's going to be really cool!
I brush my teeth, and wash my face. Then think of what to dominate.
I think, and think, and say breakfast will be great!
I run downstairs, eat my breakfast and "Time for school, time for school this day is going to RULE!!!"

Shulammite Siltan, Grade 5
Woodlawn Elementary School, VA

The First Ski Race

Wax up your skis
　　Today is the big day
　　　　The day of the race
　　　　　　Now click your skis on — pole straps too
　　　　　　Ride up the lift
　　　　　　　You're at the top
　　　　　　　　Zip off your pants — show your suit
　　　　　　　　Take off your coat
　　　　　　　　Jump to stay warm
　　　　　　　　　You're next, get in line
　　　　　　　　　Listen for the count down
　　　　　　　　　And Go! Fast fast
　　　　　　　　　You're half way through
　　　　　　　　　Go to the left
　　　　　　　　　To the right
　　　　　　　　　Tuck, tuck
　　　　　　　　　You're done
　　　　　　　　　The crowd cheers
　　　　　　　　　The butterflies are gone
　　　　　　　　　Phew.

Ali Nelson, Grade 5
Rye Elementary School, NH

The Past

The memories are vague, but remembering the past helps me in life. Learning your mistakes from the past teaches you in life that ignorance is bliss. Choosing not to acknowledge your mistakes can come back to haunt you in life. We must know not to live the past, but to reflect upon the mistakes we made. Every time we get knocked down we must get back up. So we must live the present, and embrace the future.

Christian Fernandes, Grade 6
Prince of Peace Catholic School, SC

Ruby Bridges

Ruby
Brave, smart, curious, and awesome
Daughter of Mr. Bridges
Lover of baseball, school, and friends
Who feels lonely because she was the only one in her class at school,
Happy when she got friends, and sad when she gets yelled at and threatened
Who needs friends to support her, Marshals to keep her safe, and her mom and dad to help her
Who gives love to her family, prayers to people, and happiness to her friends and family
Who fears the mob, dying, and Jimmy's mom
Who would like to have kids go to school with her,
Go to school without Marshals, and have no more protesting
Resident of Tylertown in Mississippi
Bridges

Nicole R. Edwards, Grade 4
Hope Valley Elementary School, RI

My Sister, My Friend!

She is my favorite toy when I am bored.
She is the soda and I'm the popcorn.
She is my favorite book when I am sleepy.
She is the sunshine on my cloudy day.
She is a mountain and I'm just a hill.
She is the road and I'm the fast car.
She is the dance and I'm the music
She is the basketball goal and I'm the basketball.
She is the game board and I'm the game piece.
She is the bread and I'm the cheese.

Lauren Tombs, Grade 6
Boiling Springs Intermediate School, SC

Rain

Rain is such a pain
I wish it would go down the drain
I guess I can't complain
About the rain
The rain that drives me insane.

Sarah Michaelis, Grade 5
Courthouse Road Elementary School, VA

The Mountain

The wind blows on my face
People always stomp on me
I tower over all my surroundings
The snow pounds on my face
The rain drops on my feet
Waterfalls rush down my side
I stand still all my life
The sun smiles at me
The moon winks at me
The bright lights of the city shine below me
I don't shine at all
I stand still all my life
I smile back at the sun, and wink back at the moon
As I stand still all my life
My surroundings never change

Jacob Naimark, Grade 5
Rye Elementary School, NH

Life on the Dark Side

Life is dark when depression is here.
That's what I have with my eyes filled with tears.
The softest touch may even hurt,
It hurts a lot when it came at first.

Sometimes you lose sleep and start rolling around,
Sometimes you want to fall down on the ground.
You may feel yucky and want to drag,
You may even wear something that looks like rags.

So when you have depression,
Get out, go out there and get in the right crowd!

Anna Singleton, Grade 6
Holbrook Middle School, NC

A Flower

Aren't thou so pretty,
Just swaying in the wind,
Never get tired from showing off your petals,
Red, blue, green, or pink,
Always so graceful for show,
Sitting, swaying, or putting on a show,
You sleek, powerful flower,
Always caring or loving for me.

William Belock, Grade 5
North Windy Ridge School, NC

My Many Colored Days

On my many colored days,
I don't know what to do.
There are so many different
color hues to choose.

On my fire hydrant red days,
are my hot in the head days.
That makes me want to dread days.

On my forever blue days
are my think of you days.
That colors my face with hues days.

Spacious green days
are my carefree days.
And I can dream dream dream days.

Gruesome gray days
are my sad sad days.
Those are my stay at home days.

Now you saw my many color hues.
Now you know why it's so hard to choose.

Abby Mann, Grade 5
Clover Hill Elementary School, VA

Rain Drops

Pitter patter goes the rain
Falling on the window pane
Making lots of enormous, gigantic puddles
So I can splash in them with my pet puppy Cuddles

Pitter patter goes the rain
Pouring through the gutter frame
Watering the flowers in the nearby flower bed
So that they can blossom in the days ahead

Pitter patter
Pitter patter
Pitter patter
Goes the rain

Barbara M. Euripides, Grade 4
Olde Providence Elementary School, NC

Christmas Is Coming!
Hang up your stockings!
Put up your trees!
Santa don't dawdle
I'm begging you PLEASE!!
Today is March 3rd?
Is that what I hear?
Sigh it's gonna be a long year.
Matthew Harrison, Grade 5
Rye Elementary School, NH

Walrus
Walrus
Fat and has tusks
Cute and really funny
Eats fish and can rip you to shreds
Fat glob
Ben Lensenmayer, Grade 4
Waller Mill Fine Arts Magnet School, VA

Smiles
Tastes like a strawberry
Looks like a sunset on the beach
Sounds like a nice laugh
Feels like a rosebud
Smells like a rose
Smiles are beautiful!
Anastasia Mann, Grade 4
Waller Mill Fine Arts Magnet School, VA

Spring
Spring is so bright
You have a delight
The grass is green
I am sure you have seen
With ladybugs to grasshoppers
I am sure you will go bonkers
Brittany Heath, Grade 4
Riverside Elementary School, VA

Gum
I chew gum
When I play my drum.
I want some
And I chew every crumb.

Gum tastes good
I knew it would.
Have some gum.
You'll enjoy it a ton.

Gum is gooey
Gum is chewy
Gum is yummy
But not for your tummy.
Anthony Perdomo-Cantillano, Grade 4
Bensley Elementary School, VA

Somewhere in the World
Somewhere in the world, a little boy is dying.
Somewhere in the world, a little girl cannot find her way home.
Somewhere in the world, a cat is shivering in the cold.
Somewhere in the world, a tree falls.
Somewhere in the world, a baby is crying.
Somewhere in the world, an elephant is being killed by a poacher.
Somewhere in the world, a forest is being cut down.

Somewhere in the world, a little boy is laughing gleefully.
Somewhere in the world, a little girl is playing hop scotch.
Somewhere in the world a man is recycling his water bottle.
Somewhere in the world, a woman is fighting for wildlife conservation plans.
Somewhere in the world, a baby is laughing as he drinks his warm milk.
Somewhere in the world, a newborn turtle finds water.
Somewhere in the world, a family is watching the new special on television.

Then I think. While all this is happening, what am I doing?
Aslan Bakri, Grade 6
Wakefield Forest Elementary School, VA

Invaders
I look outside, to the saturated grass.
Scanning the front lawn to see if they had struck again.
Ah-ha!
There it was, a long dilapidated line of dirt that had been dug up.
Like a giant snake had slithered itself through the dirt.
Then I saw him.
Its little furry head popping out of the ground in which the line had connected to.
Seeing its little beady eyes staring up at me with fear,
and then in that very second I saw his head go back down into that endless hole.
He disappeared, disappeared like he wasn't even there.
Sara Knudsen, Grade 6
Manchester Elementary/Middle School, VT

Suffering Is…
Suffering is your heart when someone you love dies.
Suffering is an animal when someone kills it just so they can eat.
Suffering is tears when you have cancer.
Suffering is your kids when they leave for college.
Suffering is sadness and fear.
Brittany Shook, Grade 5
Northside Elementary School, SC

Blue
Blue is the sound of a waterfall falling
Blue is the taste of a blueberry pie
Blue reminds me of a blueberry
Blue smells like the ocean
Blue is like the ocean that is singing
The blue sky is like a sapphire flower
The earthquake shook the blue water and the water disappeared
The color blue is like a Carolina blue T-shirt
Blue is the color of the beautiful sky
Blue is the color of the sweet smelling pie
Alyssa Gray, Grade 4
Tabernacle Elementary School, NC

Winter

Winter is like a snowball
Winter is like a fluffy white cloud
Winter is like the feeling of hot cocoa running down my throat
Winter is like children shouting "NO SCHOOL!"
Winter is like Candy Cane having fun
Winter is like friends and family getting together
Winter is like Santa
Winter is like the touch of love
Winter is like a winter wonderland

Kendra Smith, Grade 4
Tabernacle Elementary School, NC

The Cool Color

Green is the sound of crickets chirping
The taste of fresh salad he splashes on
Stop lights pulls down on grass
Wraps himself around trees and curves on limes

He is independent but has so many friends
He loves to play tennis; hates to play football
He loves to eat at sweet tomatoes because they have
Green vegetables. Me and green have some things
Alike and some things different
Green is a cool color

Talaysia Pettiford, Grade 4
Youngsville Elementary School, NC

Psalm 1

The waves of the sea are no match
for your strength.
The sun's warmth is no match
for your love.
O Lord, You are the foundation
of my life.
O Lord, You are my shelter
from the storm.
O Lord, You are the net
that catches my fall.
And You are the shield
protecting me from the sword of death.

Nicholas DiMeglio, Grade 5
Trinity Christian School, VA

The Black

My beautiful black Morgan
Loves to trot proudly
Black is affectionate
Loyal
Powerful, Proud, and beautiful
Black has a shiny black coat
Black is like my best friend
When Black is in the field he is the happiest
"I love the black"

Victoria A. Ricci, Grade 6
St Rocco School, RI

You Can't Do the Wash Anymore!

I can't believe you *shrunk* my clothes
and turned them green and blue
just promise to be CAREFUL
or else I'll be MAD at you

You did it again
except now my clothes are pink
and green and blue
no not again how could you
now I'm really MAD at you

I have no clothes now
you *shrunk* them all
and turned them colors I cannot recall
you CAN'T do the wash anymore!

Paige Miltenberger, Grade 5
East Mooresville Intermediate School, NC

My Strict Parents

I do not understand why my parents are so strict
I do not understand why they have rules
I do not understand what they make me do
I do not understand why I have chores
But I do understand that they love me

Hannah Church, Grade 5
Blaney Elementary School, SC

I Like/I Hate

I like books because they are funny.
I hate books because they cost money.

I like winter because it snows.
I hate winter because it stuffs up my nose.

I like pools because my body it cools.
I hate pools because they have too many rules.

I like school because I can go out and play.
I hate school because we don't get out until May.

I like my house because I have a roof over my head.
I hate my house because I have a lumpy bed.

Darius Gibson, Grade 5
Northside Elementary School, SC

Grass

Green grass
sharp but smooth too
green in the spring gold in the fall

lives and dies but always comes back

and grows up as tall as the sky
and gets cut down

Seth Stafford, Grade 5
East Mooresville Intermediate School, NC

I Used to Be…

I used to be a leaf
but now I am a flower
I used to be a baby
but now I am a grown girl
I used to be a picture book
but now I am a chapter book
I used to be flat water
but I am a beautiful flowing waterfall
and now I am just me.

Emily MacLeod, Grade 5
Quidnessett Elementary School, RI

Football Player

football player
cool, popular
running, catching, tackling
unbeatable, happy, mad, awesome
hall of fame

James Layher, Grade 6
Floyd T Binns Middle School, VA

My Life

What do you want with my life?
Please don't hurt me
What do you want with my life?
As you can see

I need more family
What do you want with my life?
I can see all the things carefully
What do you want with me life?

You can take me
Away from the evil
Be there to flee
So you need to believe

What do you want with my life?
What do you want with my life?
What do you want with my life?
Leave me alone.

Soren Spangler, Grade 5
West Hartsville Elementary School, SC

Fireworks

F un to watch
I mage of bursting colors
R eady for it to begin
E veryone in awe
W onderful colors
O oooooaaaah
R eally excited
K nowing it will end
S miles on faces

Travis Tetreault, Grade 6
E Taylor Hatton School, VT

Hamster

So cute
Cuddly
Adorable
Little wheel
Big cage
Plastic ball to run in
Nibble on some wood
Sleep in my home
I'm a cute and cuddly hamster

Jessica Firaben, Grade 4
Grace Miller Elementary School, VA

Life, Death, Sadness

Death is a part of life,
dramatic and emotional.
Especially a loved one.
You don't want them to go,
but there is always a reason.
We miss them so…we sob and cry,
Sometimes we need to say bye.
They know there is a place in
your heart just for them!

Francesca Corsinetti, Grade 6
St Rocco School, RI

Cub/Bear

Cub
cute, small
growling, jumping, climbing
cuddling, teething — fighting, killing
feeding, defending, biting
large, grown up
Bear

Beau Smith, Grade 6
Floyd T Binns Middle School, VA

Jeans

I am comfortable
and I am made of denim.

I am from Madagascar,
but my cousins come from places
all over the world such as:
China, India, and Pakistan.

I fit nicely around people's legs.
I can be fancy or casual.

I zip up or button up.
Most people like zipped.

People love me!
Life is good!

Madeline Lathroum, Grade 6
Homeschool Plus, VA

Horses

Horses are so cool
You fly and fly
You don't even notice
Time going by
They move so fast you
Better hold on to your seat
They run so fast
On four feet

Cadence Tootle, Grade 4
Queens Creek Elementary School, NC

Spring

Spring is so shocking,
Now I know why it's named,
Spring is so eye popping,
Not because of the animals and plants,
Not because of the bees and ants,
Spring is called spring,
For I found,
Because everything,
Springs from the ground.

Christen Venable, Grade 6
Lake Norman Charter School, NC

Pumpkin/Gourd

Pumpkin
Sunset orange
Round, heavy, lined
Always good to eat
Dusky sienna
Gourd

Nicole Muth, Grade 5
Lighthouse Christian School, DE

Segregation

Segregation
Evil, unfair
Waiting, sitting, thinking
Poll taxes, schools, jobs, people
Boycotting, marching, speaking
Unjust, unacceptable
Separation

Da'Quan Lewis, Grade 5
Cooper Elementary School, VA

Summer Is Back

School is out
The bright sun is here
Great friends are near
Go to the beach
Splash in the pool
Have some fun
Summer is back

Felicia Pagliarini, Grade 6
St Rocco School, RI

Larry the Cable Guy

There once was a man named Larry the Cable guy
He loves to say GIT-R-DONE, then let one rip
Who loves to make fun of people

Mike Jacques, Grade 6
Monelison Middle School, VA

The Old House

In Virginia,
It was peaceful.
A house lived on a hill,
Suddenly the house felt a big chill.
The Civil War had sadly begun,
Now the house knew this wouldn't be fun.
Men were running up and down the hills
One man named Robert E. Lee made a lot of kills
On the last day the house knew it was the end.
Then the house will write a letter he will have to send
That person is the president, his best friend.

Devin Fields, Grade 5
Cooper Elementary School, VA

Crushed

I am crushed, my hopes and dreams are flushed
I feel my life out of touch with society

People tell me I am nothing
And my heart isn't even full of loving.

Don't let the smile fool you
I am all changed and I feel like crying.

Everything that is gold
When I touch it turns to brown.

Every child I look at that has a smile
Suddenly gets a quick frown.

As you see I am crushed
And my life is going
    Down
       Down
          Down!

Imani Marshall, Grade 6
Benjamin Syms Middle School, VA

What Is Yellow?

Yellow is the color of a duck
Yellow is the color of a star
Speeding by like a race car
Yellow I can see it on my friend's head
Yellow I can feel on a cat's fur
Yellow is the color of the sun
Like a huge light bulb in the sky
Yellow is many more things than one little object

Bridgette Carman, Grade 4
Olde Providence Elementary School, NC

My Dog

My dog runs and sounds like a horse.
My dog plays ball, and sounds like a pig.
My dog barks and shakes the whole house.
But best of all my dog sleeps like a baby.

Abigail Acors, Grade 5
Riverview Elementary School, VA

Human Trees

The forest is a crowd wanting to see the lights
that light up the silent night.
The trees want to listen to the wind
like we listen to a rock band.

The mountains and the forest are the trees' home
and what do we do to their home?
We destroy their home to make cities.
What should we do?
Save the tall trees and our mountains!

The trees can be as tall as the Empire State Building
or as small as a 5'2" person.

Trees feel like us only in a different way…
They hear like us but don't register the sounds.
They drink water like we do

That is why I call them *Human Trees.*

Angela Eucker, Grade 5
Manchester Elementary/Middle School, VT

My Land

In my land
I think the birds are clouds
Soaring in the wind
And the grass is my extravagant pillow
Filled with many little seeds

In my land
Nature is the ocean
Above everyone's beautiful locks of love
And you are the sky above me

In my land
Freedom is not everything
For it is the only thing
The only thing that can bring everyone peace
On this planet called earth

In my land
God is the sun
And everyone is one plant
Forming the dance of photosynthesis
For everyone, especially me

Morgan Grimes, Grade 5
East Mooresville Intermediate School, NC

Keeping the Beat

Keeping the beat here in my seat.
It's just me keeping the beat.
Feeling the beat under my feet,
Warms my body just like heat.
It's just me keeping the beat
When I'm playing a beat,
It makes me feel like a professional athlete!
That's why I'm still keeping this beat!

Ayanna Sims, Grade 5
Courthouse Road Elementary School, VA

Air

One day I will make my own gloves,
They will be called AIR!

Some day they will be rare.
They will be so nice they will glare.

Some will look at the gloves
and they will stare!

People who love them
will buy seven pairs!

Claude Ziegler, Grade 5
Woodlawn Elementary School, VA

If I Ruled the World

I would be president.
Candy would grow on bushes.
Money would grow on trees.
Animals would be free.
Schools would be fun.
Kids would drive.
There would be a chocolate fountain.
The lakes would be soda.
There would be peace.

Libby O'Hara, Grade 4
Vergennes Union Elementary School, VT

American Flag

Oh flag oh flag oh flag
Of mine.
So bright and fine.
Red and white
Or blue and white.
Stars or stripes? Don't really care, oh flag of mine
Flowing around in my face
Red for love
And blue for hugs.
Oh flag oh flag oh flag
Of mine
You'll stay mine for
VALENTINES!!!

Caroline Corrigan, Grade 5
Sanford Creek Elementary School, NC

Best Friends

Friends are there when you need them.
Best friends are always there.
You're like a flower when they're the stem.
They'll always know what's fair,
Even in a bad affair.
Sometimes you'll fight,
Sometimes you'll cry.
But best friends are always there.
When you are down they'll cheer you up.
When you are sad they'll make you happy.
They share your interests and never get jealous.
You can always have fun, even when you're down.
Always together,
Never apart,
Best friends forever,
Siblings at heart.

Alexandra Maghear, Grade 6
School of International Studies at Meadowbrook, VA

Reading Teachers

They are big and mean!
They are crazy when they don't have their coffee!
Mine is 82 years old.
She has eight legs.
She is not nice.
She is an octopus!!!

Hunter Jenkins, Grade 4
Grace Miller Elementary School, VA

Animals

I love my mink,
She lives in the sink.
Her favorite color is green,
She isn't very mean.

I have a dog,
But I want a hog.
He loves going on walks,
He is a jock!

My mink and dog,
Sleep like logs.
They eat meat,
They smell like feet!

My dog and mink,
Like skating in the rink.
They both play ball,
But they also like going to the mall.

My mink and dog,
Love going through the fog.
They love going to camp,
They even slid down a ramp!

Mary Hutson, Grade 6
Our Lady of Lourdes Catholic School, NC

I Like Cheese

I like cheese, yes I do
Cheese is great, I can hardly wait.

Cheese is good and cheese is tasty
Come get your cheese and please be hasty.

Cheese is delicious and sweet too
Don't let it melt or it will be goo.

Cheese is soft and yellow or white
Taste it now by taking a bite.

Day or night eat your cheese.
If you're allergic, it will make you sneeze.

Aleyah Cary, Grade 4
Bensley Elementary School, VA

On and Off

Her personality's like a lamb,
Gentle and nice.
I kid around with her,
Tell her jokes and she laughs.
She's a pushover,
When you hit a vase.
Like a switch,
Being pushed back and forth.
It short circuits,
Falls over.

CRASH!
All those pieces clutter the floor.

This is when you don't
Want to see her.
She's like a lion growling,
Roaring at you.
Her fur sticking straight up.

Glaring across the room at you.
She whispers in a scarce voice,
"Uhh Sarah go take a break!"

Sarah Marcus, Grade 6
Manchester Elementary/Middle School, VT

Colors

Red is a crisp, ripe apple.
Blue is the cloudless sky.
Green is newly grown grass.
Yellow is a blooming sunflower.
Orange is the sun setting.
Black is a newly paved road.
White is a new piece of paper.
How do you think of colors?

Mark Phillips, Grade 5
C Hunter Ritchie Elementary School, VA

Leonardo

Newborn cousin,
Leonardo Joseph.
Hair is like dark brown velvet,
When hungry.
Cries and scrunches face,
With full belly peacefully falls asleep.
Until wants to play with Ma-Ma and Dada,
Until a diaper change!!
Then watches patriots with Dada,
While his father screams go team!
Then it's time for dinner,
Tonight is meat night.
Not for Leo he needs baby food,
Then it's time to play for a couple of minutes.
Then a shower comes along,
Time for a story.
Goodnight Leo says Ma-Ma and Dada,
Time for bed!

Gabriella Valente, Grade 6
St Rocco School, RI

My Room

My room sings to me at night
When I turn off the light
It squeaks and it snores
When I open the door
It's so clean it's like a giant vacuum cleaner came through
Cause that's how much I love my room
My room is like paradise
Green and bright it's so nice
My favorite, fun, friendly, place
The only one for my pace
My room is where I love to be
It's better than the eye can see
Where I can run to hide my fears
Because it listens to me with all ears
It's where I can spend my life
And where I'll be even when I'm a wife
To me it's heaven but I'm only eleven
And shouldn't think about that too much
But right now I feel I have luck
To have a room like mine
Where my world can shine

Ariana Barrett, Grade 6
School of International Studies at Meadowbrook, VA

Mean?

Why do they call the mean in math mean?
Does he bite?
Does he hurt you?
Does he have claws?
Is he dangerous?
Or is he just a
Math PROBLEM?!

Julia Roesler, Grade 5
Sanford Creek Elementary School, NC

Green Grass

Tall, green, blazing grass
Dances in the little breeze
I love the color
Colin O'Brien, Grade 4
St John Neumann Academy, VA

Intelligent Horses

Horses run really fast
   they run as fast as the wind
they are wild and free
   and a humans best friend
especially mustangs
   especially ponies
   they have beautiful names
they get along well
   and protect each other
from danger around
horses have a leader
   horses have a leader
who they listen to
   their leader is smart
and knows what to do
   horses know when you're sad
and make you feel better
horses are great!
   horses are great!
Christina Zaikina, Grade 5
North Windy Ridge School, NC

Spring

Spring is when everything comes alive
water moving
plants growing
birds hatching
Children laughing.
Sun so bright.
Sky so blue
I love spring!
How about
You?
Jeanny Altera, Grade 5
St Mary School, RI

My Big Feet

My big feet
can quietly creep
around the corner
and down the street!

I put my big feet
under the sheet
and while I sleep
I count my sheep!
Maddie Browder, Grade 5
Pocalla Springs Elementary School, SC

A Plant Is My Friend

Friendship
Is a plant
Never say never
Never say can't

Friendship
Can die
It can be small
Or it can be high

Friendship
Can grow
I hope
You know

Friendship is beautiful
Sarah Vogt, Grade 5
Rye Elementary School, NH

My Dresser

Up we climb,
On top of my dresser.
"You first,"
"No you."
We
Fall
Down
Together!
Instead of my bed,
We fall of the floor.
"Ouch, that hurt,"
Let's do it once more!
Emma Pugh, Grade 5
Sanford Creek Elementary School, NC

Feathered Friend

My feathered friend was green and small
My feathered friend could not talk at all.

My friend had stripes and a long beak,
He was so unique.

On a misty morning
We sat and cuddled in a big puddle.
Nick Carey, Grade 4
Edwards Elementary School, SC

Division

B ehavior
C an
D ivide
E veryone
F orever
Malik Millidge, Grade 4
St Helena Elementary School, SC

Obama

O ptimistic
B rave
A frican American
M ichelle
A new leader
Parker LaCourse, Grade 5
E Taylor Hatton School, VT

Fire

Nipping at the air
Chasing away all the chill
And yet so deadly
Nathan Troutman, Grade 5
Trinity Christian School, VA

Books

Books, books, books
They're in crannies and nooks
They're everywhere
And made to share

There are mysterious books
Funny books, even ones about crooks
There are many you could choose
And they will be bad to lose

You can read them while eating a cherry
And most come from a library
Some, you might have caught
Or maybe you just bought

So while you're reading books
That come from crannies and nooks
Relax your body and don't fret
As you read this couplet
Camden Campe, Grade 5
Olde Providence Elementary School, NC

My Dad: My Hero

After his clock strikes 6:00.
He runs
To get dressed and get
Into his car. He speeds over
To his job.
At his job at Duke Energy,
He works his hardest.
Until 5:30 he goes home and he turns
From a working man
To a family man and takes care
Of us.
At 10:00 he goes
To bed
To do it all over again.
Joseph Edgar, Grade 5
Northside Elementary School, SC

My Favorite Place

My favorite place
Is in New York
A house like squares and triangles.
My favorite place.
It is in a town called Carle Place.
The street is a walk, long as life
In Long Island New York.
My favorite place.
The trees around it are like people
Moving their arms in the breeze.
The house is like the sky.
Cookie cutter houses surround it.
My favorite place.
The sky is blue.
The ground is brown and crunchy
Big and rocky.
My favorite place.
The door opens two people are there
My grandparents
My favorite place
I have one more thing to say, Carle Place is cool!

Zach Frank, Grade 5
East Mooresville Intermediate School, NC

What Green Is

Green is grass
Whispering in the wind
While the parrot snake slithers silently
Green is moss
Growing on trees
Green is money
Hiding in the wallet
It is emerald
So beautiful and bright
It is luck
For anybody who needs it
Green is the green thumb
Digging into the earth
Green is the smell
of a spring breeze
The sound of green
is a water droplet
So delicately light
GREEN IS AWESOME!!!

Corina Gudinas, Grade 4
Atkinson Academy Elementary School, NH

Colors

Orange is the pumpkin that the farmer grows.
Red is the newly wed.
White is the color of the stars in the night sky.
Black is the color of the new moon.
Gray seems to be just a bore.
What is your favorite color?

Bailey Delacruz, Grade 5
C Hunter Ritchie Elementary School, VA

The 2008 Beijing Olympics

The Olympic Games of 2008
They were very, very great.
   In Beijing they took place
That was surely the case.
   I loved the ceremony signaling they'd begun
My, that was so much fun.
   There was Michael Phelps with eight,
Usain Bolt was also first rate.
   Some contestants should get credit
And some had follies they wish they could edit.
   Overall, they were very exciting
They made the television look very inviting.

Gibson Preston, Grade 5
Trinity Christian School, VA

A Promise

A promise is a friend.
You keep it.

A promise is a ball.
It comes back to you.

A promise is the sky.
It is always there.

A promise is an egg.
When you break a promise, the egg breaks.
If you keep the promise it doesn't break.

Lindsay Coté, Grade 5
Holy Cross Elementary School, DE

June

June is the color blue
Like a nice cool swimming pool
June feels like warm cookies just coming out of the oven
It sounds like laughter and screams of excitement
It smells like chlorine and salt water
June tastes like a nice cold cup of lemonade
I'm always excited when June comes around

Alyssa Thomas, Grade 5
Vienna Elementary School, NC

Briana

Beautiful, moody, caring, lovable
Daughter of Karen and Robert
Lover of family, pizza, and friends
Who feels shy, talkative, and happy
Who needs family, God, and support
Who fears spiders, lizards, and roaches
Who gives love, good advice, and treats
Who would like to see India, Bahamas, and Heaven
Resident of Saint Helena Island
Pope

Briana Pope, Grade 4
St Helena Elementary School, SC

The Monster

There is a monster
going up the street.
This is no ordinary monster
because he loves to eat.

They say he came from the Amazon,
or near Virginia Beach.
Wrecking shops and eating things
are the things he likes to do most.

The monster was a curious one,
and looked into the shops.
He saw terrified storekeepers
and numerous items and props.

The creature started to look around
and when he saw the bus,
he kicked it and pushed it over
causing a great ruckus.

When he finally reached the shore
that is finally when
the creature dived into the water.
He was never seen again.

Jonathan Lee, Grade 5
Oak View Elementary School, VA

My Very Very Stinky Feet

My very very stinky feet
If you ever smelled them you'd flee
Just wait until you see

Collin McKenzie, Grade 5
Pocalla Springs Elementary School, SC

The Tree

A while ago
when slaves were free
once was a tree
named the
emancipation
proclamation tree.
The oak
is known
in history
as a cool tree.

Tafari Bailey, Grade 5
Cooper Elementary School, VA

Hamsters

Hamsters
Furry, lovable
Runs through tubes
They feel very soft
Friend

Lauren Kim, Grade 4
Trinity Christian School, VA

The Poor Flower

There was once a flower
It was lonely each hour
Because of the drought
This poor flower was sad
There was no water which was bad
It was impossible for more hope
And there was no way to cope
Nobody was there to glare
Or have some water to share
So unhappy it would be
To watch this flower die you can see
"What a surprise I hear"
"Now I have no fear"
Finally there was somebody here to help save
That was definitely kind and brave
There was more water to hold and grip
Happily the flower can sip
No more problems for thirst
Everything is perfect the way it was at first
There were no more troubles to face again
This jolly flower was not droopy anymore and it was as shiny as a gem!

Siri Doddi, Grade 4
Colvin Run Elementary School, VA

If You Come Home

Go, leave. Leave everything that stands in your way.
Conquer them, they mean nothing.
You are your own person.
Feel no regrets, but do feel that someone is looking for you.
Longing for your return, crying at night for you
Awaiting the day that you will admit defeat and come home
But you won't, you never will
They think they know you, but they don't
As much as you hate to say it, you have to
They make every day better
Every second you spend with them you feel more like yourself
You feel that you can be yourself and they won't judge you
You're just too stubborn to open your eyes and see it
You ponder every so often on what could have been
Then you remember all the rigid things they said
All the terrible tear-jerking memories you have of them
Then you end up where you started
Alone, cold, and wishing you had gone back, but it's too late now
All your hopes and dreams are gone
And all you can do is hope that they are happy with someone
Who will do what you didn't do, which was love them

Anha Bradley, Grade 6
Monelison Middle School, VA

A Girl

A girl is a woman that stands up for the people
A girl is a winner that stands proudly
A girl has been a leader for a long time
But one day that proud winner will soon be a successful woman!!

Katelyn Futrell, Grade 5
Four Oaks Elementary School, NC

Colors

Blue is for a clear sky.
Black is when the moon is high.

Yellow is for a sunny day.
Gray is for rain that needs to go away.

White is for the snow.
Orange is for the sunset glow.

What do you think about colors?

Luke Miller, Grade 5
C Hunter Ritchie Elementary School, VA

Camp

Calm water
Drifting pine trees
Giant rocks bulging from the Earth
Fast motoring boats
Swimming gold fish
Soft wet sand
Warming sun
Darkness from trees
Tubes rubbing sounding like scraping ice
Waves crashing
Rain making puddles
Spots of mud comes
Down on wet sand
Very peaceful
Very nice
Love the bulging rocks
Rocks
Rocks
Rocks

Kyle LeBlanc, Grade 4
Maple Wood Elementary School, NH

I Wish Upon a Star

I wish...
I wish...
I wish I could live in Maine.
I could accomplish so many things.
I wish I could live in a log cabin in Millinocket.
I would work at Baxter State Park as a ranger
Or at the local paper mill.
I would climb mighty Mt. Katahdin
And be on the top of the world
Looking out on a blanket of trees
While climbing Knife's Edge.
I could snowmobile in winter
And ride an A.T.V. in summer.
Best of all I would be surrounded by nature 24/7.
I wish...
I wish...

Matthew Lamarsh, Grade 6
Wyman Elementary School, RI

Spring

I walk down a narrow path dressed in purple and orange
As my day dream begins
The world seems quiet
But some how the wood speaks
Of whistling trees and cracking twigs

Pixies dance purple spins almost as fast as the pixies dance
Their skirts flow with the wind
I'm captured by their beauty

I sound like I have forever
But if forever is just enough time to blink
Then I have forever!

Madeline Gage, Grade 4
Brewster Pierce School, VT

The Canary

I love canary yellow birds
Whose hymn-like songs are always heard!
The boys, I've read, sing better songs,
The girls, instead, get their notes wrong.

Their yellow heads are soft like down.
They also wear a greenish-brown.
Their eyes are beady, beaks are small —
Don't think they're weak because they're small!

These birds, they say, were used in mines.
They warned of gasses, and they shined.
They kept the miners safe from harm
'Cause they sang loud like an alarm.

Even pop stars sing of them —
Sting sang his own canary hymn!
But since I can't sing well in tune,
I hope to buy my own bird soon.

He'll live with me in his own cage,
And sing like my mom on a stage!
You might think that they are scary,
But I love a good canary!

Walker Lozaw, Grade 6
Our Lady of Lourdes Catholic School, NC

Scissors

Scissors are a baby lynx opening its mouth,
A giraffe eating leaves with his sand paper tongue,
Scissors are a nut falling to the ground,
The waviness of the wave,
Scissors are a nuthatch calling,
Scissors are the sound of the burning coals,
Scissors are a butterfly calling,
Scissors are the dove flying into the sunset of colors,
Scissors are a stealthy owl peering at its prey.

Kelsey Voss, Grade 5
Rye Elementary School, NH

To a President

Martin Luther King Jr. had a dream that the people of the world would discover a way to live together.
I, too have dreams.

I'm a student who dreams of a nation that doesn't contribute so much to global warming
and is benevolent to others who are in need.

I dream of a state that is known by other states like New York and California. I don't want to be an unnoticed state.
So far we have just been the first state to end slavery.

I dream of a community in which people have freedom of speech. No one should have to sit on the sidelines
thinking of new ideas that are bubbling up.

I wish for a world where everyone is equal in respect, wealth, have the right to believe
and have no criticism for religious beliefs.

I wish for a home with heat and people with full bellies.
I wish for a classroom with the necessary school supplies, and a decent education.

I'm a student who supports you and your ideas.
I am a person who thinks of ideas for a better nation, state, community, and the world.

Yes, Mr. President, I can help you create popularity.

Seth Herz, Grade 6
Main Street Middle School, VT

12 Months

January: when lots of snow falls and I love to throw snowballs.
February: on the 14th a boy can shine and give a girl a valentine.
March: is when the rain will bring the new flowers of the spring.
April: the 9th couldn't be colder because my dad becomes another year older.
May: a month when it starts to get warmer. Probably not too much fun if you are a farmer.
June: is the month when the end of school comes. Now for the summer we can sit on our lazy bums.
July: 4th is when we become free of Great Britain's monarchy.
August: is the end of summer, wouldn't it be cool if my parents bought me a Hummer?
September: is the month my parents got married, they will be together 'til they are dead and buried.
October: is the month when we dress in costumes, the masks stink of nasty fumes.
November: is when we eat our turkey, sometimes I'd rather have beef jerky.
December: is when I like to be sledding, I hope to the playoffs the Redskins are heading.

Kade Schreiber, Grade 5
C Hunter Ritchie Elementary School, VA

The Ocean Blue

Sailing the ocean blue, Dolphins swim around my boat, ships floating above the deep blue sea, my anchor sitting in the bright
yellow soft sand, the four long yellow flags blowing in the gentle winds, while I become pale and tired of steering, it becomes
night, stars come out with their lights in the night, while the ocean's tides hit the shore some more, while the waves of the
ocean lighten my soul with great joy.

Anthony Merola, Grade 6
St Rocco School, RI

Love

the bright silver moon hits the waters of paris, creating a romantic glow upon the water.
the stars are bright and shining through, on a first date with a first kiss.
rain falling hard on her, as he is down on one knee.
it is their 25th anniversary, and still every day is like their first years together.

Leanna Morris, Grade 6
Beech Springs Intermediate School, SC

Blue

The sky is blue
Like shimmering pools of blue
Having fun with the waves of blue
It shines like the water and the sun
Having a time on a great day, so stay for a day
We'll have a great day in the blue filled water
Sowing the blue shall be with me

Nigee Watson, Grade 4
Riverview Elementary School, VA

Life

Don't let a grudge set you ablaze for revenge;
Just let the fact that it's life and they chose the path.
Only carry love and forgiveness.

Josh Sexton, Grade 5
Queen's Grant Community School, NC

Death

Death is like an eternity of unwanted silence.
Death is like a black hole in ones heart.
Death is like a fate of grief for your loved ones.
Death is as if you are forever nothingness.
Death is like a sickening twist in the stomach.
Death is like many tears, newly shed.
Most of all death is a never-ending
pain in the heart for those whom
you were loved by.

Katie Marshall, Grade 5
Queen's Grant Community School, NC

My Dad and Me

My dad likes to tease me,
Like I have a beard.
I just tell him,
He has a pokey beard.
When I went to ballet,
He called it boyllet.

My dad calls me Fatalaide or Madalaide,
I call him Fatadad, or Madadad.
He lets me stay up and watch TV,
I love him, and he loves me.
And that's all that counts,
My dad and me.

Adelaide Burgess, Grade 4
Courthouse Road Elementary School, VA

I Love You the Yellowiest

Dad, I love you the yellowiest
I love you the color of the sun lighting up the world
I love you the color of smiley faces brightening your day
A blooming flower
A pencil
A bucket full of sand

KK Willoughby, Grade 5
Blaney Elementary School, SC

Disney World

As I enter Disney World
A place of excitement
Full of rides and freedom
It was a forest of never ending dreams
To do what you want, like a dream

But the excitement doesn't
Dance to you, you go in it.
This is a wonderland that plays
The dream that lives with you
A time to live in it for yourself

The family will enjoy.
The many wonders you seek are there
Disney World is where we have freedom
For the families to know the excitement
Disney World is a friend that stays.

Disney World will never leave
This wonderland will dance for us
It is like a home for people who need it.
It is a palace of peace
Many wonders are there.

Oscar Basualdo, Grade 5
East Mooresville Intermediate School, NC

Finding My Home

As I run through the water
And flip my feet,
I feel a great rush in a lively beat,
The seashore sings
With a sad mourning,
As I walk to the shore to start a dreadful morning.

As I run through the streets of Beverly Hills,
The smell of wind gives me chills.
My feet cry for water
But I know I won't bother,
For I have found my home.

Katherine Le, Grade 5
Rosemont Forest Elementary School, VA

Colors

Blue is the sky, way up high.
Purple is so royal, my oh my!

Red is a grouchy crab
Green gumdrops in a bag.

Orange sun is shiny and bright.
Yellow stars glow in the night!

Colors are so meaningful!

Emily Hogge, Grade 5
C Hunter Ritchie Elementary School, VA

Marines

They fight for us victoriously
We praise them all when we see
That they have now set us free
But some may mourn to the loss
Of faith and glee when they see
the horrible black Mary
for they bring the bodies
of dead family they say "Sorry
but remember them in your heart
for they've given all they've got"
Hannah Whisman, Grade 5
Queens Creek Elementary School, NC

The Sea

Sail boats, running crabs
rolling waves
sunny
bright white sand
loud kids playing, running
Splash…Splash…Splash…
crashing over and over
crashing sea shells
on the beach
this is
relaxing
peaceful
fun and
happy at
the Beach.
Abby Smith, Grade 4
Maple Wood Elementary School, NH

Kittens

Kittens purr loudly,
And meow softly,
Have a ball at night,
Sleep during the day,
They have the power,
To see at night,
And to lie down
in the hot sun.
Kittens
Libby Marks, Grade 5
Clover Hill Elementary School, VA

Food/Drink

Food
yummy, starving
chewing, making, loving
ribs, pizza, 7 up, coke
drinking, swallowing, toasting
thirst-quenching, ultimate drink
Drink
Jada Harris, Grade 6
Floyd T Binns Middle School, VA

Soldier

I dreamed
I was a soldier
On a battlefield
Defending my country
Sadly.
Richard Kellenberger, Grade 5
Cooper Elementary School, VA

My Little Star

My little star I saw so bright
said to me on faithful night,
"I wish I could fix the ozone layer
to conserve electricity.
I wish to watch the other stars glisten!
I wish to watch the moon sparkle!
I wish I could fix the ozone layer now!

I wish to end war so please make peace!
I wish to end hunger, so please feed!
I wish to end depression, so please give!
I wish to end war now!"
Brittneigh Nicole Chapman, Grade 6
Wyman Elementary School, RI

Running

Running
Quickly
Joyfully
Gracefully
Softly
Safely
Running
Under the trees
With her friends
With her feet
On the pavement
In her workout clothes
Running
As if she were an ostrich
Because of the ice cream man
While wishing she was faster
While she was talking
Because she loved it
Running
Jennifer Lapinski, Grade 6
St Mary's School, SC

Sound

I dreamed
I was a drum
In a parade
Beating
Rhythmically.
Kaylah Moseley-Pressley, Grade 5
Cooper Elementary School, VA

Softball

Softball is the best
Hit, swing, catch, throw, batter out
Finally we won
Katlyn D'Alessandro, Grade 5
North Windy Ridge School, NC

Space

I like to look at outer space
The man in the moon makes a face
One planet is red
It dizzies my head
And the Earth is the humans' home base.
Jonathon Moore, Grade 4
Battlefield Elementary School, VA

A Lie

A lie is a backpack
because it weighs you down
and it's hard to carry.

A lie is a shadow
because it follows you where ever you go
and stays with you

A lie is a plant
because it keeps on growing
and never stops till you tell the truth

A lie is permanent marker
because you can't erase it easily.
Marissa Johnson, Grade 5
Holy Cross Elementary School, DE

Good Times

I'm walking through the city
with bags in my hands
When I see a little baby
with a grown man.
The man seems weak
I wonder what's wrong.
Then he puts down the baby
then leaves it all alone.
I walk to get the child,
tears in its eyes
turns out it was my brother
no need to cry! The man was
my uncle, Uncle Bobby Black
he said he was testing me
turns out it was a fact
he was testing on my courage
my compassion too
he said that I passed
My heart is pure and true.
Paige Leary, Grade 5
Queen's Grant Community School, NC

Ode to a Volleyball

Volleyball, oh volleyball
You are so round
I love it when I hit you and score a point
You are bouncy and squishy
I love playing with you
You can be yellow or green sometimes blue
You can hurt my hands
But that's ok
Just try to be more gentle
You are the best sport ever.

Alyssa Cefaretti, Grade 5
Vienna Elementary School, NC

My World

In this world,
I am a girl.
A normal, everyday girl.

But in my world.
I am a queen.
A marvelous, special queen.

I am the queen where the fairies fly.
I am the queen where the clouds go by.

I am the queen where the mermaids swim.
I am the queen where the fish wave their fins.

I am the queen where the woodland animals dwell.
I am the queen where the bird's voices sing as clear as a bell.

My world is where I can reach it easily
It is in my imagination
I close my eyes, draw a breath
I am there.

Louisa Sholar, Grade 5
East Mooresville Intermediate School, NC

A Visit to the Sea

As I sit on the shore with my eyes gently closed,
I listen to a wave as it comes and it goes.
The salty wind rushes right through my hair,
As I pick up a shell so plain and so bare.
Above me a gull flies its wings pearly white,
It soon disappears right out of my sight.
I see children playing and having fun in the sand,
One has a shovel clamped in his hand.
The reeds are rustling up on the dunes,
And I hear the sound of nature's own tunes.
The sun's warm rays feel nice on my skin,
I'm sure it's the best place I've ever been.
There really is nothing better to me,
Than sitting and enjoying a day by the sea.

Lucy Willis, Grade 6
Cape Henry Collegiate School, VA

The Roller Coaster

As I walked anxiously to the seat
I felt like I was going to hurl
BANG!
BOOM!
The brakes dropped and we all slowly pulled away

The clanging cracking clumsy metal chain hit the metal bar
PING!
PONG!
PANG!
I was BLINDED by a bright flash

I was BLINDED by another bright flash
I hurled to the ground faster than you can say WOW!
My stomach dropped every second it could
Heart beating harder than ever
Hands held higher than ever

Four rough rapid rugged more turns
I was on land or I thought so
Slowly I took my seatbelt off and when I looked up
The car had already started to leave the station
So I just went one more time

Zack Nantz, Grade 5
East Mooresville Intermediate School, NC

Being a Floor

Oh how I hate being a floor
I should've been a door
I get stepped on constantly
I wish I could plea
But they won't listen to me
Oh how I hate being a floor

Leah Dyer, Grade 5
Courthouse Road Elementary School, VA

Proud to Be

I'm proud to be me
a person called me
sometimes I climb a tree
And when I go down, I say, "Whee!"

My name is Savannah
but I've never been to Havana
My nickname is Banana
which are rarely found in the African savanna

Sometimes I collect rocks
and I've never had the chicken pox
Sometimes I don't have matching socks
I also like to sit on the docks

There's somebody I'm proud to be
and that special person is called me!

Savannah Bunch, Grade 5
Riverview Elementary School, VA

What Is Red

Red is the taste of
hot peppers and apples.

Red is the smell of fire and
strawberry ice cream.

Red is the sight of leaves
in the fall and the American Flag.

Red is the touch of a book
and a rug.

Red is the sound of fast cars
and a kick ball.

That is red
to me.

Johnathan Feeny, Grade 5
St Mary School, RI

Friends

Friends
Loving, encouraging
Shares with you
You think they're loyal
Companions

Julianne Cobb, Grade 4
Trinity Christian School, VA

A Bunny

I am a bunny.
All small and sweet
And like a frog
I shall leap.

Surrounding me
Are forests and trees
And busily, busily
Buzzing bees.

I am a bunny
All small and sweet
And like a frog
I shall leap.

Grace Ray, Grade 4
Crestwood Elementary School, VA

Forest

Forest
green, beautiful
rain falling down
peaceful, quiet, relaxed, calm
Nature

Michelle Lescano, Grade 6
Floyd T Binns Middle School, VA

Rain

I could hear the rain
in my room.
Pitter patter,
splash poosh
it went,
as it hit
my window.
Then a couple
of big drops came.
Pish, posh
they went.
Then it
slowed up.
Shhhh.
I could still hear it,
but just barely.
Tick. Tick.
And then poof!
It started back again.

Brandon Roby, Grade 6
Monelison Middle School, VA

Flowers

Flowers begin as a seed
Over time they grow
Like a child growing up
They are everywhere you go
They always blossom out
Just like a child

Sara Beth Napper, Grade 5
Blaney Elementary School, SC

The Log

The cold log cracks
Sparkly snow blankets it.
Lightly, snow falls on the log.
A porcupine scratches fiercely at the log.
Looking for dinner.

Cold wind dries my mouth.
I sink in the snow,
As white as a tissue
Deer delicately walk on snow,
Leaving behind fresh, light prints.

Shae Gordon, Grade 4
Bethlehem Elementary School, NH

Chewing

Chewing
Food, noise
Open, close, swallow
Full, drowsy, sleepy, snoring
Eating

Danya Abutaleb, Grade 6
Floyd T Binns Middle School, VA

Winter

Warm hot chocolate
Over glossy cup's red sides
Spills on my fingers

Cameron Galligher, Grade 6
Midlothian Middle School, VA

The Quiet

The quiet is —
So loud.

I cannot —
Concentrate.

It's like a —
Sonic boom
Concealed in my head.

I need —
Something to distract me.
A tune,
A tumble,
Anything —
Will do.

Books drop.
Everyone —
Laughs.

Noise —
Sweet —
Noise.

Mallory Hahn, Grade 5
Oak View Elementary School, VA

Summer

Playing in the pool,
Out of the sun,
Keeping cool,
Having fun.
No school!
Drinking lemonade,
My energy tool.
Swim team starts,
A swimming duel.
Summer.
Each year is a new whirlpool.

Cameron Darr, Grade 4
Oak View Elementary School, VA

Spring

Hooray spring is here
Children playing on the ground
The sun glazing down

Halie Josey, Grade 5
Pocalla Springs Elementary School, SC

Summer

Summer tastes like popsicles dripping down my face
Summer smells like fresh grass being cut
Summer sounds like birds chirping in the sky
Summer makes me feel like a flower
Summer looks like grass and clouds
Summer is as big as the Earth
Summer is tears of rain dropping out of the sky
Summer is the best season

Tyler Salisbury, Grade 4
Tabernacle Elementary School, NC

The Wonder of the Seasons

The waves come up and down,
The snow's fluttering sound.

Autumn's passionate leaves,
And spring's buzzing bees.

Winter's cool colors,
And sunny bright summers.

Spring's merry flowers,
And autumn's leaf showers.

Oh, the wonders of winter,
And the happiness of spring.

Summer's picnic baskets,
And cookies and cupcakes to bring.

There are the wonders of the seasons.

Samantha-Hope Brouillet, Grade 5
Rosemont Forest Elementary School, VA

Cat

Cat
Furry
Funny
Adorable
Swift
Attentive
Cat
With a silky coat
With begging eyes
With pleading meows
With contented purrs
Between my mom and me
Cat
Sprawling all over the desk
Staring intently at birds
Perking up at the slightest noise
Meowing and chirping without enough petting
Following us as we go upstairs
Cat

Paul List, Grade 6
St Mary's School, SC

Purple

Purple is the moon on a sunny day
Purple is the romantic dinner at a fast-food restaurant
Purple is the smell of walking into a fresh shoe store
Purple is the lone tree on the mountain summit
Purple is the color that lives inside me.

August Vitzthum, Grade 6
Main Street Middle School, VT

The Scent of Herbs

The whiff of rosemary in the air
The smell of thyme in animals' hair
Spring's gentle wind bringing out the scent
Across the countryside it went
Now the beautiful fragrance is revealed
With glory, springtime makes the curtain be peeled.

Kayleigh McCoy, Grade 4
Charlottesville Waldorf School, VA

Mountains

I love going to the mountains
That feeling in my stomach
The hills and thrills.
We go bumpty, bump
Clunky, clunk.

I get out of the car
Then the wind whispers,
"The trees are happy to see you."
I run to my happy place.
My cousin and I are Indians
With our pretend spears
Catching fish in the water.

I lay by the river.
It takes away my stress
Like when a bear goes to sleep for the winter
Thinking about nothing.

I hate leaving the mountains
That sad feeling in my stomach
No hills, no thrills
We won't go bumpty, bump
Clunky, clunk.

Zoey Bumgardner, Grade 5
East Mooresville Intermediate School, NC

My Snowflake

I sat at the window of my house at the lake,
I see slowly but gracefully a dancing snowflake.
I run outside to touch it,
But it melted away.
I was getting chilly,
But I wish I could stay.

Emily Lund, Grade 5
Wakefield Forest Elementary School, VA

All About Me

I am short
you are tall
let's get together
and have a ball!

I am good looking
and you are not
so back off
and go cry a lot

It is good to be lazy
because it is fun
and leave me alone
because I have a water gun

Zachery Crawford, Grade 5
Pocalla Springs Elementary School, SC

My Grandmother, Laura

Laura was my grandmother.
She loved me like no other.

To me it was shown clearly,
she loved me dearly.

She lived at a lake
and she loved to bake.

Her food was so good.
She cooked like no one else could.

Oh yeah, she loved to fish.
If I could have one wish…

It would be
for me to see…

Her smiling face
and just in case…

Tell her how much I love her
and miss her like no other.

Ariana Peniston, Grade 6
Camperdown Academy, SC

Spring

Sunny and warm
Few showers
Flower buds start to come up
Everything starting to get green
A little chilly
Late spring pool opens up
Feels happy and exciting
No more bundling up
Springtime is here!

Thomasin Coffman, Grade 6
Wakefield Forest Elementary School, VA

Oh Mr. Easter Bunny

Oh Mr. Easter Bunny you tickle me funny because I'm excited for Easter
and I wish I could see you one time and that would be fine
Oh Mr. Easter Bunny you are so nice but since it's spring and its hot don't you need ice
Oh Mr. Easter Bunny you hide too much I really want to see you in person.

Stephanie Davalos, Grade 4
Courthouse Road Elementary School, VA

Books!

What takes you on a journey to a not-so-distant land? Books!
What can be big or small, skinny or tall? Books!
What can be about life or death! Books!
What can make you feel good or bad, sad or mad? Books!
What can be long or short? Books!
What can have characters like me or you? Books!
What can be an adventure or a mystery? Books!
What can be about beans, blimps, or black bears? Books!
What can give you a better understanding of something? Books!
What can have an animal that talks? Books!
What can teach you how to publish poetry? Books!
What can be about a hare or a hippo who likes Heath Bars? Books!
What can teach you how to cook waffles, make wafers,
Grow watermelon, or make wasabi? Books!
What can show you the way to go? Maps!

Nathaniel Rendell, Grade 5
East Mooresville Intermediate School, NC

Dreams and Secrets

Dreams cannot be seen.
Only by the lips may they be told.
Only by the pure in heart may they be secure.
Only by the ears may they be heard.
Dreams are things we set our standards to.
Dreams can be beautiful in any way you can imagine.
Secrets cannot be seen.
Only by the lips may they be told.
Only by the pure in heart may they be secure.
Only by the ears may they be heard.
Secrets are the things we all tell our friends that they keep close.
Secrets can be good or bad, big or small.
Dreams and secrets we have all imagined and told.

Keely Wilson, Grade 6
Chapin Middle School, SC

I've Learned That…

I've learned that there are two paths.
I've learned which one to take.
I've learned what they both mean.
I've learned to treat others the way you would want to be treated.
I've learned that friends like you for who you are.
I've learned that family will love you from the beginning until the end.
I've learned that there will always be someone there to catch you when you fall.
I've learned to make the right decisions.
I've learned to do what I need to do in my life that's right.
I've learned that school makes you smart.

Brandi Collins, Grade 5
Northside Elementary School, SC

White

White is a blank page waiting for pencils and lead
White are graceful doves flying over your head
White is the winter snow that blinds your eyes
White are the clouds that vary in shape and size

White is the innocent color of your grandma's hair
White is the hunted tiger that has become rare
White is the cap of a colossal mountain
White is water splashing down a marble fountain

White is the marshmallow that plops in your cup
White is the suit of a runner that never gives up
White is the continent at the bottom of the globe
White is the heavenly color of an angel's robe

Grace M. Speas, Grade 5
Symonds Elementary School, NH

The Child

The child is a *butterfly*.
The child starts as something *small*
Then grows into something beautiful,
In which everyone wishes to be,
All of the children are different and *unique*,
In their very own special way.

Celeste Carberry, Grade 5
East Mooresville Intermediate School, NC

Winter

Winter is as cold as ice water in my glass
Winter tastes like snow
Winter smells like a marshmallow being cooked over a bonfire
Winter looks like a fluffy cloud
Winter sounds like a bird chirping
Winter is a touch of my cold breath
Winter is fun because I can go sledding
Winter is snowy because it gets real cold
Winter is my favorite time of the year
Winter is my favorite time of the year

Hunter Hamby, Grade 4
Tabernacle Elementary School, NC

Steven

My brother said, "Number three is even."
I said, "Something's wrong with you Steven."

Then he went into his room.
And I said, "What are you doing with that broom?"

He said, "I am going to chase you around the room."
I said, "Don't you hit me with that broom."

As I kept shouting, "Three is not even."
Mother came in and said, "Something's wrong with you Steven!"

Mikala Glover, Grade 4
St Helena Elementary School, SC

Realization

She pulls the old rowboat back into the sea grass.
The golden sunset turns a dragonfly
into an iridescent crystal as it skims the waves.
With a grin, she realizes how content she is with her life.

Tyler Wilson, Grade 6
Wakefield Forest Elementary School, VA

Tatyanna

Lazy, independent, happy, silly
Sister of Fajour and Jah'nyia
Lover of cheerleading, dancing, and singing
Who feels sweet, funny, and safe
Who needs friends, family, and love
Who fears deer, alligators, and bugs
Who gives clothes, shoes, and gadgets
Who would like to see Lil Wayne, T.I., and Mickey Mouse
Resident of Canopy Lane
Fripp

Tatyana Fripp, Grade 4
St Helena Elementary School, SC

My Little Girl

Some little girls are nice.
Some little girls are sweet.
Some little girls are fun.
But my little girl is all that combined in one.

Abygail J. Romero, Grade 4
Courthouse Road Elementary School, VA

Lee-Lee

Lee-Lee is my pet
I haven't found a better one yet.
She got stung by a bee
she came running for me to see.

Lee-Lee likes to eat meat
to her it is a very special treat.
She is also very clean
and sometimes can be quite mean.

Lee-Lee loves to go for a ride
she would rather be in a car than stuck inside.
She doesn't like to share her toys
with other dogs girls or boys.

When you brush her hair it becomes a fight
if you don't stop she is probably going to bite.
She means the world to me
I wish she was here for all of you to see.

Now I am going outside to sit on a log
and spend some time with my dog.
Just watching her run
and having some fun.

Melia Roberts, Grade 5
Forrest W Hunt Elementary School, NC

Animals

A pes climb
N uthatches fly
I guanas sit in the sun
M onkeys eat bananas
A rmadillos hide
L ions roar
S nakes bite with sharp teeth

Christina Arnold, Grade 5
Blaney Elementary School, SC

Swiftly Swinging Swing

I dreamed
I was a swing
On a school playground
Swinging back and forth
Swiftly.

Victoria Jones, Grade 5
Cooper Elementary School, VA

Spring Is Here

Glamorous blue skies
Bright bugs on blooming flowers
All because spring's here

Deondrae Cisse, Grade 5
Pocalla Springs Elementary School, SC

Sports

Football
Cool, tough
Tackling, tiring, running
Demanding, outdoor, indoor, exciting
Shooting, dunking, rebounding
Heat, powerful
Basketball

Stephon Chaplin, Grade 5
St Helena Elementary School, SC

Nana*

N ice as can be
A lways giving hugs
N ever will be forgotten
A lways will be loved

Kyle Brown, Grade 4
Robertson School, RI
**In loving memory of my Nana*
who died 5/10/08

Obama

O bama is the first
B lack man to become President of
A merica and it's going to
M ake amazing
A nd incredible things happen.

Willem Morin, Grade 6
Forestbrook Middle School, SC

Love

L iving up to it every day
O dd moments
V ery rough, but at the
E nd, it all pays off!

Alex Massey, Grade 6
Forestbrook Middle School, SC

Waves Crashing on the Shore

Waves crashing on the shore
Makes me wish for many more
Sleepless nights when I cannot rest
Makes me feel all depressed
Until I go out to the shore
That makes me wish for many more.
Kids splashing on the shore
Makes me wish for many more
Playful days and joyous nights
So it won't be such a fright
When I go out in the night.
Kids playing on the shore
Makes me wish for many more.

Erin Underwood, Grade 6
Chapin Middle School, SC

Gothic

Cantering so hard
Gothic flies through the air
He has won first place

Evan Moxley, Grade 5
Northside Elementary School, SC

Clock

'Tis a clock, tells time
It tells you if you are late
Only if you look.

Mitchell Whalen, Grade 6
Main Street Middle School, VT

A Book

I am a book
All smooth and nice
And like an elephant
I hate mice.

Surrounding me,
Are shelves and desks
And all the children
Taking tests.

I am a book
All smooth and nice
And like an elephant
I hate mice.

Melanie Chow, Grade 6
Crestwood Elementary School, VA

Green Is Lucky

Green is a lucky feeling you get!!!
He's a patch of 4 leaf clovers
He's the stem of a flower
Green is the frosting on a birthday cake
He's a leprechaun

Green means go
Green is always joyful
He is worst at being mean
He collects luck
Play with him, he won't bite!
He's spreading luck
He loves to find shamrocks
He's everywhere you go

He hates green beans
But loves fruit
He's what you always wanted!
His friends are orange and pink

He's always kind
He dodges all trouble
Green's my mom, lucky and happy!

Haley Zamorano, Grade 4
Youngsville Elementary School, NC

Sleeping

Sleeping
unendingly
gracefully
dreamily
wonderfully
thoroughly
Sleeping
on her bed
with her dog
after dinner
during a movie
with her favorite pillow
Sleeping
as if she would never wake up
while dreaming happily
when she shouldn't be
since she was so tired
where she wanted to
Sleeping

Laura Franco, Grade 6
St Mary's School, SC

Butterfly

Butterfly flutters
Across the moonlit river
Daintily landing

Meredith Jennings, Grade 6
Cape Henry Collegiate School, VA

Colors of the Earth

Earth's colors spinning all around,
Colors in the sky, the colors on the ground.
The sun, yellow as thy
Reminds me of lemon meringue pie.
Blue peaceful and just,
Having blue is a must.
Orange almost as bright as yellow
Is also worn by big, friendly fellows.
Pink the colors ladies adore,
Boys are wearing it more and more.
These colors to name a few,
There are more colors around you.

Taishai Fauntleroy, Grade 4
Riverview Elementary School, VA

A Wonderful Woman

J oyful when it comes to spending time with Holly and I
A wesome when it comes to snuggle time
N ever give up on me
I nstead of missing school plays you come to them
S ometimes you let me watch American Idol

R ight on my birthday, you serve me breakfast in bed
E ven when you're mad, you still love me
N ever miss any Doctor shows
F ight for your children to behave
R ight after school on Fridays, you take me to Girl Scouts
O ver the weekends, you let me have sleepovers
W ow, mom!

Sarah Joy Renfrow, Grade 5
Trinity Christian School, VA

The Holocaust and I

A man named Adolph Hitler murdered many innocent Jews.
He disliked them and felt no sympathy for them
When they were killed, he seemed not to hear their cries.
Today I'm glad there is no Holocaust

If there were
Many more would die!

MiKayla Molina, Grade 5
Pembroke Elementary School, NC

Our Trip

One cloudy morning
I woke up to noise
My mom yells, "Hurry up or we'll miss our flight!"
I rushed downstairs and opened the door
And then the rain started to pour.
And when we got to the airport
our flight was canceled
I was really mad
but I was glad
It was all a dream…

Esi Oyofo, Grade 5
Woodlawn Elementary School, VA

Blue

Blue is the color of the sea
The color of the sky
The paint on my paintbrush
It is the candy in my mouth
Blue is how I feel when I am sad
It is the ink in the container
It is the very hot fire from the burning wood
Blue is the ice in the North Pole
It is my veins
It is my favorite color
That is blue!

Stetson Gardin, Grade 5
Jonesville Elementary School, SC

Months

July
Hot, sunny
Grilling, swimming, fishing
Vacation, firecrackers, Christmas, presents
Snowing, skating, sledding
Cold, windy
December

Javion Watson, Grade 5
St Helena Elementary School, SC

Yellow

Yellow is the color of the sun,
it is very light and that's what's fun.
Yellow is cool, big and bright,
it's that big bright bulb that lights up the night.
Yellow is the color of a flower,
the smell that has such great power.
Yellow is the color of the Pittsburgh Steelers,
also the color of my big four wheeler.
Yellow is the color of a book,
the peppers I love to cook.
Yellow is the color of a juicy lemon,
and it tastes like you're floating in heaven.
Yellow is the color of the New Mexico flag,
and it waves like a tail wags.
That is why I like yellow.

Thomas Vessella, Grade 5
St Mary School, RI

Catnap

I'm napping quietly.
I'm napping soundlessly.
I'm napping softly.
I'm napping silently, peacefully.
I'm napping calmly, gently, tranquilly.
I'm napping tenderly, serenely, restfully, noiselessly.
I'm napping hushed, subdued, muted, unvoiced, still.
I'm napping quietly.

Isaac Wolfe, Grade 4
Blacksburg New School, VA

Harriet Tubman

Harriet
Brave, strong, outgoing, believer
Daughter of Old Rit
Lover of her rag doll, having freedom, fighting in the revolt
Who feels the need to have rights, be treated respectfully, forced to do what is wrong
Who needs to help black people, love everybody, feel loved
Who gives great ideas, a chance for freedom, as much support as she can
Who fears getting killed in the revolt, being a slave again, not having the same rights as everybody else
Who would like to be free, have back her rag doll, always be General Tubman
Resident of Maryland
Tubman

Jayna Ryan, Grade 4
Hope Valley Elementary School, RI

Where I'm From

I am from the clean streets of Montpelier, Vermont.
The roads packed with cars.
I am from the dark blue sky in winter.
Snow drifting.
Hitting my nose.
Melting.
I am from the garden growing tradition in the summer's sun.
I am from Main Street Middle School, Union Elementary School and the Family Center.
Schools that gave me education.
I am from a mentor who came to my house every day to teach me manners and educational work
before I went to preschool.
I am from the dreams that make me, me.
I dream about Harvard University.
Getting my teaching degree.
I am from the Chinese-food-smelling house as you enter.
My family's Chinese restaurant I work at.
I am from Hong Kong where my extended family originated.
I am from the memories of eating bunny poop at the age of one or two.

Christina Tang, Grade 6
Main Street Middle School, VT

The Longest Bike Ride Ever

The longest bike ride ever is the ride of life,
Filled with scenes of courage, fear, and strife.
There are hills going up and down, and times you want to turn around,
But you know that's life.
You may fall off once or twice,
And there'll be times you'll have to make a sacrifice.
But there are signs that help you move along, reminding you to stay strong,
But you know that's life.
As you reach the end of the curving pass, you smile while riding in the grass.
You watch the struggling animals around you, and are reminded of all you went through,
'Cause you know that's life.
As you stop under the maze of trees,
You feel the wind in your hair, and see the falling leaves.
And simply love the world around you, taking pleasure at the beautiful view,
Because you now understand the meaning of life:
To always strive to be your best,
And to follow the right path on this joyful, Bike Ride Quest.

Tamra Nebabu, Grade 6
Queen of Apostles School, VA

I'm Like a Good Person

I'm like a butterfly; I fly so high
I'm like a computer; I get tapped every day
I'm like a cat; I'm so puffy
I'm like a lion; I get a loud noise
I'm like a cloud; I blow some good wind
I'm like a glass; if I lose control I will break
I'm like a tree; I'm still
I'm like a camera; I take a picture

Judith Valdez, Grade 5
Four Oaks Elementary School, NC

Friendship

Friendship is a wave,
Playfully toppling ones that come near it.
Enjoying the fun that the surfer is having with it.
Tickling the sand and rocks that laugh and play below it.
Helping a different surfer win a competition.
As storms and wind make it bigger and bigger,
It sighs and creates new friendships with the
Lightning, rain, wind, and clouds.

Isabelle Hanna, Grade 5
Rye Elementary School, NH

Anger Is…

Anger is not getting the toy I wanted.
Anger is not having a party to celebrate the day you were born.
Anger is not getting treated fairly.
Anger is not getting to watch my favorite show.
Anger is getting blamed for something I didn't do.
Anger is eating beans instead of cheese pizza.
Anger is not having recess at school.
Anger is not getting to play outside on a sunny day.
Anger is when your face turns the color of magma.
Anger is not fun at all.

Alexus Grant, Grade 5
Northside Elementary School, SC

Feed Me

Ginger bread, ginger bread,
Tasty when hot,
Eat it and tell me you like it a lot,
Make it,
Then bake it,
As tasty as can be,
Then hop down the road and give it to me!

Claire Forehand, Grade 6
Homeschool Plus, VA

Apple

An apple like a bomb,
with a stem and a core
a blast of deliciousness when you bite
always making you want more!

Dominic Vicharelli, Grade 5
East Mooresville Intermediate School, NC

Tyasia

Happy, mean, helpful, lovable,
Daughter of Eddie and Tenekia
Lover of TV, cheerleading, and my friends
Who feels shy, scared, and safe
Who needs friends, a family, and help
Who fears tigers, death, and snakes
Who gives candy, love, and toys
Who would like to see Disney Land, family, and New York
Resident of South Carolina
Gadson

Tyasia Gadson, Grade 4
St Helena Elementary School, SC

I Wonder

I wonder what my sister was like
Did she get frights during the night
Did she cry before she died
Was she a baby of delight
Or a baby full of fright
Maybe so
Maybe no
Because I never got to meet her
But I know she is up in the sky watching down on me
So when I die I'll be able to greet her
And finally get to meet her
It will be a great time just to get to know her
And to show her
A wonderful time as we take our places in the sky

Andrew Seegulam, Grade 6
Dr Edward Ricci School, RI

The Jungle

A place where it's hot like the sun
and the tiger is the lion hunting for food in the tree,
so tall and wet,
the prey runs like a man in the Olympics.

The animals are loud and calm
and so are the tall twisted trees
but men hunting animals, all but one hide
it is the tiger in the grass watching the men go by.

The jungle is a wonderful place with many magnificent animals
like the swift cheetah
and the mindful monkeys
and the beckoning birds.

Gannon Teunissen, Grade 5
Manchester Elementary/Middle School, VT

My Cat

My cat goes meow meow when she is hungry,
Her name is Fluffy.
She is a fat cat and lazy too,
I say to her how I love you.

Hailey Melton, Grade 4
Edwards Elementary School, SC

The Nice Guy

M ysterious
A mbitious
T rustworthy
T houghtful
H appy
E xciting
W onderful

Matthew Flores, Grade 6
Benjamin Syms Middle School, VA

Sister

Sister
Helpful, caring
Running, hopping, jumping
Nice, like no other
Friend

Madison Totty, Grade 4
Appomattox Elementary School, VA

Volcanos

Active volcanos
Erupt hot as red peppers
Aren't they breathtaking?

Brian Alexzander Arredondo, Grade 5
North Windy Ridge School, NC

Lion

Lion
huge, golden
attacking, stalking, pursuing
watching and waiting silently
King

Abby Culver, Grade 6
Floyd T Binns Middle School, VA

Acadia

Warmth of the fire
Drifts up to my face
Blazing
Blazing
Blazing
Feet pattering on rocks
Children giggling
I'm chasing them
Passing tents
Fun
Fun
Fun
Summer stars stare down upon us
What does Acadia look like in the fall?
I sit down by the fire
Joyful
Joyful
Joyful.

Sadie Burgess, Grade 4
Maple Wood Elementary School, NH

Alone

The wind is pushing me away from the one place I want to be.
Home.
Back home.
Where my friends and I laugh and play, but they are gone with the east wind.
As I am gone with the west wind.
My friends said that I would be with them, but it feels as if I am not.
I am lying, crying, and thinking about my place.
Home.
Back home.
I am going to think about my friends every day.
Will they about me?
Or leave me to wonder in a path of darkness.
They say I am strong.
Very strong.
I am at my new home.
Home.

Abbey Folk, Grade 6
Berry Shoals Intermediate School, SC

The Extraordinary Man

I met the most extraordinary man today.
Something familiar about him just drew me to him like a magnet.
Although, the stress and strain of his past was visible in his face,
he had a beauty that was undeniable.
His eyes were bright and inviting.
His smile was brilliant and sincere.
He spoke of his dreams as well as plans for the future.
He was so focused and determined.
He was a survivor and risk-taker.
Independent and strong, he was.
He was all that I longed very much to be.
About twenty minutes into class,
I realized that extraordinary young man that I met today, was ME.

Jonathan Eskew-Martin, Grade 6
CrossRoads Middle School, SC

I Have to Do My Best

I am an ant. I search for food for my colony and me.
I seem to rest too much and not look enough. I have to do my best.
I also must defend myself from anything that attacks me. I must watch.
I am scared of my surroundings and don't want to fight, but I must do my best.
I have to stay focused and complete my job. My colony is waiting for me.
I must continue and not quit. I have to keep going. I have to do my best.

Brantley Crile, Grade 6
Berry Shoals Intermediate School, SC

New York

As we ride through the state of New York
I see tall buildings as we're zooming by.
I also see rain on the cars.
I hear water splashing on the ground and the loud sounds of the cars' engines.
I feel the wet cloth of my clothes and the slipperiness of the door knobs.
I taste the rain water and the good Jamaican food.
We all smell the gas and the rain and it smells bad.

Nyree Andrea, Grade 6
Crestwood Elementary School, VA

War

War is full of danger and violence
There is no end; there is no silence
We all know there is a lot more
Sometimes it ends with a knock on your door
Once you hear that horrific news
You know in war, we really all lose

Christopher Ebbecke, Grade 4
Mary Walter Elementary School, VA

Where I'm From

I am from football to basketball
From baseball to soccer

The ball I used to play is as round
And as hard as a rock

I am from pizzas to delicious tacos
YUM! I can eat 100 slices more

I am from impressive birthdays
To incredible vacations

I am from T.I. to Fat Joe
And oh yes, R. Kelly

I am from a magnificent and small town
With a lot of wonderful dogs
The dogs are as beautiful as if it was a sunny day

That is where I'm from

Cristian Noriega, Grade 4
Whittaker Elementary School, SC

Yellow Eyes on Halloween

Creeping into the black night forest
I saw shining yellow eyes
Staring straight at me
My insides filled with buckets of fear
I took a step back
Into a withered cornfield

Gaining back my courage
Into the forest I went
Trying to ignore the scary sounds
Of loud, hooting owls
Out my hand went
Carefully to touch the yellow-eyed figure

Frightening they were
Those wide yellow eyes
I shut my own
Before the terror held me back
My hand finally reached the figure
I was surprised it was my costumed friend!

Briana Bernstein, Grade 5
Olde Providence Elementary School, NC

Mother Nature

She paints the leaves every fall
She nurtures the flowers to be tall
She designs the snowflakes in every design
She makes the grass straight as a line
She nurtures the babies every spring
She teaches them to use their wings
This is Mother Nature

Brenda Rios, Grade 6
Prince of Peace Catholic School, SC

David Norris

David
Responsible, nosy, honest, friendly
Son of Crystal Johnson and David Norris
Lover of math, pets, and chocolate
Who feels sad when your pet dies,
excitement when you hit the ball,
friendly when you are around kids
Who needs thinking time, recess, and privacy
Who gives hope, help, and time
Who fears tornados, lightning, and snakes
Who would like to see no more murder,
cure for sickness, no more violence
Resident of Four Oaks, NC
Norris

David Norris, Grade 5
Four Oaks Elementary School, NC

My First Camp Out

By the lake
Beneath the trees
Feeling that soft summer breeze
Playing Kingdom like kids
With swords and knights
We were being children
My dad and I

We played even more
My dad and I
Like a Tennessee logger at the state fair.
Digging his face into a chocolate pie.
Roasting hot dogs all night.

We told scary stories
And caused great fright.
And finally
Returning to our tent
To retire for the night

When I thought the day was over
When I thought it was done
My dad said let's play some poker
One round, just one

Trey Laws, Grade 5
East Mooresville Intermediate School, NC

Stick Figures

Stick figures are easy to draw.
Stick figures are easy to make.
Can you make them wear a shirt.
Can you make their name be Kurt.
Can you make them wear a coat.
Can you make them on a boat.

Nick Clark, Grade 5
Courthouse Road Elementary School, VA

PT23

Whenever I walk on a b-ball court with fans
My heart and mind pound like 10 huge marching bands
When we tip-off to start the game
My whole body only has one aim
I will not stop
Until I drop
When I get that perfect steal
I roll like my legs are wheels
If somebody gives me a dish
When I put it up I bet all you hear is swish
When they guard me man to man
I wave them off like a fan
When they go up for a block
They stand their like a broken clock
They're so dazed
Even I'm amazed
In the end
It all depends
But at least they know
I can't be controlled

Patrick Tape, Grade 5
Queen's Grant Community School, NC

Cats and Dogs, Two Different Stories

Mean as the Siamese, smart as the shepherd
Pretty as a calico, keen as the Labrador
Sly as the minx, witty as the poodle
Clean as a rag doll, shy as a Chihuahua
Cats and dogs, two different stories

Savannah Dudley, Grade 5
Four Oaks Elementary School, NC

'49 Goldrush

Out to San Francisco many a man sailed,
To see what he could find, the stone, his ax impaled.
It's called the San Francisco gold rush of '49.
When every stone near was turned into a mine.
The people went to see if the story was just lore,
Or to see if they could find themselves some shiny gold ore.
Some found riches beyond compare,
While others found nothing, to their great despair.
This was a great time in history,
And that is no mystery.

Alyssa Curcio, Grade 5
Trinity Christian School, VA

Ezekiel

Athletic, handsome, smart, funny
Son of Val and Ezekiel
Lover of football, basketball, baseball and driving
Who feels happy, sad, and mad
Who needs Grandparents, Mom, and Dad
Who fears big head boys, bears, and Ms. Sweetenburg
Who gives love, toys, and books
Who would like to see New York, Alabama, and Las Vegas
Resident of Ann Fripp
Miller

Ezekiel Miller, Grade 4
St Helena Elementary School, SC

Colors

Blue is a high blue sky.
Red is a fiery fire.
Orange is a ripe pumpkin
Brown is dried out grass
Yellow is shiny fine gold.

What's your favorite colors?

Hunter Schultz, Grade 5
C Hunter Ritchie Elementary School, VA

Brown

Brown looks like the soft dirt after rain.
Brown sounds like dead pine needles in the wind.
Brown smells like hot chocolate on a cold day.
Brown tastes like chocolate ice cream after dinner.
Brown feels like an oatmeal raisin cookie before you eat it.

Ewan Malenfant, Grade 5
Holy Cross Elementary School, DE

10 Little Bunnies

Ten little bunnies waiting in line,
One ran away now there's nine.
Nine little bunnies went to skate,
One fell down now there's eight.
Eight little bunnies went to see Kevin

Cheerleading

Jumps, kicks, even splits
I love cheerleading

Stunts, punts, and a lot of fun
I love cheerleading

Screaming girls, ponytails curled
I love cheerleading

I put away my problems and bring out my pompoms because
I love cheerleading

Olivia Nappi, Grade 6
St Rocco School, RI

I Bought a Leprechaun

I got onto my school bus.
I sat down in my seat.
A kid says "Do you know what today is?"
"Prepare for a beat."
I say "Today is St. Patrick's Day
but what does beat mean?"
"Today is St. Patrick's Day
and you're not wearing green."
I jumped out of the bus
before it drove down the road.
I hopped onto my bicycle
and to the store I rode.
"1 leprechaun please!"
I say to the cashier.
Now no one will pinch me
because I have this green thing here!

Kailyn Marshall, Grade 4
Courthouse Road Elementary School, VA

Kittens

Some cute little kittens sitting in their dens
Licking their paws
Some asleep and some awake
Some happy and some mad

Some orange, black, and white
Some small and some tall
But I pick up one
And come back with five more
They purr on me one by one as I rub them
Hours go by as I have rubbed them asleep
Then five minutes later it seems I have joined them

Resting on the couch with six little fur balls
Piled on top of me purring asleep
They're cozy and warm
But most of all they're my six kittens
And they're all as great as my life

Tess Pollard, Grade 5
Manchester Elementary/Middle School, VT

Cat

She curled against me,
a ball of fuzz.
She looked at me,
and I gave in.
She was the one!

Katrina Stepanek, Grade 6
East Mooresville Intermediate School, NC

Spectacular Red

Red is my favorite color.
Carolina Blue is his friend, Duke blue is his enemy.
Crimson is his twin brother.
They get along 100%. They smell like cinnamon.
Red is the inside of a juicy grapefruit
Also a sweet ripe plum.
It's better than any kind of color.
Red is strawberry cool-aid on a hot summer day.
It's an apple.
Red loves to eat at Cici's
Pizza and cinnamon buns.
Red is the blood running warm in our veins.
Its NC State,
The Boston Red Sox.
Red is the color of my future NC State jersey.
Red means get out the way because NC State is coming.
Red is the king of colors.

Chris Tilley, Grade 4
Youngsville Elementary School, NC

Smoking Lungs

My dear uncle,
I know you were weak,
but why go that far,
and be so stupid?
I thought you were smarter than that.
I guess I was wrong.

Why?
Why did you have to let those orange and white Winstons,
Camels Carltons, filtered and unfiltered butts
get the best of you?

disgraceful
evil
revolting
deadly
bad-for-you
death-causing
cancer sticks!

Death…suicide
You were highly intelligent
Yet you let yourself get that bad —
and have smoker's black lungs.

Ana Doyle, Grade 6
Main Street Middle School, VT

Anna

A nna's
B rother
C ameron
D ances
E verywhere
Jordan Johnson, Grade 4
St Helena Elementary School, SC

Christmas Is Near

Sparkling snowflakes falling.
Hanging the beautiful mistletoe.
The sound of rustling wrapping paper.
The smell of glowing minty candles.

Hanging the beautiful mistletoe.
"Did you hear that?"
The smell of glowing minty candles.
Making delicious gingerbread houses.
"Did you hear that?"

Feeling steam from the glowing fire.
The sound of rustling wrapping paper.
Playing with cousins.
Sparkling snowflakes falling.
Jessica Baron, Grade 4
Hope Valley Elementary School, RI

Birthday

It's my birthday,
now I'm ten.
I invite
my good friends.
It's in spring.
It's my birthday again.
Audrey Haynes, Grade 4
Grace Miller Elementary School, VA

Vermont

The snow is bitter
But it is adaptable
When you love Vermont
Devin Tetreault, Grade 5
E Taylor Hatton School, VT

Lady Bug

Small and round
With polka-dots,
They eat leaves
And sit a lot,
You will find,
Them on some trees,
Especially when it is
Spring!
Tara Biernacki, Grade 5
Good Shepherd Catholic School, RI

Carolina Mall

I went to the Carolina mall
When I got a phone call
It was my mom
I had to go home

When I got home
She was fast asleep
So I left to the mall
I got another call

So I went back home
I went to help my dad
I saw him eating mac and cheese
I went to the mall again

This was my last call of the day
It was my sister with an airplane delay
She wanted me to do some errands
It was my last trip of the day

The problem was I never got to shop
Christmas for my family
I went home to sleep
But I didn't find 1 gift
Fidel Roldan, Grade 6
East Albemarle Elementary School, NC

The White Bengal Tiger Cub

Soft white and black fur
Yellow eyes staring at you
Teeth sharp as a knife

Cute as a button
Swims as fast as the river
The playful cub speaks

His beautiful face
He gets bigger every day
An amazing thing
Taylor Lincoln, Grade 5
Rye Elementary School, NH

Yellow

Yellow looks like a bright light bulb,
lit with a new idea.
Yellow sounds like a "Tweetie" bird
singing its song.
Yellow smells like a hot cake
that just came out of the oven.
Yellow tastes like butter,
moist and warm.
Yellow feels like the soft quilt
on my new Vera Bradley bag.
Madeline Carlson, Grade 5
Holy Cross Elementary School, DE

A Dolphin

I dreamed
I was a dolphin
On the beach
Flowing through the water
Gracefully.
Briana Pittman, Grade 5
Cooper Elementary School, VA

Civil War

I dreamed
I was a drummer boy
In the Civil War
Trying not to get shot
Angrily.
Vincent Collins II, Grade 5
Cooper Elementary School, VA

Smeago

Smeago is a cat,
Who is very fat!
He tried to go down the stairs
And went SPLAT!

When he got back on his feet
He let me know that is was time to eat.

Crunch, crunch, crunch
He ate his lunch.
Then he tried to drink my punch!
Katie Kopacz, Grade 4
Edwards Elementary School, SC

Spring

Flowers blooming, buzzing bees
Wearing pants above your knees
Raining, raining
down
down
down
Bugs creeping, crawling
Without a sound
Leaves are sprouting on the trees
Allergies are coming
Cover your sneeze!
Kolby Tracey, Grade 4
Memorial School, NH

Spring

Spring
warm, sunny
blooming, playing, climbing
picking, tanning, watering, growing
May
Makayla Gough, Grade 6
Floyd T Binns Middle School, VA

To a Prez

Dr. Martin Luther King had a dream, well, I have one too:
I am a kid who dreams of a nation where there is no crime.
I dream of a state where there is no racism.
I dream of a community in which we all can have fun.
I wish for a world that everyone can be treated the same.
I wish for a home that does not bicker all of the time.
A classroom that has two goals: to learn and to have fun.
I am a student who wants world peace.
I am a person who maybe one day will bring peace on Earth.
Yes, Mister President, I can help you create a nonviolent world.
My words to you are that I believe that if you try you can.

Nicholas DeCoteau, Grade 6
Main Street Middle School, VT

Interesting Birds

One white woodpecker was wrestling wiggly worms.
Two titmice twittered trills.
Three hermit thrushes thought their chicks were lost.
Four finches fed hungry chicks.
Five flickers frantically foraged for food.

Sebastian Seifert, Grade 4
Blacksburg New School, VA

The Christmas Day Attack

On Christmas Day, December 25, 1776, George Washington
Lead an attack against the forces of Britain
On the Hessians, too!

It was an icy walk across the forest floor.
The ice brutally slicing their feet and making enormous gore.
The American soldiers took over with ease.

If you listen you can hear…
People shouting at the Britains with a sneer.
As we cursed them with all our strength.

It gained us our freedom through their fear.
We gave the British sorrow and humiliation to be here.
This is why Christmas Day is important to all of us.

Will Voss, Grade 6
Camperdown Academy, SC

The Jabberwocky

J umbo and monstrous creature is he.
A driot in his battles against monster and man.
B attles and wars fiercely fought and with much cleverness.
B lazing and piercing eyes, glaring at his prey.
E xtremely quick and strong.
R esists you and eats you plain without seasoning.
W anders around his territory like a guard.
O bstructs you as you try to cross the line… which,
C uts between him and you.
K een eye looking out for his dinner…now who would that be?
Y ou!

Ryan Cranston, Grade 5
Trinity Christian School, VA

I Am Following the King to Graceland

I love to shred on my awesome guitar
My legendary skills helped me go far.

With my bandana on my crazy fro'
I will be singing songs like, "Hey Joe"

I am following the King to Graceland
Searching for something to use in my band

This trip is so long, it is a big pain
Not playing my guitar drives me insane

I'll borrow the King's moves like his shaking
He might add a dance in the cool making

I'm looking forward to his appearance
I'm all ready for his experience

I'm finally there, just as stiff as logs
As they say, it ain't nothin' but a hound dog!

Kian Lari, Grade 6
Beck Academy, SC

Voice of Light

My pillow is soft from the light of the moon.
My window is open so voices can be heard.
An angel's voice awakes me,
leaving me breathless.
A poem of love,
taking home a friend.

Meghan Howe, Grade 5
Wakefield Forest Elementary School, VA

The Black Pig

I'm laying in the grass
Just looking in the sky
I'm falling asleep
So I close my eyes

Next thing I know
I'm wide awake
Then I look around
Oh! for Pete's sake!

To come to my attention
I see a black pig
I had the feeling to dance
So we did a little jig

The day was long
The day was hot
I finished the jig
But he did not.

CJ Glover, Grade 5
Rosemont Forest Elementary School, VA

Blowing in the Wind
I dreamed
I was a tree.
Outside
Blowing in the wind
Gently.
D'Shawn Creque, Grade 5
Cooper Elementary School, VA

Mountains
Mountains, oh strong mountains
How were you made?
Where did you come from?
Do you get cold in the winter
Or hot in the summer?
Mighty mountains, can you be hurt
Or taken down?
William Richards, Grade 4
Sangaree Intermediate School, SC

Unicycling
hold, mount, pedal,
mount, pedal, turn,
pedal, turn, jump,
turn, jump, dismount,
jump, dismount, finish,
dismount, finish, bow.
Claire Théfaine, Grade 5
Queen's Grant Community School, NC

Sleepy Lilly
I don't want
you to pat my blondish soft fluffy fur
I don't want
to go outside in the freezing air
I don't want
to play frisbee in the yard
I don't want
to go to the vet to get a shot
I don't want
to sit on the hard tile floor
I'm sleeping, sleeping, sleeping
Annie Sedoric, Grade 5
Rye Elementary School, NH

A Walrus's Wish
Tusks and blubber
Whiskers and fat
Brown body with flippers
The creature just sat
Breathing and blinking
Eating lots of fish
Laying around in the sun
A walrus's wish
River King, Grade 5
Blacksburg New School, VA

Night Time
I see a desert
I smell the cold breeze
I hear a frog croaking
I feel cold
I taste the wind
I think it is night time
Tyler Banner, Grade 5
Blaney Elementary School, SC

Hawk
I am a hawk
Flying swiftly as an eagle
the sky is my home
They keep me safe from predators
The wind is like my father
It keeps me safe from hunters
So come and see where I live
The wind is my home
Come with me
And see where I glide
I am a hawk
Flying swiftly as an eagle
The sky is my home
Bryant Bonzali, Grade 4
St Christopher's School, VA

Oh Shadow Oh Shadow
Oh shadow oh shadow I see on the wall,
   sometimes you seem somewhat small

Oh shadow oh shadow I see on the wall,
   sometimes you are quite tall

Oh shadow oh shadow I see on the wall,
   you are my best pal of all
Logan Maurer, Grade 5
Cool Spring Elementary School, NC

I Miss You Sadie
You left me with no goodbye.
You lied.
You said you would stay by my side.
I miss you so.

Why did you have to go?
She was like a sister.
That's why I missed her.
I missed you all those days.

But now we go our different ways.
You were the best.
I just had to confess.
I miss you and love you Sadie.
Gina Sterling, Grade 5
West Hartsville Elementary School, SC

Portabella Me
Summer breeze
Making me sway
I am stuck in one place
I want to move around
But instead
I am stuck in this cluster
Of my kind
The sun is setting
It's getting much colder
But I am distracted
By the pink and purple sky
When the sun is fully gone
I realize it's so cold
I huddle with my siblings
And wait for the next sunrise.
When the sun comes up again
I want to move around
But I am still stuck
With my dreams inside me
Every night I dream of running free
But every morning I wake up the same.
Spencer Schwartz, Grade 5
Rye Elementary School, NH

Bear
Brown haired animal
Ready to attack his prey
With terrible friends
Montana Gleason, Grade 4
Grace Miller Elementary School, VA

My Dog Snowflake
My dog Snowflake,
Woof, woof, woof,
Wags her tail.
She is so white when it snows.
You could steal her barkish bark,
Bark, bark, bark
When it's cold.
She sniffs the bone and puppy chow.
When and when you come,
She jumps and swirls around,
As you feed her or play with her.
My dog eats anything that's
on the floor,
on the ground,
or anywhere around.
She gets sick from eating my ice cream.
We play ball.
I throw a tennis ball,
She bites it and gives it to me,
All wet and soggy.
My dog Snowflake.
Kissiah Redmon, Grade 4
Cool Spring Elementary School, NC

Him
How do you know he's the one
I most certainly set limits

He'll know how to make me smile
And I'll get the feeling of warmth and comfort

If he's the one he won't run from love
If he's the one he'll have to be a gentleman

If he's the one he'll know I need time until I say I do
We'll need to have sweet Kodak moments until…I do
Lindsay Smith, Grade 6
Pilot Mountain Middle School, NC

James
Kind, friendly, helpful, and prompt
Son of James and Marlene
Lover of Mom, Dad, and Grandma
Who feels great, loved, and glad
Who needs food, love, and shelter
Who fears snakes, frogs, and wolves
Who gives gifts, clothes, and kisses
Who would like to see lakes, rivers, and mountains
Resident of Seaside Road
Young
James Young, Grade 4
St Helena Elementary School, SC

The Run from the British
Don't pack up your bags,
There's no time for running!
Just load up your guns,
'Cause the British are coming!

The British are coming,
To take you dead or alive.
So run, my friend, run!
There's no time to hide!

Let's hurry! Let's hurry!
The British are here!
So don't just sit there,
And cower in fear!

Run away! Go!
It's better than here!
Look!
There goes Paul Revere!

Good bye for now, my friend!
I should hope to see you again!
I wish you luck on your journey. Embark!
You will always be in all of our hearts.
Brenna Buckley, Grade 6
Our Lady of Lourdes Catholic School, NC

Black Mamba
A roller coaster is a 12 ft black mamba.
Slithering up and down hills.
Twisting and turning night and day.
Looping around mountains and valleys.
Hissing past trees and fields.
Giving you a scare as they curve around.
Sneaking up on flips and mice.
They come to a stop when it's all over and done.
KayAnna Hall, Grade 6
CrossRoads Middle School, SC

My Cat
I have a cat her name is Squeaky.
We're glad she's ours.
Only she steals our socks and hides them
under Mom and Dad's bed.
My friend slept over
when she woke up…
found a sock on her head.
Named Squeaky because of her squeaky meow.
Best cat ever, special!
Allie Palacz, Grade 4
Maple Wood Elementary School, NH

April
April is all different colors.
It is the colors of Easter eggs.
April feels like candy going down my throat.
It sounds like my family singing happy birthday to me.
It smells like blooming flowers.
It tastes like cake.
April is a long month.
Ben Ngo, Grade 5
Vienna Elementary School, NC

Stone Angels of the Night
On top of a tower, covered with fright,
Stand the guardians of the night.
Grotesque and beautiful, they wait for dark
As the mark of stone dissipates.
When the moon rises and light fades,
They go and fly away.
With wings and claws flying about they might have a bout.
Scales of red, black and yellow
They go and bellow to their friends.
A screech like lightning and a call so cold,
As the night goes as foretold.
When daybreak comes and the creatures stand,
I know that they are gargoyles from their stone tan.
All day they wait for their prison to dissipate.
When the younglings scoff and laugh at the hidden beauty,
The gargoyles silently plan their flight for night.
And when the bell rings for midnight,
There go those stone angels of the night.
Duncan Watson, Grade 6
Watson Home School, VA

Full Moon

The beacon through the long dark night
With rays of majestic white light
As it glides across the star speckled sky
It entrances the world as it flies by
But that bright disk begins to wane
And I cannot wait to see it again.

Clair Huffine, Grade 5
Mary Walter Elementary School, VA

Queen's Grant

Q ueen's Grant Community School
U nique in lots of great ways
E xcitement around school
E ducating every student
N ever giving up
S o cool

G o Knights
R eally friendly
A wesome school
N ever gets boring
T he school rules!

Deanna Foster, Grade 5
Queen's Grant Community School, NC

The World

It spins round and round
Such a lovely place to be
A wonderful sight

Elisabeth Harris, Grade 4
Trinity Christian School, VA

The Quiet Pond

The hot sunny day
brings people together
The quiet pond awaits.

The peaceful day
has brought me there
for me to
relax the day away.

In the distance I hear dogs bark
I mumble to myself
about the remarkable place
quiet, quiet, quiet.

The waves are lapping
the geese are honking
They're welcoming me
to the lively place
The quiet day
Will end.

Alexis Desmarais, Grade 4
Maple Wood Elementary School, NH

Red Birds

Flowers red to yellow
Smell the fresh air
Water flowing
Birds chirping
But in the night
Beware of the great howl
Where it stares at you
By every step
Running won't help
Sprinting won't help
What to do
What to do
But soon the great
Red birds appear
Behind the horizon
The wolf fled
Like a vampire with garlic

Seongtaeg Kang, Grade 5
Oak View Elementary School, VA

Spring Is Here

The breezes of spring
Are blowing the ripple astray
Along the water —
Today they will surely melt
The sheet of ice on the pond.

Renato Rios, Grade 6
Berry Shoals Intermediate School, SC

Blue Bird

I see them Blue Birds way up in the sky
flying by and telling me what to do next.
They see me sitting on stairs waiting for
my prince to come.

Brieana Dial, Grade 4
Barnardsville Elementary School, NC

Homework

I had so much homework,
I need a pick-up truck
To carry all my books home!

Jonathan Williams, Grade 4
Edwards Elementary School, SC

Little Puppy

I have a little puppy
She's very, very cute
I would like to take her everywhere
But my parents say, "No!"
Once I took her to the store
Then I found that pets are not allowed
So I sneaked her into my purse
She was very, very loud.

Blaine Taddesse, Grade 4
Angelus Academy, VA

Tyler Choate

T errific
Y elling when losing control
L earn from mistakes
E ager to play
R eady to learn

C atching the ball
H ates broccoli
O ver tries, sometimes
A lways loved basketball
T hankful
E very March 18, my birthday

Tyler Choate, Grade 6
Wakefield Forest Elementary School, VA

They're Gone

I will never know why
But he took them away
Just the other day
They asked me to play
I feel sad,
But also mad
Sometimes I wish
He never had.
In shame to walk,
Never wanting to talk,
Never wanting to go home.
Now knowing (They're Gone).

Tia Glover, Grade 6
Saint Pauls Middle School, NC

Roxy

My name is Roxy
Beautiful, yellow, and soft
I love my dog, Rox.

Taylor Otto, Grade 5
North Windy Ridge School, NC

My Precious Box

I will put into my precious box
The love of my family
The pleasure of my video games
The care of a handshake
The view of the beach
The experience of riding my bike
And precious sounds of TV

I will not put in my box
The violence of unkind people
The hard ships of starving people
The unawareness of dying soldiers at war
The scared people at war
The brutalness of homeless people.

Patrick Andrews, Grade 5
Four Oaks Elementary School, NC

Childhood

Brown, coiled fur,
Worn out
From the many times in the wash,
The many times I was sick.
Nose,
Barely a nose,
Ripped and ragged
From the many times I chewed on it
As a kid,
The many times I was scared.
Ears,
Attached by only one thread
Thin and delicate
Like a piece of straw.
But yet, he still survived
All of these days
All of these moments.
I carried him everywhere
As a kid,
Afraid to lose him,
Afraid to lose my childhood.

Samantha Somple, Grade 6
Manchester Elementary/Middle School, VT

Ocean Boom

The ocean stretched as far as the eye can see
Like the sky on a clear day
The colossal waves crashing
I hear the sound,
It's the boom of thunder.

Dive into the water
Down to the ocean floor,
Where the crab crawls
Like leaves on a breezy day.
Where the fish swims
With its slimy scales
Like jelly.

Waves take me under
I tumble like a washing machine
They crash with me
It makes a sound,
It's the boom of thunder.

Deirdre Walsh, Grade 6
Manchester Elementary/Middle School, VT

Pride Is...

Pride is when you feel light as a feather.
Pride is when you can do something others can't.
Pride is when you make someone sad feel better.
Pride is when your heart feels sane.
Pride is when you feel as if you can soar,
And there is not a thing in the world that can touch you.

Sara Perrero, Grade 5
Northside Elementary School, SC

Camp Gundalow

Finally I've arrived!
Camp Gundalow's grassy fields, and numerous tall trees,
And rarely, but possibly, the buzzing bees!
There's all kinds of green
But being on the topic of the bees,
Be careful where you go, 'cause they can be mean.
There's swimming and painting,
Canoeing and arching.
Choose what you like,
And there's a pretty good chance,
You'll meet a kid that you'll like!
Like me and Riley B.
We're both pretty mischievous
Him and me,
But what really stunk was that,
He got stung by a bee!
Good thing only once,
And at least there's a nurse.
But besides all that, it's the end of the day.
But there's more to come, it's only Monday.

Darius Fink, Grade 5
Rye Elementary School, NH

Thanks Sammy

Thanks for all the encouraging hugs.
Thanks for giving me sisterly love.
Thanks for being my real, true friend.
Thanks for a relationship that will never end.
Thanks for always backing me up.
Thanks for lifting my spirits up.
Thanks for all those sleepover nights.
Thanks for always leading me right.
Thanks for little notes I will always treasure.
Thanks for friends that will last forever.
Thanks for standing beside me.
Thanks...
for everything.

Kristin DiBello, Grade 4
Sangaree Intermediate School, SC

Blue

Blue can be happy
Blue can be sad
Blue is the roaring ocean waving in the sunlight
Blue is the taste of sweet blueberries just picked
Blue hides when other colors are running around playing
Blue is what a person feels if they have been hurt
Blue is the color of people's tears
Blue is more than a color it's a feeling
Blue is a sloth slow and always sleeping
Blue stands on the Tar Heels side during a game
The color blue only cries Wa Wa Wa
Blue is the color of sad eyes crying

Nikki Kelleher, Grade 4
Tabernacle Elementary School, NC

Fall

Golden leaves fall to the ground,
as the wind goes round and round.
The day is dusk, the ground is frosty,
I'll go in and have some toffee.
The leaves are falling off the trees,
I'll pick them up, if you please.

Anna Valentine, Grade 4
Brewster Pierce School, VT

To Do List for a Crazy Life

Brush my teeth with chocolate milk
Put on day clothes inside out
Mess up my hair
Get the cat out of the rat
Feed my mouse its tasty lizard
Eat my orange juice and drink my cereal
Kick my mom good bye
Wait for the bus forever
Remember that it's Saturday!

Mary Grace McKusick, Grade 5
Olde Providence Elementary School, NC

My Brother

My brother is the sun.
He warms me when I am down.

My brother is a blanket.
He keeps me warm when I am cold.

My brother is a rare jewel.
I protect him because he is four.

My brother is a clown.
He makes me laugh a lot.

Akhil Patel, Grade 5
Holy Cross Elementary School, DE

Winter

W hite
I cy
N ice
T winkling
E legant
R arc

Colleen Burger, Grade 4
Angelus Academy, VA

Nightmare

You lay there and try to sleep
But you can't seem to
Finally you fall asleep
Scary ideas fly through your head
You wake up relived, and scared
But then you're faced with sleep again

Nicholas Spardello, Grade 6
Metcalf School, RI

Baseball

B rown dirt streaked across home plate by a runner's foot
    while sliding into home on a close play at the plate
A nticipating the call of the umpire on the first pitch of the game
S peed and rotation of the ball on every pitch
E nergy of the roaring fans as a home-run ball leaves the stadium
B oos of the crowd at Yankee Stadium as the Boston Red Sox take the field
A bag of fresh roasted peanuts with the shells being thrown under my seat
L istening to starting lineups announced over the PA system
L emonade quenching my thirst on a sweltering hot summer day

Blake Gershon, Grade 6
Cape Henry Collegiate School, VA

Ode to My Harry Potter Books

My Harry Potter books rest each day after I read a chapter or two.
They are like my best friend.
I bet each night it comes to life and relives everything I read.
Sometimes scary, sometimes funny, but always very adventurous.
My adventurous, magical Harry Potter books are very special to me.

Kayln Ellenburg, Grade 5
Faith Elementary School, NC

Howling Cries

At night you hear howling and cries from nearby woods
It sounds close
The next morning, nothing,
So you go and play

Night falls like a blanket
And you hear nothing but howling cries from the nearby woods
Next morning you hear nothing
Zip, zero, goose egg, no evidence whatsoever

The next night nothing
But howling and more cries,
But then all of a sudden, silence falls quicker than a cricket could chirp
Then all of the sudden howling, louder than a girl in a horror movie
The next day, you go outside to find that the howling has come from a wolf
Lying on the ground with her six puppies.

Madison Scott, Grade 5
Manchester Elementary/Middle School, VT

Swirls

The sunset is covered by the swirling clouds,
Like the swirls of clouds, the river snakes through the valley,
Like the river snakes through the valley, the mountains have winding ravines.

Water created the snaking rivers,
Water created the swirling clouds,
Water created the ravines in the tan glazed mountains.

Color makes us see the swirls,
Shades of gray and brown in the sky,
Shades of orange, black and brown in the valley and the mountains,
Lots and lots of swirls!

Hunter Borwick, Grade 5
Manchester Elementary/Middle School, VT

Ocean

The ocean's water goes splish splash!
Seagulls flying overhead
Mussels and clams from the sea are thrown against the sea wall
The lighthouses ding
The dogs bark
When I am here
I know that I'm free
Wouldn't you love to know
That the ocean is a state of mind?
Because when I'm here,
I'm in mine.

Mackenzie Lafond, Grade 4
Heron Pond Elementary School, NH

A Soldier's Life

A soldier's life
I hear the silent boom
I see the light growing dimmer
I hear the yell of the others in pain
I feel as if I can help but I also am lying here
I try to get up but I am seeing the light of heaven
This is a soldier's life

Alexandria Cumbo, Grade 5
Queens Creek Elementary School, NC

Daddy's Little Girl

The time has come for you to go
To the place where no one knows
I know you miss me and I miss you too
But I understand what you have to do
I think of you every single day
And I cry and cry to get my way
Without you here it hurts so bad
And sometimes it really makes me mad
Just to think what if you don't make it
What will I do? And if I could make it through without you
I know you try to make ends meet while fighting over in Tikrit
You are the best daddy in the world
And I'm proud to say I'm "daddy's little girl."

Aryan Davenport, Grade 5
Manchester Elementary School, NC

Fall

Fall feels like the leaves crunching on my feet
Fall looks like people picking just right apples for us to eat
Fall sounds like trees shaking from the wind
The leaves stomp on the ground
Fall smells like apples that have fallen to the ground
Fall is like a cold chill rushing down my back
Fall tastes like a round red apple
Fall is me getting ready for Halloween
Fall is the pumpkin we made into a jack-o'-lantern
Fall is us walking around and getting all the candy I can eat

Suzie Church, Grade 4
Tabernacle Elementary School, NC

What Is Red?

Red shouts and shrieks to the other colors like a demander
Red races down the stage like a fashion model
He doesn't let people's eyes go off him
People can't resist him
He always catches people's eyes
Red is a cherry red race car using boost to win the race
Red roars a loud roar that is so loud it can cross the Earth
Red is energized as if just coming from birth
He blows flames out of his hand like he's the fire master
Red is a mighty color
Red is a fierce tiger chasing its prey
Red is proud to be the man of all colors
Red is as strong as your heart
Red tastes like a shiny fresh picked cherry straight from the vine
Red is red hot lava coming from a tall steaming hot volcano

Red is red

Skylar McAdams, Grade 4
Tabernacle Elementary School, NC

Swimming

I am sitting at home
Thinking of something to do
My friends are going to the pool
Sounds cool
Think I will go to

I arrived at the gate
Through the bars
The pool is like
A shimmering lake
To jump in, I can't wait

I tested the water
With my big toe
It was as cold as ice
I shivered
And said oh no

I jumped in the pool
I had a good time
My friends and I laughed
When the waves
Waved good bye

Sommer McCracken, Grade 5
East Mooresville Intermediate School, NC

Fall

The leaves are red, yellow, brown and orange;
The wind lightly blows;
Thanksgiving is coming;
Pumpkins and corn are growing;
People are dressed in costumes for Halloween;
Churches rejoice on All Saints Day.

Jonathan Austin, Grade 5
St Anne Catholic School, SC

The Forest Sounds

The wind blows the trees. Whoosh! Whoosh! The deer steps on the brightly colored leaves. Crunch Crunch! The squirrels chomp on all sorts of nuts. Chomp! Chomp! The birds sing a beautiful tone. Tweet! Tweet! The daytime is so sweet. Then the sun fades away and it becomes dark. The owls scream out. Hoo! Hoo! The crickets chirp repeatedly. Chirp! Chirp! And the wolf howls over all the sounds Ohhhhhhh! The forest sounds are precious and peaceful. Too bad it is my bedtime. Sweet dreams.

Kara Ward, Grade 6
Monelison Middle School, VA

Fins for Swimming

Watching, as her legs stick together. Forming a majestic aquamarine tail, she swims out in to the crashing waves. Her shimmery blonde hair sparkles in the moonlight, as she sits on her perch, combing her hair with her coral brush. She dives into the water, going deeper to find her playground. Finally, she arrives, smiling happily to herself. The ceiling was made out of mother-of-pearl and floor made out of sparkling diamond. The ship's name wrapped her up. Majestica, the most beautiful ship of all! Sadly, as she climbed back to shore, she thought to herself, "Another night of pleasure, yet more night to come."

Marissa Levis, Grade 6
Eagle's Nest Christian School, DE

Why

Why must life be filled with problems why do we have to face the fact things happen for a reason why do we choose to do wrong why must dreams fall why can't we forgive and forget why must we hurt the world why do we live up to stereotypes why can't we get change why can't we strive to do good why must we turn against each other why can't we be one nation why do we have violence why must we hurt each other why can't we get along JUST ASK ME WHY!!!!!!

Taylor Biles, Grade 6
Seaford Middle School, DE

Love

Love is not just a feeling,
    It is a feeling that takes your body with it.
    Love is not just something that happens to you,
        It is a special feeling that you feel with all your heart.
        Love is something some may never feel,
            So embrace it and don't let go if it is true.
            Love that is true should never be overlooked,
                Take true love by the hand and never let it go.
                Love even has an important day or special day,
                    Valentines Day is its special day.
                    Love is very important but some don't agree,
                        Most that don't have never felt.
                        Love is not to be fooled around with,
                            So believe in it with all your might.
                            Love is something you can go on and on about,
                                So this is just a piece of what love is.

Autumn Robinson, Grade 5
Courthouse Road Elementary School, VA

A Second Chance of Life

Pleasure turns to the pain of the lesson learned form the strain of questions that burn in my brain, about whether love remains in this touch. These voices are like salmon swimming up stream into tears. A second chance of life.

Fighting occurs, hurt kills more and created by drama of our peer of emotions. Arrive because of the pressure of emotions; life has been unplugged from vessels of our undying evaporation, separations. A second chance of life.

A distance between our minds is no longer passed by the demons that have been over seers of my statement to your lies, the deceiving of these lies are rooted so deeply they have cracked the foundation of what we've once shared, allowing faith in us. I have a second chance of life. I have a second chance of life.

Davon Joyner, Grade 5
Macedonia Elementary School, SC

Wood

Wood can be strong or soft.
Wood can be sawed or drilled.
Wood can help you sail the seas.
Wood can give you a seat and a place to eat.
Wood is soft or light and sometimes has bark.
Wood can give you a special place to call home.
Wood gives us fires that keep us warm at night.
Wood gave me paper and a pencil to write this poem.

Brad Fessenden, Grade 5
Rye Elementary School, NH

Lisa

Lisa,
Loving, friendly, intelligent, and different
Mother of Casey
Lover of God, family, and ballet
Who feels happy, hopeful, and tired
Who needs to be loved, cared for, and helped
Who gives love, happiness, and joy to the world
Who fears the Lord
Who would like to see her children succeed,
Husband content, and Jesus return

Casey Danowski, Grade 5
Vienna Elementary School, NC

Friendship

F aithful to each other
R ushes to each other when they are down
I 'll be there to hold your hand
E veryday friends will hold each other tight
N ever says anything that will make you want to fight
D on't let anyone come between your friendship
S how your respect for your friends
H elp them whenever they need a friend
I 'll look after you day and night
P lace yourself in a good position with a friend

Tyashia Toler, Grade 6
Monelison Middle School, VA

The Berlin Wall

The Cold War was a nuclear standoff.
America and Russia were enemies.
Across the world, they were afraid of a blastoff.
Leaving a destructive breeze.

Once, Gorbachov and Reagan were both a leader.
Russia with Gorbachov did thrive.
Reagan, America's President the voters prefer.
As both countries ran into a war to strive.

A barrier, as hard as rock.
You can never see your family, friends at all.
Blurred with dust, it falls down.
It's a countdown to the end, the end of the Berlin Wall.

Anderson Hunt, Grade 6
Camperdown Academy, SC

Red Bicycle

Red bicycle, red bicycle it sits on my porch
when you look at it closely it's as bright as a torch.
Red bicycle, red bicycle it goes very fast
when you first get on it's like a blast.
Red bicycle, red bicycle I love you to death
I'll take you everywhere and make the best.
Red bicycle, red bicycle sometimes I don't see
but I know in my heart we were meant to be.

Madeline Pierce, Grade 5
Queens Creek Elementary School, NC

Green

Green is my anole
Running through the grass
While eating asparagus
Green is March
With clovers everywhere
Green is the forest
With bugs in the air
Green is the wind
Whistling through the grass
In the morning
Green beans are good
With Celtics shooting baskets
Green is awesome

Michael Parigian, Grade 4
Atkinson Academy Elementary School, NH

Summer Days

Climbing trees
Was like climbing a rope.
Climbing all the way
With stars and hope.

When we jumped rocks
We were Kangaroos
Jumping with glee.
The wind soared too.

The sky was a blanket
A blanket over wind.
The grass was dancing,
But also prancing.

Now the bugs of light
Lit the sky as they flew.
Flying their greatest flight.
Soaring through the night.

When I wake up,
The sun is up high
I run outside
Happy and full of life!

Hannah Killian, Grade 5
East Mooresville Intermediate School, NC

A Lie

A lie is a shadow
because it follows
wherever you go.

A lie is a plant
because it gets bigger and bigger
the more you have it.

A lie is a cave
because it is dark
and you feel alone and dark inside.

A lie is a backpack
because the more books you put in it,
it starts to weigh you down.

Maura Gast, Grade 5
Holy Cross Elementary School, DE

School

I walk into school
People think it's cool,
But I hate it, it's dumb
It's annoying
Super boring
And school makes me a bum.

Jacob Henry, Grade 4
Grace Miller Elementary School, VA

Lord of Mercy

L ord, your mercy is greater than earth
O thers may think differently
R eally, Lord, it's very, very true
D emons may think very differently

O ur Father above
F ind mercy in us

M y God help me
E verlasting God help me to
R eally show mercy, merciful God
C ould you show mercy if I did wrong?
Y es, because you are Lord of Mercy

Connor Ames, Grade 4
Trinity Christian School, VA

Ice Cream and Cookies

Ice cream
Yummy, cold
Eating, melting, freezing
Sprinkles, freezer, chocolate chip, milk
Munching, breaking, crumbling
Warm, yummy
Cookie

Parker Rhee, Grade 4
Waller Mill Fine Arts Magnet School, VA

The Hotdog

Life stinks!!!
You never know when
Someone's going to eat you.
All day long
People just dump mustard
And ketchup on you.
Once they sliced up my friend
Mr. Pickle and poured him on me,
It's horrible what they do to us!!!
You just never know
What's going to happen
When you're a hotdog.

Robert Neitz, Grade 5
Rye Elementary School, NH

School's Out

School's out get ready to shout,
Throw all those old papers out.
School's out!
There won't be a doubt
When school's out
That I'll go wandering about.
Blooms start to bloom
Some people are gloom.
I say don't be a gloom
We have all the summer afternoons!
Plant gardens,
Pretend to be Martians
There shall be more to do.
When we play we laugh
And some cry
But hey sometimes the cry
Just flies by.

Kameron Coffey, Grade 4
Appomattox Elementary School, VA

Roses

Roses can wilt and die.
Roses have thorns
that tease and prick.
Roses make some people really sick.
Roses are red never blue.
Roses are beautiful just like you!

Javier King, Grade 4
Bensley Elementary School, VA

My Grey Kitty

Ash plays with me
She is a grey kitty
Ash plays with me
She is shy, but so friendly
She is playful, loving kitty
And she is all mine

Samantha Paige Sadowski, Grade 5
Cool Spring Elementary School, NC

Out of the Park

Crack! the ball
made contact with the bat
Now the ball is out of the park
All of the
Whoo-hoo's and yeah's
in the crowd
The ball sails
Through the air
Safe! Yelled the umpire
The crowd went wild
That's the day the ball went
Out of the park

J.T. Melton, Grade 4
Edwards Elementary School, SC

Stray Dog

Needing a home out in the cold
Waiting for someone there
Waiting for a bite to eat
Someone spots him there
They see him shiver
And call him over
And showed the dog they care
They take him to a safe new home
With friendship, and love to share

Lauren Rampenthal, Grade 5
Good Shepherd Catholic School, RI

Soccer

The wind rustles my hair,
I'm about to shoot the ball,
The crowd is cheering me on,
I pass to my teammate.

She shoots,
She scores,
I love soccer,
I love it!

It is the fourth period,
We are down by one goal,
I play this period,
My teammate, Ashley does too.

She passes the ball to me,
I'm the only chance,
I have to make the shot,
The ball went in!

We won the game!
Now we go out to eat,
We celebrate,
We had played soccer!

Claire Bublitz, Grade 5
Queen's Grant Community School, NC

Grandmas Are the Super Heroes

Grandmas are always there to cook you something nice,
it could be salad,
dessert,
pizza,
or rice.
Their specialties are to clean and to cook,
they are nice and lean and read you books.
Grandmas are the ones who come to the rescue every time,
that is why I am writing this awesome rhyme.
Those Grandmas are just plain old fun,
they laugh,
run,
and play in the bright,
blazing sun.
Papas eh' they're fun too,
of course the take you out to EAT,
but all they like to do is sit in that comfy seat.

Gisele Iafrate, Grade 6
St Rocco School, RI

Turtles

Turtles poking their heads out of the pond
Tiny fish swimming
Sun burning down on my skin
Crickets chirping
Birds singing
Flies buzzing in my ear
Why won't the fish bite?
Hey what's that on my pole?
What?
A turtle
Turtle, turtle, turtle
No fish caught today.

Thomas Bonneau, Grade 4
Maple Wood Elementary School, NH

Alec Is…

He is short cake when I'm a 10 layer wedding cake.
He is the neon yellow in my grayness.
He is the cream in my coffee.
He is the crayon in my crayon box.
He is my friend.

He is the desire my heart has longed for.
He is the deer I'm hunting in the woods.
He is the mansion in my small neighborhood.
He is the excitement in my boring class.
He is my friend.

He is the door to all things adventurous.
He is the key to all fun things.
He is the swift bandit in my favorite movie.
He is my friend.

Sharriff Moore, Grade 6
Boiling Springs Intermediate School, SC

A Boy's Psalm of Life

Playing video games and watching TV,
Listening to music on CDs.
Boys like to do many different things,
Listening to Karaoke while your best friend sings.

Laughing and goofing around with friends,
And hanging out like the day never ends.
Boys like to do many different things,
Like playing guitar on a new set of strings.

Fixing sports cars and running them fast,
Tuning them up to make them last.
These are the things that boys like to do,
But don't forget eating tons of junk food!

Connor Ryan, Grade 6
Homeschool Plus, VA

The Dream

One night I fell asleep in bed;
All of a sudden, my room turns red.
I can't find the door,
But I hear a loud roar;
Then, over there, appears a doorway;
I enter it, and it's the middle of May.
The children are happy, school will be out;
They kick and play, scream and shout,
But wait, what's that across the yard?
A forest bigger than a barnyard!
I go to explore the forest all over,
But before, I eat an apple turnover.
Suddenly, I am high in the treetops:
Oh no! I feel a few rain drops!
Then I'm on a fluffy cloud, riding the night sky,
Floating past the moon up above the world so high.
Suddenly, I'm back in my bed,
In a room of pink instead of red.

Madison Decker, Grade 5
Clover Hill Elementary School, VA

A Book

A book is like a television inside your head
When you're thinking really hard
you start imagining instead

All the aliens and monsters
end up coming true,
and when they are coming for you
there's nothing you can do.

So think a book is a TV
and come and read with ME.

Listen, learn, and understand
then if you stop flying; you'll finally land.

Gracey Dorsey, Grade 6
Salem Church Middle School, VA

A Little Pea

I'm a little pea
Squish, splash, splat
I am on a plate
Waiting to be eaten
But then when
The family is done
The mom makes the kid
Eat the pea
The pea screams
"Please eat!
I'm not the best
But I'm good for you.
If you won't eat your peas
You won't
Grow up
Big and strong."

Matt Wolf, Grade 5
Rye Elementary School, NH

Empty

I can't
I can't think of anything
I am a leaf on the fall ground
I am an empty bottle
I am empty
I cannot find my heart
I am lost and broken
I am not me
I am someone I don't want to be
I am different
Only the kids at school don't know me
Only who am I
I am the only one who knows me
I am special in every single way
I might not be cool or popular but I am
Me

Rachel Jurus, Grade 5
Rye Elementary School, NH

Civil War Soldier

I dreamed
I was a Civil War soldier
Sitting high in a tree
Aiming for my shot
Skillfully.

T'Niya Hutchinson, Grade 5
Cooper Elementary School, VA

Teacher

Teacher oh teacher
so nice and so kind
though this year has come to an end
I'll never forget to remember you

Destiny Mozingo, Grade 5
Four Oaks Elementary School, NC

All About Me

Madison
It means weird, funny, and different
It is the number twelve
It is like a Hawaiian beach
It is going to Universal Studios
It is the memory of my granny
Who taught me how to do word searches
When she sat at the table
My name is Madison

Madison Ervin, Grade 5
Blaney Elementary School, SC

Snowstorm

As we ride the four-wheeler
through the Virginia forest,
the cold, crisp air smells like
gasoline exhaust
on the damp, frigid earth.

Snowflakes, are nickels,
spiraling on the chilly breeze.

I hear the "shushing" of the snow falling
and the "puttering" of the four-wheeler.

My stiff, frozen cheeks cringe
as the vehicle vibrates
across the mantle of pine needles.

Hot coffee scalds my tongue
as the aromatic vapors
swirl their way to my nose.

The forest embraces us
as we meander down her paths

Mrs. Bivins' Class, Grade 6
Crestwood Elementary School, VA

My Mom Ate My Homework

My mom ate my homework
She said she loved division
My mom ate my homework,
not a good decision.

I took my homework to school
with three bites out of it,
I hope my teacher's in a good mood
I should of called in sick.

My mom ate my homework
Shouldn't have left it on the floor
I guess now it's my fault…
That my mom's a dinosaur.

Trey Perry, Grade 5
Woodlawn Elementary School, VA

I Am a Knight

I am a knight
My sword in one hand
My shield in the other
Hiya! Hiya!
I will defeat you dragon!
Hiya! Hiya!
Whoops!
I broke a vase

Will McKinnon, Grade 5
St Christopher's School, VA

Puppy

Puppy
pretty, small
cuddling, running, playing
barking, cool, hyper, big
sleeping, eating, jumping
mature, biting
dog

Owen Van Krimpen, Grade 6
Floyd T Binns Middle School, VA

Peace

Peace is all over the world.
There are peace signs all swirled.
There are many ways to show peace.
Handshake is a peace symbol.
White doves flying
In the world peace signs are everywhere.

Rhiannon Frye, Grade 5
Moyock Elementary School, NC

My Favorite Place

My favorite place to be
Is not in the city or by the sea,
It's not by the ocean at high tide
Or a paradise that makes me sigh.
Some say it's ugly,
But that is a lie,
You can't tell a book by its cover —
You have to look inside.
Some say it's a nasty place to be
but it's perfect and beautiful to me.

It's the swamp
That captures my heart.

All the grazing herds of deer
And the lush forest very near,
Many flying, diving, swimming ducks —
Silent but alive, no loud cars or trucks.
It's a place where I can get away
From life and my troubles of the day.

Patrick Bradley Lancaster, Grade 6
Farmville Middle School, NC

Squash

Hands sweating
Goggles getting foggy
And whole body dripping with sweat
Desperately waiting for the ball to get served
SSSWWWAAACCKK
The ball comes flying at me
I use my forehand to hit the ball
It was a hard shot
And it hits the back-glass
It is too far away for the opponent to reach it
I await the championship trophy

Thorn Wilbanks, Grade 4
St Christopher's School, VA

Winter

As I walk down a chilly, snowy mountain
With lots of trees covered with so much
Snow it looks like white frosting.

After a few hours I get sleepy and very cold
As I walk my way back home
Where my nice fireplace is crackling.

My mom makes me warm hot cocoa with marshmallows
As I lie in my cozy bed under a comfy quilt
Waiting for a new day to begin.

Kiara Cepeda, Grade 4
Bensley Elementary School, VA

In the Forest

I saw it in the forest
It moved just by the trees
It made me that much frightened
I fell down on my knees

Just before I saw it
I heard a little squeak
I thought it was a mouse
Because mice are just meek

And then it just swooped
With talons and a beak
This is how I saw it
Big, smart and sleek

It picked the mouse right up
And flew right out of sight
I thought it would be back
To come and get a bite

It was a fierce bald eagle
Now they are really fast
So if I tried to run
I knew I wouldn't last!

Jerard Dean Hernandez, Grade 5
Rosemont Forest Elementary School, VA

The Beach

The beach is very exciting,
The sand is hot from the sun's lighting.
The roar of the ocean,
In the same flowing motion,
You can build a sand dominion,
And the sand looks like crystal, that's my opinion.
The cool ocean spray,
And in a chair you could lay.
The shells for collecting on top of the sand,
On a hot day you may want to be fanned.
You may prefer a calmer place like the bay,
But as for me, I would prefer the ocean any day.

Deborah Jensen, Grade 5
Trinity Christian School, VA

Thanks

When I see the homeless,
The needy, and the sick,
I'm thankful for what I have…

My family, who loves me
Like there's no tomorrow,
And hangs on to me
Like an autumn tree
Clinging onto its last leaf.

I'm thankful for my house,
With the smiling garden,
Welcoming me with its sweet scent of brownies
And sheltering me
From the outside world.

And I'm thankful for my good health,
For without it,
I'd be like a fish out of water.

So when you pass the homeless, the needy,
And the sick,
YOU should be very thankful
For what you have.

Sara Veera, Grade 6
Wyman Elementary School, RI

Obama

In 2009 we got a new president
Finally a new white house resident
His name was Obama
A man without drama
And finally a hope for lots of good karma
His daughters Melia and Sasha live with their mama
Michelle Obama
Their grandma S. Anne Soetoro
I hope Obama will be a modern day hero

Diego Maness, Grade 5
Queens Creek Elementary School, NC

A Bright Future

I dig and dig
and dig all day.

I just can't
seem to find
my way,

I try to scoop,
I try to see,

the big path in
front of me,

Suddenly, I see the light,
now I know my future's bright!

Maria Caramadre, Grade 5
St Mary School, RI

Departed

Departed
A simple word
So much to do
With so little time
Now that's how
He is
He lies there, frozen
Always frozen
Always beautiful
But in a bittersweet
Way
I would give anything
Anything to have
Him here, alive
Next to me
Alive and
Warm
Really
Anything…

Willow Barbero, Grade 6
Main Street Middle School, VT

My Pet Butterscotch

My name is Butterscotch
I was the first
My ears are small and round
I wheek for snacks
I burble when I'm happy
I chutt chutt when I walk around
I have black and tan stripes
I look like I am part tiger
I'm small, I'm cute and I'm fluffy
I'm very very sweet
I need lots and lots of love
I am a guinea pig

Katie Henry, Grade 5
Salem Elementary School, VA

Water

I am water, peaceful and easygoing.
More mighty than Neptune or Poseidon.
Cool and refreshing like an aqua colored dream.
I am a waterspout, stinging like a trident with the strength of a god.
When I am calmed down I become a gentle mist.
A sky blue mirage in a puddle.
I am water.

Garrett Lien, Grade 5
Wakefield Forest Elementary School, VA

Where I'm From

I am from the horizon,
From where the sun meets the sea and where you walk along the shore.
I am from where the land meets the sea.
From the seagulls flying around.
(Waiting until food ends up in their mouth.)

I am from 3 amigos and skateboards,
From Daniel and Isabel.
I'm from "Be good" and "Take care."
I'm from salsa recipes that I make when we run out,
I'm from my uncle and aunt's ranch,
From the goats and the geese that play with me when I'm lonely.
I am from those moments —
That have brought me here and made me who I am.

Adan Gutierrez, Grade 5
Central Elementary School, NC

Springtime Oh, Springtime

The spring is so beautiful when all the flowers bloom and the air is so cool.
The leaves on the trees start to bloom and you see all the animals looking for food.
The grass is happily moving side to side.
And the seeds are happy because they are going to the water slide.
The water is peaceful and calm and some water is on my palm.
Every day the bees go to the flowers with their beautiful sound.
Springtime oh springtime I love you so much.

Nicole Concepcion, Grade 4
Courthouse Road Elementary School, VA

Where I'm From

I am from moving around.
From Maine, Texas, and California.
I am from where you walk along the stars.
Where the streets are filled with lights.
I am from riding into the sunset and
the big old cherry tree that grows with me.

I'm from the wishing well and the pennies that rest on the bottom.
From Alicia and Mark,
I'm from those days dad sent me flowers.
From "rise and shine" and "turn that frown upside down"

I'm from fetch with Hannah and swimming with Ally.
I'm from the journey of my life and the childhood that led me there.

Rebecca Chryss, Grade 5
Central Elementary School, NC

Ode to Tigger

Oh Tigger oh Tigger you are so sweet
I picked you out when you were just a kitten
You were so weak and small from the others
You accepted me right when I picked you up
And now you sleep with me every night
You never bite or growl at a single thing
You never fight with things in your territory
You show affection to anyone who comes in
When toddlers pull on your tail you know better
When you are scolded you never do so again
You are the neighborhood cat
Oh Tigger I love you so.

Claire Gainey, Grade 5
Vienna Elementary School, NC

The Snowy Pine Tree

The birds were singing on the pine trees.
Their tails, soft and fluffy blow in the breeze.
The people's houses are as smoky as a dust bunny.
Pine trees are as green as money.

The kids were playing,
While the adults were laughing.
It was as snowy as cotton balls,
as all of the fluffy snow falls.

Haley Stone, Grade 4
Bethlehem Elementary School, NH

Ocean Waves

Ocean waves make the world shimmer,
Though no one sees it in the winter,
Riding down on the summer bumpy roads,
To the beach there we go but no one knows.

Swimming in the ocean waters,
Now here's my car sick sister, but that's just her,
To me this is the road to adventure!
Here we go up the hills we'll be there just you see.

Oh man, I love summer,
Too bad school starts in August, what a bummer,
I can't wait for ocean waves,
Live life to the fullest, that's what I always say.

Here we are at the cozy beach house,
While we unpack things are quiet as a mouse
Look at the other beach houses big and wide,
Look at the other beach houses side by side.

On the beach we go oh man, oh man,
Can't wait to stick my toes in the sand,
Look at the beautiful ocean waters,
This is what I call a vacation to explore.

Morgan Hargett, Grade 5
Queen's Grant Community School, NC

My Color Days

Some days are lazy yellow some days are tropical green,
some days I feel a boy needs to scream,

Some days are orangey red
and I want to stay in my soft white bed,

Some days are mixed with purple and blue
and those days I always learn something new,

Some days are café brown
and I say where is my shiny crown,

Some days I feel plain white
and I want to fly a kite,

And on one specific day
I want to bounce and play,

Unfortunately on a black rainy day
my heart beats and runs away.

Adam Aboelmatty, Grade 5
Clover Hill Elementary School, VA

Red

Red is the feel of lava hot anger in you
Red is the sight of a red rose thorn
Red is the feeling of anger running through you
Red is the smell of burning lava bellowing out
Red is the sound of stomping feet
Red runs up you angrily
Red breathes out anger
Red is the feeling of anger when you don't get your way
Red is the feel of a bee's painful sting
Red hisses when it's angry and stomps around

Ronnie Hall, Grade 4
Tabernacle Elementary School, NC

Lazy Lion

In a field,
a lion rested on a bed of grass,
his fur, shining like the sun.
But when he wakes up, he won't be so fun.
He'll shout his ferocious roar.

But until then, he'll sleep like a baby,
letting his wife do all the work.
His pride is too high for doing nothing,
and his sense of the wild too low.

But even so,
he's called the king of the jungle,
and that's just the way he likes it.
The lazy lion does nothing at all,
yet nothing can ever stop him.

Tristan Lalor, Grade 5
Manchester Elementary/Middle School, VT

Grass

Grass is everywhere
Forgotten like pavement
On the street.
Beautiful
Luke Demers, Grade 5
Good Shepherd Catholic School, RI

Love

L ove is very special
O ut of reach when you want it
V ery close when you need it
E ven though love hurts the most,
 it's the best and that I know.
Chris Burwell, Grade 6
Benjamin Syms Middle School, VA

Passion

Love
 Since the beginning
Peace
 Another way of living
Feeling
 To tell it all
Passion
Karen Adkins, Grade 5
Sanford Creek Elementary School, NC

Colors

Warm
Red, orange
Heating, warming, exciting
Flaming, burning, freezing, frosty
Relaxing, calming
Purple, green
Cool
Dayjia Capers, Grade 5
St Helena Elementary School, SC

The First Song of the Housekeeper!

I'm poor and I'm old,
My hair has gone to gray,
My robe is nothing but patches,
My sash is made of hay.

The fat god of luck,
Never enters our door,
And no visitors come around,
To drink tea anymore.

Yet I hold my head high,
As I walk through the town,
While I serve such a master,
My heart now bows down.
Elvira Negron, Grade 6
Benjamin Syms Middle School, VA

The Greatest Game

Baseball is an awesome game
My favorite team has this name:
Red Sox, Red Sox, go go go
Yankees, Yankees you're so slow!
To be a Yankee is a shame!

Slider, spitter, fastball, curve
Schilling throws it, watch it swerve.
The ball is hit back to the wall
A fielder leaps, a diving fall
A Red Sox doesn't lose his nerve!
Nathan Hubbard, Grade 6
Home School, NH

Soccer

Soccer
Hot, sweaty
Running, kicking, sprinting
It's my favorite sport
Shooting, dribbling, passing
Tiring, energetic
Soccer
Taylor Bird, Grade 5
Blaney Elementary School, SC

Ocean

Ocean
big, blue, and cool
smashes down in the sand
I'm going to the beach today!
Sandy
Anna Sing, Grade 4
Waller Mill Fine Arts Magnet School, VA

Sister

Sister
Smart, awesome
Spelling, loving, caring
Easy to make laugh
Girl
Sean Murray, Grade 4
Appomattox Elementary School, VA

Grasslands

Grasslands that go on forever,
Snakes slither through the land,
the sun burns down
Upon the tiny cricket,
and the trees wallow in the sun.
All of the animals in the grassland
look for shade
Under the basking tree.
Julia Mahon Kuzin, Grade 5
Oak View Elementary School, VA

Lightness and Darkness

They course through us all.
The lightness and the darkness.
The good and the evil,
The light and the dark,
They collide to fight in us
They both course through me
Burning through my soul
Our soul isn't good, or evil
Neither is the earth God made.
Neither is the life
Some of us might live.
We shall be gone in the end
It might be torment
Or it could be happy.
Maybe it is full of fright,
As I turn around.
Billy Ford, Grade 4
Appomattox Elementary School, VA

Grilled Cheese

Bread, cheese, butter,
Cheese, butter, pan,
Butter, pan, stove,
Pan, stove, HOT!
Stove, HOT!, sizzle,
HOT!, sizzle, flip,
Sizzle, flip, done,
Flip, done, place mat,
Done, place mat, napkin
Place mat, napkin, plate,
Napkin, plate, lemonade,
Plate, lemonade, grilled cheese
Lemonade, grilled cheese, YUM!
Benjamin Dodson, Grade 5
Queen's Grant Community School, NC

Citrus

Citrus is tangy and sour bittersweet too
 puckering is the thing to do
 it is similar to the flower rue
 citrus will come and get you
Olivia Markowski, Grade 5
Clover Hill Elementary School, VA

Hockey/Lacrosse

ice hockey
fun, hard
playing, checking, trying
ice, sideboard, grass, mud
jumping, passing, running
fun, hard
lacrosse
Karl Jessen, Grade 4
Waller Mill Fine Arts Magnet School, VA

Dear Teacher You Rock

Dear teacher you rock my socks right off,
You're there for me when I need you most.

You're always willing to give a helping hand
No matter where you go

You're nice to everyone you meet
You're pretty kind but most of all, sweet

And dear teacher, that is why
You rock my socks right off.

Brooke Robertson, Grade 4
Courthouse Road Elementary School, VA

Water

I am water
Swimming through life.
Blue with happiness
Blue with sadness
Raining, running, streaming
Cold like ice
Warm like oceans
Puddles of tears, tantrums like monsoons
Laughter like tsunamis
Soaking into sponges
Not too deep in life
Only wading
I am water

Millie Cunningham, Grade 6
Wakefield Forest Elementary School, VA

The Circus

I watch in wow
As a clown rides a tricycle
The clown takes his bow
And rides along a monkey on a bicycle
I sit and watch the circus

The acrobats fly through the air
The man on stilts standing high
The wind blowing through their hair
I wave as they go goodbye
I sit and watch the circus

Roar goes the lion
A little car goes around the ring
And boom goes the canyon as a man goes flying
The horn goes bling, bling
I sit and watch the circus

Flips and turns
A man breathing fire
I hope he doesn't get a burn
The circus is what I admire

Aleksandra Daws, Grade 6
East Mooresville Intermediate School, NC

Emotions

Relieve
Comfort, console, ease, lighten
When I'm relieved I'm sometimes frightened.
Scared
Panicked, horrified, startled, frighten
When I get scared my hands will tighten.
Surface
Exterior, cover, covering, mass
When I run on the surface I'm so fast.
Master
Servant, mastermind, genius
My master is devious.

Annie Francis, Grade 5
Olde Providence Elementary School, NC

Spot

I have a dog that is a bone
When he barks
I can hear his tone

I feel really bad
That he is sad
He better be good
In his new neighborhood

Your love is lost above
Your love cost more than anything
I would do anything to keep you
Oh Spots, oh Spots I wonder where you are!

Stacie Selvey, Grade 5
Forrest W Hunt Elementary School, NC

A Clock Song

Looking upon her desk of the one and only ball point pen,
Thinking of her faithful mailmen,
Sits the wide-eyed teacher
As her mail-like thoughts are drowned
In the loud, unpleasant sound
Of the clock songs of the students impatient waiting.
Tick-tock, tick-tock
The clock is working slowly!
Ms., do mind fixing it
So we can all go home?!
Slumped over their desks
Trying to figure out how to deal with their naughty pesks
Though their thoughts are packed away
When they hear the teacher say
That they soon will not have to stay
So the clock song rises again.
Tick-tock, tick-tock
The clock is working slowly!
Ms., do mind fixing it
So we can all go home?!

Katherine A. Kane, Grade 5
Fairhill Elementary School, VA

Man's Best Friends

Big-eared, identical, entwined dogs
Possessing the cozy chair
Adorable, brown, cute but only together
Hiding and scared of the unknown
Could it be sadness or fear lurking out there
Sharing compassion for each other
Big-eared, identical entwined dogs
Possessing the cozy chair.

Nathan Johnson, Grade 6
Main Street Middle School, VT

The Monster

Cross his threshold and you're sure to become toast,
For this little monster is not a gracious host.
Clicket, clackety, clicket, trap.

Like a tribe of angry bees who knows who stole their honey,
So comes this horrible monster as swift as a bunny.
Clicket, clackety, clicket, trap.

Closer and closer comes that dreadful sound,
Closer and closer like a howling hound.
Clicket, clackety, clicket, trap.

Know him and fear him and run for your life,
This malicious monster is about to cause strife.
Clicket, clackety, clicket, trap.

There it is, it's about to devour you —
It's only the vacuum cleaner, it always seems to cower you.
Clicket, clackety, clicket, trap.

Abigail Coberly, Grade 5
Ocean Acres Academy, NC

I Am a Butterfly

I am a heart; full of love
I am a star; always shining
I am a butterfly; I spread my wings
I am a diary; secrets are kept with me
I am a bunny; get scared easily
I am a phone; people can talk to me
I am a pencil; used all the time
I am a teddy bear; friends can cuddle up with me.

Emmaline Mejia, Grade 5
Four Oaks Elementary School, NC

Tigers

Green eyes stalking prey
Big paws leaping in the air.
Stripes brushing against the bushes
Roaring and mumbling across the air.
Giant paws sinking in the mud,
A wet tongue licking the small helpless cubs.

Brianna Turner, Grade 4
Olde Providence Elementary School, NC

About Me

I am a diary; all secrets stay inside of me.
I am a river; I flow along with everything.
I am an aunt hen; I protect my little ones.
I am a gardenia; strong and keep coming every year.
I am a heart; always show love.
I am a bottle; I keep my feelings inside of me.
I am a garden; full of wonder and laughter.
I am a snowflake; I fluttered in the air.

Alicia Enriquez, Grade 5
Four Oaks Elementary School, NC

My Brother

I'd like to talk about someone who's really sweet,
And someone you would surely want to meet.
He likes to play games; he likes to do puzzles,
But sometimes I wish I just put him in a muzzle.
All in all he's really funny and very kind.
Hopefully somebody out there would be lucky to find,
A brother as great as mine.

Courtney Nicholas, Grade 6
Benjamin Syms Middle School, VA

Civil Rights

We have rights
that are very bright and well right
so be fair and use them right.

We have had sit-ins, meetings and greetings,
so please just give into the present and later into the past.
And at last we get our freedom, legacy, and freedom of speech
so…redeem the usual.

Acaysha Clark, Grade 5
Cooper Elementary School, VA

Hate

Is the feeling of loathing inside,
A burst of flames, rage anger
Tries to befriend all,
Once left alone
It might just get one more thing out of you —
A smirk makes you into a jerk
Harsh weather it makes out of a sunny day,
Making your life a burning flesh of feeling,
Your tree of happiness, joy and laughter is cut down.
But the way you deal with it is how hate can be gone,
Otherwise hate will turn your loathing day
Into your loathing life.

Sarah Wade, Grade 5
Rye Elementary School, NH

Summer

Surfing the fast waves
Falling into deep water.
The best season yet.

Drew Wilkers, Grade 5
C Hunter Ritchie Elementary School, VA

My Guardian Angel

How does it feel,
To lose someone you love?
Well, how does it feel,
To love someone you lost?
Ever wondered what they were like?
Or, ever wanted to be by their side?
I lost my brother, and I can't believe why.
He got cancer,
And just had to die.
I never met him,
But I can feel him inside.
He's just like me,
Inside and out.
He's my guardian angel,
ALWAYS
by my side.

Maria Gil, Grade 6
St Rocco School, RI

Bart Simpson

I'm a 10-year-old boy my hair's spiky
My shoes are both blue, but I hate Nike

I go to school, but I do not like it
Principal Skinner is such a dimwit

I wear a red T-shirt and wear blue shorts
I fool 'round in class then get bad reports

My name is Bart, I pick on my sister
She's smarter than me, I'm stronger than her

My dad's name is Homer, sleeps on the job
His punishments are good, to be a slob

I always have one thing, my one slingshot
I'll take it with me, I'll use it a lot

Max Ferney, Grade 6
Beck Academy, SC

Snakes

Snakes are the devils and demons sent from the underworld.
Who lurk around every corner waiting to drain the innocence
Out of your very soul by striking fear into it.
Just lurking, just waiting in the shadows.
With just knowing you will scare.
So just watch yourself be aware
For you will never know what
Is around the next corner
And just waiting to strike
Fear into your
Soul.

Mariah Dutil, Grade 5
Rye Elementary School, NH

Looking Outside

Everything is gray
The white snow is melting
Acres of trees staring at me
The gray sky stands alone and cold
It's getting darker
It seems like time has stopped

Peyton Durkee, Grade 4
Atkinson Academy Elementary School, NH

The Huge Hustling Husky

A huge hustling husky hates hypnosis and hyenas.
While humoring a hummingbird a horsefly hit his heart.
Hospitalization had helped his hurting heart.
On his hottest house boat a horsewoman had her
horse help the huge hustling husky.

Christian Luck, Grade 4
Edwards Elementary School, SC

The Waves

The winter waves are sad and lonely
There are no children in the water
No sun shining down on them
No playful dolphins splashing in the waves
With cold, hard chunks of ice on its back
Just moving back and forth
But then the nighttime comes
The crashing waves look sadly up at the moon
And they see the moon shining down on them
And then they feel better again.

Madeline Bachmann, Grade 5
Rye Elementary School, NH

Rain

Heavy rain falls on my bedroom window,
Pitter patter sound of rain synchronize with my heart beat,
Gazing at the ceiling,
Sleeping, Dreaming,
Dreaming of what tomorrow will bring,
Rain awakens me from slumber,
staring out my window,
Ground wet and slippery,
Sky dark and depressing,
Sun creeps out of clouds,
A new day begins.

Meghan Buerman, Grade 6
St Rocco School, RI

Blue Is Cool

Blue is the color of the sky
it makes me so cheerful I want to fly
I hear the ocean waves crashing
and the children laughing
I taste the salty water being at the blue sea
I feel refreshed as the waves crash on me

Abigail Duffy, Grade 5
St Mary School, RI

Julius Peppers

Julius,
Strong, athletic, loves football, and nice
Player for Carolina Panthers
Lover of football, meat, and his teammates
Who feels good while playing football, strong while tackling a player, and weak while being tackled
Who needs food, water, and shelter
Who gives bruises, cuts, and broken bones
Who fears death, being sick, and losing a game
Who would like to see another championship, the team he is playing lose, and a player of the year award
Resident of Wilson, North Carolina
Peppers

Dylan Dameron, Grade 5
Vienna Elementary School, NC

Pencils and Pens

Pencils with colors so bright and sketches so tight and paintbrushes so thick
Drawings so good just use a pencil or pen you should just use one on paper
Then you will have a nice pencil or pen you should use one on paper
Then you will have a nice picture made with a pen or a pencil with lines so nice and neat
And with bright colors like red, blue and orange too
So just pick up a pencil or pen and then just let your hand do all the work
Like a poor little pet who went to the vet or draw a painting or two
The more you draw the better you'll get and the better you draw the more you will do.

William Cather, Grade 4
Courthouse Road Elementary School, VA

12 Months

January is when my sister was born, after she opens the present the paper is torn.
February is the month that has Valentine's Day, what more do I have to say?
March is the month where everybody wears green, sometimes the leprechauns are mean.
April is when the weather gets warm; and the bees start to swarm.
May is when the flowers start to grow and finally we get rid of the snow.
June is when we get out of school; man that is really cool.
July is when we see the lights in the sky; boy, they are really high.
August is when we go back to school, man do I feel like a fool!
September is when the leaves start to brown, and then they come down.
October is for cats and mummies, and all the candy goes to our tummies.
November has the turkey day and I eat whatever I may.
December is when Christ was born, and we open up presents Christmas morn.

Jordan Leone, Grade 5
C Hunter Ritchie Elementary School, VA

Chase

Chase
Friendly, joyful, caring, historical
Brother of William
Lover of animals, hamburgers, and cinematography
Who feels happy when someone agrees, worried for his wild temper, and respectful of others
Who needs a better mind for math, listening, and shooting
Who gives help, explaining, and understanding
Who fears death, space, and poisonous snakes
Who would like to see the American dream, go hunting for boars, and the NASA Space Center
Resident of Pfafftown, North Carolina
Cunningham

Chase Cunningham, Grade 5
Vienna Elementary School, NC

My Funky Skunk

Once there was a little skunk
He always smelled like some kind of funk.
We thought it was a black cat
But we didn't see it eat any rats.
We were lucky we didn't have a black vase
It might have been the skunk in case.

Ciera Fox, Grade 5
Riverview Elementary School, VA

Summer

See all the flowers
Stuffed with color
And fill the air with a fragrant scent.
IIear the soothing sound
Of rushing streams running
Throughout the forest.
The buzz of bees
Collecting pollen from flower to flower.
Fireflies skimming the water
With their delicate wings
Leaving a drizzle of water behind
That gets bigger and bigger until it fades away.
Looking at the big creamy clouds floating in the sky
Reminds me of fluffier nuttier
Filled with warmth and taste.
I can just reach into the sky and pull a piece off.
A sun setting on top of the hills,
It's filled with shades of colors
Then it just fades away.

Ryder Ferrone, Grade 6
Manchester Elementary/Middle School, VT

Ode to a Grapefruit

Sweet yet sour citrus fruit,
healthy pink citrus loot
Evil citrus, squirt my eye,
make it sting and make me cry!
Now I must eat you —
Die die, DIE!

Pungent taste,
I won't make waste.
I take a bite —
I lose my sight!
Evil citrus, you squirt my eye!
You made it sting — I should have had pie.

Katherine Wojcik, Grade 6
Boiling Springs Intermediate School, SC

Love

Love is a pillow because it is comfort on a rainy day.
Love is rain because it comes and goes.
Love is a tree because you can lean on it.
Love is a freckle because it stays with you.

Marisa Schilling, Grade 5
Holy Cross Elementary School, DE

I Am

Who am I do you ask?
I am the sand on the beach,
the waves in the ocean,
the leaves on the trees
and the grass below your feet.
I am much more than a simple rose petal,
more than a single dew drop,
more than a cloud floating in the magenta sky.
I am as soft as the first snowfall
and as rough as an old leaf.
I am like the sound of a gentle breeze,
as heartwarming as a baby's first cry,
as adventurous as the sound of thunder.
I am Nature.

Aimee Krafft, Grade 6
Milford Middle School, NH

Old Jumping Leaves

These old jumping leaves,
From old times,
Of memories,
They remind me about playing in the meadow,
A pumpkin patch filled with jack-o-lanterns.
I was the princess,
And they were the kings and queens,
Dressed in robes and capes.
On Christmas we would take turns wearing the Santa hat,
Acting like silly monkeys,
Running around,
Going up the hill to have sled races,
Some waiting at the bottom to trip people's sleds.
People flying across the snow,
Like birds skimming across sky.
Making leaf piles out of the old jumping leaves.
How I wish I would be one of those little girls again,
Diving into the old jumping leaves.

Courtney Lynch, Grade 6
Manchester Elementary/Middle School, VT

The Knawing Biting Bunny Fudge

Dear my dearest Fudge,
Why do you knaw wildly at your cage?
Why do you ferociously lunge at me?
What does your little heart dearly want?
I'll do almost anything for you to abruptly stop.
The Hershey Kiss shaped and sized purple drops?
More precious time to be delicately held?
More fresh green hay?
More strawberry treats?
Which of those options do really you want?
I really do care.
P.S. Please listen.

Allison Jodoin, Grade 5
Rye Elementary School, NH

A Girl's Eyes

There is a young lady whose eyes
were unique as to color and size.
When she opened them wide,
people all turned aside,
and started away in surprise.

Mary Martinez, Grade 5
Four Oaks Elementary School, NC

Rabbit/Bunny

Rabbit
Fluffy, cute
Bouncing, twitching, nibbling
Hopping through grassy plains
Bunny

Maryann Adesoba, Grade 6
Floyd T Binns Middle School, VA

Autumn

The sun shines brightly
on the cool fall air,
as the harvesting farmers
pick the newly grown pears.

The leaves are falling
on the active woods,
while the animals prance
for autumn goods.

The forest isn't lazy,
just listen and hear,
the birds are calling,
for you to cheer.

The young deer are growing,
their mother by their side,
teaching them the wonders
and the key to survive.

As you watch the geese
fly south for the time,
you'll smile and realize
how autumn is divine.

Ria Das, Grade 4
Bicentennial Elementary School, NH

Softball

Bam! The ball was hit.
Whoosh! It flew through the air.
Slap! I caught the ball.

I threw the ball.
The player's out.
The crowd goes wild.
What a happy day!

Hannah Crump, Grade 4
Pocahontas Elementary School, VA

Not on the Map

Do you know how it feels to NOT be on the map?
It feels as if you're not important
Too small to be on the map
Neglected, left, forgotten
To be mentioned on the Weather Channel
It's always "Today in Portsmouth it is sunny with a 50% chance of rain."
Never, "Today in Rye…"
Maybe…it means I'm unique
So important I'm NOT on the map
And the people inside me aren't perfect, but they live their own special way
I am small but mighty
Hello
I am Rye
And I am NOT on the map

Shanley King, Grade 5
Rye Elementary School, NH

January

January is the month that it snows so very much.
My mom's in the kitchen cooking dough while I'm outside playing in snow.
January feels like hot chocolate on a cold day.
January smells like my mom's scented candles.
Snow is like clouds cascading across the sky.
January is like snow when you touch it.
January sounds like snow splashed across my back.
January looks like sleet on the road.
January is like snow that floats in the wind.
January is like hot chocolate running down my throat.

Brandon Williams, Grade 4
Tabernacle Elementary School, NC

The Day My Mom Fell into the Christmas Tree

I remember the funny Christmas.
I remember how cold it was outside.
I remember how everything smelled good,
and how my mom looked.
I remember the smile she had on her pretty face.
I remember her opening all the presents then leaving the big one for last.
I remember her smiling as she opened it.
Even as she started to fall back into the Christmas tree.
I remember her laughing as she got up out of the tree.
But my favorite memory is still to come.

Kiersten Turner, Grade 6
Boiling Springs Intermediate School, SC

Girl of the Wind

Sally is a young girl listening to the sounds of the world.
Her eyes, though she is not blind, do not see.
Her ears, like speakers for her brain, seem to be her only sense.
She sees with her ears — watching the world.
Attentively, she listens to nothing waiting for something to happen.
The silence, seeming like the key to the lock of her heart, is like her best friend.
I think she's got a secret.
A secret she was told by the breeze.

Skylar Jones, Grade 4
Olde Providence Elementary School, NC

A Loving Sister

H eart is never full
E very basketball game a good luck charm
A lways is a loving sister
T hen don't mess with her
H er smile is like sunshine
E very day she is beautiful
R eally smart

Sara Cubit, Grade 5
E Taylor Hatton School, VT

Freedom, Waiting to Break Through…

Had a bad day, take those fears away.
Telling her it's going to be fine
Just be patient,
Soon every race will shine
The gravel under my toes.
My heart beating loud, but ever so slow.
Fresh rain dripping down my face.
Segregation!
What a disgrace!
The peace waiting to come,
And all the problems over and done
The hands reaching out, waiting for freedom,
That's what it's all about!

Gina Baldassare, Grade 6
Dr Edward Ricci School, RI

Under the Cover

I tried to sneak out of my bedroom window,
But my mother said, "Put your head back on your pillow."

I grab my book by E.B. White,
And then I grab a flashlight.

I call myself a silly spy,
But I know I'm just a regular guy.

"I can't sleep," I told my mother.
She said to just get back under the cover.

Abbie Danielle Anton, Grade 5
Forrest W Hunt Elementary School, NC

Holocaust

If you have ever lost a loved one,
You won't want to hear this,
I find this very cruel although that's how it is,
The man in charge was Adolf Hitler,
I highly dislike what he stood for,
He must have had a dark personality,
You wouldn't want to step in his door,
I hope I gave you enough info.
Well I have to go!!!

Kendall Luz, Grade 5
Queens Creek Elementary School, NC

Cinderella

Cinderella once dressed all in yellow
Chef, making lots of cherry-lime Jell-O

Dreamed of shiny pink Lamborghini
On a beach with Prince Charming in Capri

It all started at a fairy-tale ball
And it ended with a fancy house call

She had traveled all the way from Greenville
With her ten bridesmaids, even some from Brazil

Her transportation is a pink bus
She's getting married in Graceland, of course

Her fiancé is a huge Elvis fan
He would like Elvis to be his best man

That young princess, with beautiful blue eyes
Her smile, beautiful as the winter skies

Tonight she is dressed all in sparkling white
For it is her very own wedding night.

Catherine Pierre, Grade 6
Beck Academy, SC

Color

As you read along
You'll find a catching song
About my many colored days
And how I spend them right here today.

Some days are new, true, and blue
On those days I'm so clueless that I could eat glue.

But others are sunshine yellow
When I feel like eating a whole bucket of Jell-O.

Some days are mean dark green
On those days I just want to pull out my hair and scream.

A lot of times they're fire red
And on those days I want to go to bed.

And those are my many colored days
And how I spent them right here today.

Gabrielle Hundley, Grade 5
Clover Hill Elementary School, VA

When I First Saw You

When I first saw you I was afraid to meet you
When I first met you I was afraid to hold you
When I first held you I was afraid to love you
When I first loved you I was afraid to lose you.

Martraivius Bristow, Grade 5
Four Oaks Elementary School, NC

My Family

I love my family
Family cheers me up
Helps me when I'm blue
Helps me along the way
Loves me so much
Lucky that I have a loving family
Have a good family
Loves and cares
Special in life

Cares so much
I love my family
Part of my life
Helps me with mess ups
Keeps me company
Loves me so much
Still loves me

Always remembers me
Always loves me
Family cheers me up
I love my family
Nicholas Vecchio, Grade 4
Hope Valley Elementary School, RI

What Is Writing?

Writing is my passion
I'll never let it go
You can't make me
You can't pay me
I'll do it for the rest of my life
I'll do it for the world
And I'll keep it that way.
Caitlyn Brantley, Grade 6
Benjamin Syms Middle School, VA

Who Knew?

Who knew that a bird could fly?
Who knew that a fish could swim?
Who knew?
Who knew that a teacher could teach?
Who knew that an author could write?
Who Knew?
Who knew that a flower could grow?
Who knew that a printer could print?
Who knew?
You knew!
I knew!
He knew!
She knew!
We knew!
Who knew we knew?
Erin Scully, Grade 5
Moyock Elementary School, NC

My Colors

Here are my many colored days
from yellow to red
I hope you like them and don't go to bed

On bright lightning yellow days
I go very fast
When I enter a race
I don't come in last

Flamingo pink days are very great
If you don't mind
I would like some cake

On gloomy gray days I am very sad
This is a day that is very bad

Rosy red days are the very best
I love them so much
I do not rest

And those are my colored days
I hope you enjoyed
I'm very glad you don't look annoyed
Laney Sanchez, Grade 5
Clover Hill Elementary School, VA

The Place

One…two…three
Ribbits
From the one man band
Mucky, mucky
Water
Wild life
Live for this place
One tree
123,456,789
blades of grass
4 plants popping
up to say hello
1 rocky beach
3 big rocks
And a lifetime of good
Memories
Rosie Boucher, Grade 6
Main Street Middle School, VT

Jobs

Jobs
Do good
Always be ready
Put in enough effort
Promotion
Katie Holt, Grade 5
Queen's Grant Community School, NC

Cougar

Cougar is my beloved horse
He loves to run the jumping course!
He's dreary when I go
But he really loves to show!
He'll always be my blue ribbon horse.
Camryn Cenderelli, Grade 5
North Windy Ridge School, NC

Summer Starts

petite bird flying
through the orange open skies
showing summer starts
Kate Parker, Grade 6
Salem Church Middle School, VA

Family

My family is an escalator
because it keeps me moving.

My family is glue
because we stick together.

My family is like a staple
because we are hard to pull apart.

My family is like a fire
because we keep each other warm.
Mark Bonnie, Grade 5
Holy Cross Elementary School, DE

Easter

Easter, Easter, Easter,
I love Easter!
There are Easter egg hunts,
Flowers everywhere,
Pretty dresses that girls are wearing,
Happy faces everywhere,
The reason why we celebrate
This happy day —
Because God rose up from the dead!
Mikayla Burgess, Grade 4
Homeschool Plus, VA

you are at the beach

waves crashing on land,
salty air all around you,
the sand between your toes,
you are at the beach.
sand castles built up high,
board walk food smelling fresh,
all the shops passing by,
you are at the beach.
Rebecca Zachry, Grade 6
Seaford Middle School, DE

Crazy Dogs

Dogs are fun to watch.
They do the craziest things…
I give her a bone,
and she grins while she chews it.
Then her sister comes…
She snatches the bone away.
Then she looks at me,
With her sad, sad eyes and then…
I give her two more.
Now she always keeps it close!

Caitlin Crawford, Grade 5
Courthouse Road Elementary School, VA

When Summer Ends

I'm savoring the sun and the wind
Because I don't want to forget them when summer ends

I'm soaking in the heat and the sand on my skin
Because I don't want to forget them when summer ends

I'm memorizing the crashing waves where I loved to swim
Because I don't want to forget them when summer ends

I don't want to forget all the odds and the ends
So I'll remember everything when summer ends

Allison Bradshaw, Grade 6
Holbrook Middle School, NC

What Is Red

Red is the taste of sweet cherries
Red is the sight of fire
Red is the sound of a firetruck
Red feels like a Coke can
Red smells like an apple pie
Red is an angry person
Red is like a fireball
Red is the sun hiding behind the white cloud
Red is a firetruck heading toward a fire ding-dong ding-dong
Red is the feel of a red heart

Ethan Brown, Grade 4
Tabernacle Elementary School, NC

Bold Blue

BLUE is sad he's bold and dashing he pours on the sky
He splashes when waves crash down.
He's always united on the American flag
He's snow flakes that melt on your tongue
Blue is a marker that can be seen
He's your clothes that you wear to school
He likes to talk. He likes to sing
I feel cold when blue is around
His favorite food is seafood
He has no friends but I love
Blue. Blue is me

Amy Nunnery, Grade 4
Youngsville Elementary School, NC

Color Days

On sunny days I think of yellow
Which makes me think of a meadow warm and mellow
On blue days I feel cool inside
It makes me think of the ocean's tide
On green days I feel very cozy
It makes my cheeks turn really rosy
On gray days I feel oh so lazy
It makes my family all go crazy
And when I think of the color red
I just want to lie in my big fluffy bed
And if my feelings were all the same
I think my world would be very plain
So I will add color to my life's light
I think it will turn out very bright

Gabby Walkey, Grade 5
Clover Hill Elementary School, VA

I Am

I am a fast boy who wants to find the way
I wonder how to get to where I wish to go
I hear my feet slapping any terrain
I see the doors opening in front of me
I want to get there as fast as I run
I am a fast boy who wants to find the way

I pretend to train for my journey
I feel I must train even harder
I touch the blade of glory
I worry that I will not find the way
I cry because people think there is no such place
I am a fast boy who wants to find the way

I understand there might not be a way
I say that this place is real
I dream that someone will come with me
I try my hardest to get where I want to go
I hope I will be there soon
I am a fast boy who wants to find the way

Matthew Kozak, Grade 5
Clover Hill Elementary School, VA

The Fish

I am a fish
Filled with glee
Let me show you my home, the sea
The sea is so blue with lots of things to do
There are reefs galore and caves to explore
But never go down too deep, where it is dark
Or you'll meet lots of hungry sharks
I am a fish
Filled with glee
Let me show you my home, the sea

Jackson Barkstrom, Grade 4
St Christopher's School, VA

Green

Green is the whole reason we are alive
So when we breathe, thank green
Green is luck on St. Patrick's Day
And goes away in May
Green is so healthy for you
And the reason cars go
Green is something to make you rich
And my very favorite color

C.J. Torcellini, Grade 4
Olde Providence Elementary School, NC

My Dog Jack

Dog
Soft, brown
Fast, lovable, crazy
He loves my hamster
Jack

Taylor Altizer, Grade 5
Blaney Elementary School, SC

Spring/Fall

Spring
Warm, bright
Blooming, singing, waking
Beaches, vacation, cold, weather
Changing, hibernating, skiing
Frosty, cool
Fall

Allison Brown, Grade 5
St Helena Elementary School, SC

Summer/Winter

Summer
hot, fun
swimming, playing, shorts
sweating, outside — cold, inside
snowing, ice, sledding
snowball, hot chocolate
Winter

Tiara Jackson, Grade 6
Floyd T Binns Middle School, VA

Sparkling Snow

Chilly to a frosty white.
You are never to know
how much you can give,
until you fall upon the ground.
With flakes that can never
match another.
Upon the ground you fall
until the earth is covered
with a new snow sparkle.

Jacob Pelletier, Grade 6
Warwick Neck School, RI

A Doughnut Bagel

A bagel could be a Frisbee
Your guinea pig's necklace
It could be the head of your dog
A pair of two glaring eyes
Sometimes used as a telescope
Or even a tire on your father's truck
A bagel could be broiled at Starbucks
Sometimes at Dunkin Donuts
It could be your breakfast
Bagels are like doughnuts

Jamie Meade, Grade 5
Rye Elementary School, NH

Christmas Tree

I want to be a Christmas tree
shimmering with orange lights.
BOOM! He is coming, but who is he?
I'm at home and scared. Is it just me?
He's got a lamp and an orange.
He puts them under me.
Then he says, "I'm off to infinity!"
He disappears and the dog barks.
Joey comes down the stairs and yells…

"Mom! He just came!"

Joshua Kinnes, Grade 5
Quidnessett Elementary School, RI

James

J oyful
A mazing
M ighty
E ntertaining
S uper

James Drouillard, Grade 4
Angelus Academy, VA

Electricity

I dreamed
I was electricity.
In the power lines
Powering up houses.
Energetically.

Kalif Anderson-Seawell, Grade 5
Cooper Elementary School, VA

The Fair Knight

There once was a fair knight.
He loved to get in a fight.
He got on his horse,
But took the wrong course,
And then he saw a big fright!

Thomas Lamb, Grade 4
Trinity Christian School, VA

Helicopter

Silver Helicopter,
Flying away,
Simply floating,
In the
Breezy wind.
Propellers spinning,
Thump, thump, thump, thump,
Rapidly rotating,
In the empty air
Bright blue sky,
Inside the aircraft,
The pilot,
Is near death
And needs help
And on the ground
Onlookers have no idea
Just a solitary helicopter
In the bright sky.

Garrett Pembroke, Grade 6
Main Street Middle School, VT

Secrets

I have many secrets
I want to share
My new discoveries
My feelings
The things I do
The things I see
My wonders, hopes and dreams
I wish to share all
I have kept many secrets
I do not know why
The secrets want out
To be heard all around
I have many secrets

Kendall Williams, Grade 6
Bull Run Middle School, VA

Depression

Depression, depression
The rich and the poor
Depression, depression
No more!
Depression, depression
Dull, gloomy, tired, and sad
Depression, depression
Makes me mad!
Depression, depression
Terrified, lonely, and old
Depression, depression
If this is not the half of it
When will it unfold?

Brandon Manchester, Grade 6
Dr Edward Ricci School, RI

The Red Bucket

The red bucket,
I'm so proud of it,
it's been ten years
since I got it
and now it's done.
After holding the
gallons of blue water,
the brown mud with worms,
the grey nails for my dad,
the tan dog treats for training,
and my rainbow school supplies.
The red bucket was the
one color out of
all those colors that I loved.

Hanna Simonetti, Grade 6
Manchester Elementary/Middle School, VT

Gingerbread Stan

I have a funny gingerbread man,
He is covered in frosting and his name is Stan.
He loves to dance and sing galore,
Stan is never, not ever a bore!
He was out for a run when he heard a jolly giggle.
It was Santa and his reindeer, they started to wiggle
Santa and his reindeer started heading Stan's way
Stan wondered what they'd do if they caught him today.
Would they eat him, greet him, or dip him in milk?
Would they put him in a box and wrap it with silk?
He finally gave up and prepared for the worst.
It turns out that Santa gave him some cider to quench his thirst!

Krystina Millar, Grade 5
Waccamaw Intermediate School, SC

I Remember

Have you ever entered a room
And saw the whole world flash by your face?
Like entering a new place
You say you've seen these walls before
Probably behind a closed door
Life comes and it goes
You walk outside and the wind blows
I can't believe how much you've grown
It's like another you I've never known
I see the big smile on your joyful face
I wish you'd walk at a faster pace
Me and you together again
Do you know how long it's been?
I remember that time
When we made up that silly rhyme
But now that your gone
I watch the deer play with their new baby fawn
I'm alone now but I still remember

Deja Gentry, Grade 6
Monelison Middle School, VA

Little Bird

Little bird, little bird,
Life so free
I wonder what it's like to be
To soar above the sky so high,
As all time is passing by
To peacefully sing my beautiful song,
For all to hear, all summer long
To travel far and near and wide
No one to run from, no reason to hide
Little bird, little bird,
Body so light
Light enough to carry by wings in flight
Bones so tiny and body so small,
Although to fellow birds, you might be tall
Life so carefree, mind so clear
No reason to worry, no reason to fear
Little bird, little bird,
Life so free,
I wonder what it's like to be

Jennifer Kondas, Grade 6
Cape Henry Collegiate School, VA

The Dogwood Tree

I climb up the beautiful Dogwood tree
Petals fly around me from the chilly breeze
Is this a dream?

Sarah Mueller, Grade 6
Wakefield Forest Elementary School, VA

Goldfish

I used to keep my goldfish in a tank
but now it's completely blank.
There were eight who had lots of fun
but now there's only one.

The first of my goldfish
ended upon my father's dish.
Now we start with goldfish number two
who got squashed with my little brother's shoe.

Number three died from greed
we found his mouth filled with feed.
The fourth's death was a disgrace
Cupid shot him in the face.

I fed number five a frosted flake
but when he played possum it was not fake.
Number six was the saddest of all
he ended upon my grandfather's wall.

Seven made friends with the cat
I think you know what happened after that.
I found out that number eight was a she
the next day I found the tank full of kids like me.

Cypress Snyder, Grade 5
Forrest W Hunt Elementary School, NC

Columbus

Christopher Columbus sailed the sea.
He had an idea probably.
He sailed from Spain.
He had some pain.
But he wanted to be in history.

Abbey LaVelle, Grade 4
Waller Mill Fine Arts Magnet School, VA

Cinnamon

Cinnamon
Red, short
Eating, running, sleeping
Fearless, mischievous, curious, anxious
Miniature Dachshund.

Taylor Biche, Grade 6
Floyd T Binns Middle School, VA

My Friend

My friend always wears a smile,
He helps me if I'm away a mile.
He comforts me when I'm sad,
He also always makes me glad.
Happy or sad, he's always nice,
Even if we have to pay the price.
My friend is always true to me,
He makes me have a place to be.

Joseph Mann, Grade 4
St Thomas More Catholic School, NC

There's a Bear at My Door

there's a bear at my door
with big claws and big teeth
I'd try to sneak past it
but it really scares me
I don't care for that dog
named "bear" anymore

Devon White, Grade 6
Monelison Middle School, VA

The Pond

Full of life and joy
Water lilies placed upon
Koi Fish dancing there.

Bailey Miller, Grade 5
Trinity Christian School, VA

Mice

Mice like to eat cheese.
Lots of mice are scared of cats.
They can scare adults.
Mice are not fun to play with.
Mice scurry in the kitchen.

Cameron McGann, Grade 4
Battlefield Elementary School, VA

Spring, Spring

Spring comes far too slow
For flowers to grow
Spring, Spring, Spring come
To run around

Spring, Spring, Spring come
Children to play around
Rainy days and
Beautiful Rainbows

Children to play around
Spring comes far too slow
To run around and
Rainy days

Beautiful rainbows
Playing outside
Spring comes far too slow
For flowers to grow

Davis Pillow, Grade 4
Riverside Elementary School, VA

Rice

I am rice
All small and white
And like an ant
I am light.

Surrounding me
Are water and sun
And little green snakes
That make it fun.

I am rice
All small and white
And like an ant
I am light.

Anthony Ing, Grade 4
Crestwood Elementary School, VA

Friends

Friends are a bra.
They are always there for support.

Friends are memories.
The ones you can never forget.

Friends are a blanket.
Soft, kind, and always keep you warm.

Friends are a brick wall.
If you run into them they won't break.

Kylie Arndt, Grade 5
Holy Cross Elementary School, DE

Colors

Blue is the sky on a sunny day.
White is Jesus as a pure heart.
Red is the sunset on the bay.
Yellow is a light bulb that is smart.
Green is the dollars you must pay.
Purple is a sweet purple sweet-tart.
Orange is a sunset ray.

Grace Weaver, Grade 5
Trinity Christian School, VA

The Sword in the Stone*

The sword in the stone,
stuck in well and deep,
no one can pull it out,
glory no one can keep.

Then comes young Arthur,
looking for a sword for his brother,
he pulls the sword out easily!
He did it like no other.

His brother sees the sword in awe,
his brother tells Arthur to keep quiet,
he fails to claim the sword for himself
for King Arthur there's a riot!

John Koh, Grade 5
Trinity Christian School, VA
**Based on the story from*
"The Story of King Arthur and his
Knights" by Howard Pyle

Little Cutie Pie*

You are my cutie pie,
And my little lollipop
You are my sunshine,
And my small doodle bop.

You raise my hopes up,
When I am sad
So sweet like syrup,
That makes me glad.

You have a pleasure to be here,
Always happy and cute
You make me hoot and cheer,
A Little Cutie Patoot.

Now that I am done,
The poem must die
At least I had fun,
My little cutie pie.

Jordan Lipinski, Grade 5
Cold Harbor Elementary School, VA
**Dedicated to my little sister, Hannah*

Love That Chicken*

I love that chicken like a cat loves to meow.
I said I love that chicken like a cat loves to meow.
Love to call him in the morning,
Love to call him,
"Hey there Chicky!"

Clint Seeley, Grade 6
East Mooresville Intermediate School, NC
*Inspired by Walter Dean Myers

That Star…

I looked up at the night sky
And saw a glimmering star.
A bolt of ideas flashed into my brain,
And I wished upon that star.

I peered out my window
And imagined my wish had come true.
I was invisible and couldn't be seen,
And I wished upon that star.

I would walk around my neighborhood
And see my neighbors play around.
But they wouldn't see me,
And I wished upon that star.

I didn't think about the consequences much,
And I had trouble getting to sleep.
So I thought about new ideas,
And I wished upon that star.

I looked at the mirror in my room,
And I couldn't see myself at all.
Now my parents think I am missing
Because I wished upon that star.

Matthew Parisi, Grade 6
Wyman Elementary School, RI

I Am

I am a baby, learning step by step
I am a ball, I travel far
I am a jacket, I get worn out
I am a bomb, when I get mad I explode
I am a football, I go high in the sky
I am ice cream, soft and sweet
I am a wall, you can never knock me down

Ryan Dawes, Grade 5
Four Oaks Elementary School, NC

Happiness

Happiness is yellow
It sounds like an honorable speech
It looks like a smile on someone's face
It smells like a golden flower in the summer
It tastes like sweet, sweet honey

Efrain Alonzo, Grade 5
Vienna Elementary School, NC

Life

Life is like snowflakes,
It's different every day.
Life is like a violin,
Waiting to be played.
Life is amazing; in its own ways,
So why do we always complain?

Life can be depressing,
During hard times.
Life can be sour,
Like sucking on a lime.
Life is like a rhyme,
Some things sound the same, but they never are.

Life is so amazing,
It's hard to understand.
We should be thankful for what we have,
And the life we live.

Erin Hickey, Grade 5
Symonds Elementary School, NH

Santa Claus

With his group of elves,
Who make toys for all the good boys and girls,
On Christmas night he sits on his sleigh
All across the Milky Way.
Ho, Ho, Ho!

Chris Rickabaugh, Grade 5
St Anne Catholic School, SC

I Can Survive!

Me, but why?
So scrawny, so weak.
What did I do?
I don't deserve this.
Or do I?
This sickness will finish me!
Is there anything we can do?
No, nothing!
But can I fight?
Yes, and I will!
I won't go down without a war!

Casey Danielle Crenshaw, Grade 6
Boiling Springs Intermediate School, SC

I May Have a Big Head

I may have a big head but I blame my father
because having a big head is such a bother
please stop my head before it grows farther
If you see that mouse
tell him don't come to my house
or I will smash it with my big head.

Tianna Brunson, Grade 5
Pocalla Springs Elementary School, SC

Sungazer Lizard
Sungazer lizard,
With sharp brown spikes on its back,
Plays dead on the sand.
Hector Rodriguez, Grade 5
Central Elementary School, NC

The Light from the Keyhole
From the keyhole
Comes a light,
In the darkness,
Shines bright

A light is on,
I wonder why,
My sister works,
The time flies by

I'm lying here,
On my bed,
I will tell you
What's in my head

Flowers, rhymes
Division, times
The color red
Is in my head

I don't know why,
Why ask me?
I can't explain
What you can't see.
Abigail Roberts, Grade 6
Linkhorne Middle School, VA

Phoenix
Fire lights the night
Blazing bird in front of me
Then gone with the smoke.
Nathaniel Elliott, Grade 4
Brewster Pierce School, VT

A Promise
A promise is steel.
It is hard to break.

A promise is a glass plate.
You wouldn't want to break it.

A promise is a bank.
It keeps treasure.

A promise is a gift.
When someone gives you something,
you treasure it.
B. Nicolo Bautista, Grade 5
Holy Cross Elementary School, DE

Ruby Bridges
Ruby
Brave, smart, strong, pretty
Student of Mrs. Henry
Lover of school, baseball, potato chips
Who feels smart when she gets something right in school,
Nervous on the first day of school, and happy when she gets a home run
Who needs friends that can play with her all the time, help if she is stuck,
And to not have white people hate her
Who gives care to others when they need it,
A chance for other black kids to go to integrated schools, effort at school
Who fears poison, big mobs, dying
Who would like to make friends with white children,
Not to get teased because she is black, be a part of history
Resident of New Orleans
Bridges
Erika Smith, Grade 4
Hope Valley Elementary School, RI

Dancer
I am a dancer.
I leap through the stiff air.
I feel the wind brush against my face.

One day my teacher said to me, "Never give up. Never give up your dream."
My shoes are as tight as rubber bands.
But I force myself to keep dancing. Let my dream come true.

If I fall, I will get back up.
In the dark, dim room I am practicing my pirouettes.
Under the blazing sun I leap into the air.
The sun smiles at me.
The grass is a studio floor.

I am a dancer.
I am strong.
Makala Wang, Grade 4
Claymont Elementary School, DE

Today, I Am Water...
Sometimes I refresh people,
And sometimes I will make you feel like you are going to drown,
But today I am clear,
Trickling from a waterfall,
I can flow around everything,
And I am brave enough to put out a fire with myself,
If I am cold, I turn into ice,
I feel good on a hot summer day,
And I like to be splashed,
I am a need to everyone,
Now I am rain dropping silently to the ground,
Then I will evaporate up to the clouds,
I am a liquid,
I am water.
Molly Gormley, Grade 5
Wakefield Forest Elementary School, VA

Blue

Blue is the sound of the crashing waves
Blue is the highlights in the mermaid's hair
Blue is the taste of the salty ocean
Blue is the clouds in the sky moving slowly
Blue is the smell of the fresh blueberries
Blue is the clue in my mind
Blue is the sparkle in my eyes
Blue is the sparkling prom dress
Blue is the silky shirt

Mikayla Morris, Grade 4
Tabernacle Elementary School, NC

Ode to Tree

It's always there
No matter the weather —
Still strong,
Still tall.
And always
Doesn't matter the situation
Its branches are there wide open,
Ready to listen to me and
What's going on in the world.
It's a tree in the Amazon jungle
And I am the monkey swinging from its branches.
A shady getaway where I can drink my grandmas lemonade.
My place where my cousins' names and
Mine are always there.
A place where no secret
Will be revealed
To any squirrel or insect that crawls on
The tree
My tree —
My outdoor escape of adventure.

Holly Turlington, Grade 6
CrossRoads Middle School, SC

Green

Green is trees with leaves flying everywhere,
Aliens appearing from nowhere,
With people that have green faces,
While frogs jump through the air.

Green is March,
With clovers on the ground,
A mini leprechaun hat on its leaf,
The Celtics always winning against the Lakers.

Green is grass,
When the crickets chirp,
When turtles move across the road,
While lizards are in the lead of the race against the turtles
When green takes over the world.

Jonathan Mace, Grade 4
Atkinson Academy Elementary School, NH

Epitaph for Auburn

Auburn lies here
She hated homework so dear
She was fed up with homework from Mr. Schmidt
She eventually had enough and threw a fit
For this homework burned her eyes,
For that, here she lies.

Auburn Howerth, Grade 5
North Windy Ridge School, NC

Soccer

Heart is what soccer is about.
You put your all into it.
The ball is like a snake you can never catch it.
Play and practice and you will get better.
BAM!
You hear the soccer ball slam into the goal.
Curve around your opponents.
You're running so much you feel like you're
        going to pass out.
You make it and it takes your breath away.
Goal!
You win.

Game over.

Schuyler Lauder, Grade 5
Sanford Creek Elementary School, NC

Gray

Gray is gloomy
It's the gray clouds
On a rainy day
It's the gray toothbrush
Inside my mouth
Gray is an elephant ready
To stomp on the ground
It is sad especially on
A gray day
Gray is the book cover
On my book
It is dolphins splashing
Water on my face
Gray is the world

Daniel Jordan, Grade 4
Atkinson Academy Elementary School, NH

Mckenzie

M icky Mouse is cute
C ats are scary
K ind girl
E cuador is weird
N eon purple socks
Z ebras make me dizzy
I ce cream rocks
E xtraordinary kid

Mckenzie Deutsch, Grade 5
Courthouse Road Elementary School, VA

Mr. Window

Mr. Window, do you like your life? No, it's dull, boring and painful. How so? I must sit through the worst of weather. What types? Rain, snow, wind and even hail!! I don't even get rewarded for sitting through this despicable weather. The only good thing is the view of the apartment I am in. It's nice and warm and the family is so happy. When I look outside though it is a mad house! All the honking horns and the smell of gas is terrible! What about sunny days? Sun, oh don't even get me started about sunny days. It gets so hot and bright! Sometimes I almost go blind! My life is absolutely horrible!

William Cole Musto, Grade 5
Rye Elementary School, NH

Miracles

Miracles surround us every day we walk this mysterious land.
We must just train our eyes to look for them.
When you do you will find yourself discovering them in the most inadequate places.
A flower beginning to bloom through the concrete,
The rising and setting of the sun and everything in between.
The miracle of laugher and the happy moments that come with it.
The miracle of pain and the tears that are always there to keep it company.
Dreams, the miracles that give us the key to the future,
And maybe the most important miracle of all true love the thing that gives us the hope to continue.
So let us attempt to focus our clouded eyes to see all the miracles that surround us.

Megan Clary, Grade 6
Boiling Springs Intermediate School, SC

Ruby Bridges

Ruby
Strong, outgoing, conqueror, historical
Daughter of Mrs. Bridges
Lover of freedom, forgiveness, and equality
Who feels hated by whites, scared of the mob, and happy to be in a good school
Who needs to have friends of all races, the same things as others, and love from others
Who gives a helping hand when in need, peace all around, and time to others
Who fears the mob, poison, and scary dreams
Who would like to have people like her, have her own rights, and set things right for all
Resident of New Orleans, Louisiana
Bridges

Elena Brunell, Grade 4
Hope Valley Elementary School, RI

Alligator Clip

My claw clip is an alligator waiting for its prey.
My hair is twisted, and the alligator's jaws are wide open.
As it bites down on my hair, I can feel the teeth scrape my scalp. Shivers run down my spine.
I know that when an alligator's jaws are shut, they will not open again, but I still cross my fingers hoping they will not open.
So now, I am ready to go hoping, praying, and crossing my fingers that the alligator will not lose its grip all day long.

Michaela Baker, Grade 6
CrossRoads Middle School, SC

Touchdown

I stood there waiting on the crowded field just hoping for someone to get open. No one seemed to be paying attention to the fact that I had a pig skin football in my hand getting ready to slip and fall to the ground, shattering my little league dreams. Then I saw standing on the fresh green grass was Jeffery the shortest of all, on our big football team, and he was open. I passed to him. It seemed to take forever for the ball to stop soaring through the bright blue sky. It finally reached him and he caught it and started running. I watched in awe as no one on the other team could catch him. He jumped for the touchdown. Yaaaah, I screamed as he softly landed in a patch of grass inside the touchdown zone. I then knew that we had the season in the bag.

Devin Thorpe, Grade 5
Queen's Grant Community School, NC

These Are My Skates

These are my skates.
My skates are white.
Look at the blade shine.
Make sure your skate is always tight.

These are my skates.
It's hard to skate the first time
But with practice, practice, practice
I get it right and feel really fine.

These are my skates.
Look how many tricks they do.
See how I spin and jump,
When I go fast it feels like I flew.

Anna Lulis, Grade 5
C Hunter Ritchie Elementary School, VA

Dress Appropriately

Summer, summer is hot
No longer cold,
so don't wear snow boots,
and don't put on lazy school shirt child.
So be a good person
and dress appropriately for the weather girls.

Jalin Parker, Grade 5
Cooper Elementary School, VA

My Teddy Bears

My teddy bears are very sweet.
Sometimes they come with treats.
Some come with a beautiful sound.
It's very comfortable to lie on their feet.
My small one was in the lost and found.
I think that some of them weigh a pound.
My teddy bears are very sweet.

Cinamyn Seward, Grade 4
Bensley Elementary School, VA

Lime Green

Lime green is cheerful and excited
She's my best friend
Lime green is a St. Patrick's Day clover
Lime green helps me when I'm down
She's my fat, silly cat
She's a smarty
Lime green is a new spring leaf drifting through the air
Lime green is my minty snack in the afternoon
Lime green is slimy spinach
She's the grass the dogs run in at the park
Her best friend is lemon yellow
Lime green is the seasons blooming
She is never jealous
Lime green is never mean
Lime green is me

Whitney Brown, Grade 4
Youngsville Elementary School, NC

Life

I am living so are you
Now spread the joy to others too
Because a couple more are coming soon
But now you know what to do.

Let's live long and forever
In a candy made shelter
With licorice for the roof
All I care is that I am with you.

Wade Hall, Grade 4
Courthouse Road Elementary School, VA

Through the Woods and Under a Flower

Through the woods and under a flower you may find a fairy,
Don't get frightened, don't be afraid,
For each of them aren't quite scary.
Some you can find nestled under a leaf,
But don't go looking,
Because you might hurt one and feel immense grief.
While we sleep they dance in the night,
Do not be judgmental,
Many of them dance all right.
Each of them are vivid and bright,
Under flower petals waiting for excitement,
If you ever find one you won't believe your sight!
People who don't believe shame on them,
Because many fairies deceive.

Lauren Garafano, Grade 6
St Rocco School, RI

The Leaves Are Falling Down

The leaves are falling down,
The leaves are falling down.
Red, yellow, orange, and brown.
The leaves are falling down.

I like when the leaves are falling down.
I am able to play with them when they are on the ground.
I can still jump in them.
The leaves are falling down.

Hayla Simpson, Grade 5
Cooper Elementary School, VA

Epitaph How I Died

Dakota Webster
1998-2009
What happened to me was not good at all
At the game not ashamed 'til the call
There I saw
It was a ball
There it thumped me right in the head
Here I lie down in the bed

Dakota Webster, Grade 5
North Windy Ridge School, NC

Spring

Fragrant smells all around,
Nature making all kinds of sounds.

Children laughing happy as can be,
Spring is a sight I love to see.
Marissa Wharton, Grade 5
St John Neumann Academy, VA

My Cat

Of course I have a cat,
And she tears up my hat.
But when I give her a call,
She comes running down the hall.
So when she purrs
I pet her fur.
And after that's all done
I hug her like she's my sis
And give her a kiss.
Christina Henry, Grade 4
Grace Miller Elementary School, VA

The Tree of Life

Out of all the trees in a cluster
One stands alone…
It's emerald leaves dancing
In the warm summer breezes
Its roots, the color of copper
Deep in the damp chestnut earth
The bark is like sand paper
To the touch of my fingers
The thick branches look up to the sky
Electric blue and blotches of milky white
Hang in the air
It stands firm through powerful gales
And striking lightning
When we are huddled in our home
When the blaring ginger sun comes out
From behind its wall of dark ash
The tree's once moss green leaves
Will darken and crumple
This tree will never die…
This tree will never die…
My tree will never die
Camden Myles, Grade 5
Rye Elementary School, NH

Llamas

Llamas
Fluffy, furry
Eating, sleeping, spitting
Very smart and intelligent
Clothing
Henry Elich, Grade 5
Blacksburg New School, VA

White

White is the color of the clouds.
White is the color of the snow.
White is the color of paper.
White is the color of the clean water.
White is the color of planes.
White is the color of our flag.
White is the color of our whiteboard.
White is the color of our trailers.
Dalton Leccia, Grade 4
Waller Mill Fine Arts Magnet School, VA

My Creek

Always in my woods,
Nice creek to wash my tears down.
Always there for me.
Sarah Gruhn, Grade 4
Trinity Christian School, VA

Dog

Chasing his tail,
not a care in the world.
chewing on it till it's soggy
and lays there, limp

Hiding under the bed,
with his tail sticking out
You can't see me he thinks
so we play around
Trying to find him
calling his name
Until he runs out and
kisses us.

Watching TV
on the couch.
Until he reaches out his paw
and changes the channel
As I scold him
he pushes it off the couch.

Chases his tail,
Not a care in the world.
Abby Holdeman, Grade 6
Chapin Middle School, SC

Winter

W hite snow
I s engulfing
N eighbors houses
T rails are made
E veryone is
R eally happy to get out!!
Taylor Blake, Grade 6
E Taylor Hatton School, VT

My Kitten Won't Stop Eating

My kitten wouldn't stop eating
She ate all night and all day
She ate apples, blueberries, strawberries
And yummy chocolate sundaes

My kitten never eats 9 Lives
She never even cared,
Only possession she counted on
Was her mouse named Bear

She waited for me to come home
And growled at my knees,
I can tell from her eyes she said,
I ate dad's car keys

I knew I was in trouble
My kitten was a big mess,
As I went up to my room I screamed,
"Lily you ate my treasure chest!"

I'll never forget that day
When Lily tried to eat her nose,
Then one minute later…
BOOM! She explodes!
Ashlin Parnell, Grade 6
CrossRoads Middle School, SC

Man on the Moon

High in the sky
Farther than the eye can see
Doing what they think is right
They're aiming for victory
Craters beyond the farthest star
As light as a feather
Beyond what you think is Mars
Having Armstrong as your brother
Is not quite the same as having
Amelia Earhart as your mother
A lot of things may happen
That you did not intend
But think of life this way
You aim for every turn and bend.
Olivia DuCharme, Grade 5
Wakefield Forest Elementary School, VA

Pancakes

Soft and yummy
In my tummy
Make me more!
Maple syrup with
A side of French toast
This is what I like the most!
Victoria Scorpio, Grade 5
St Mary School, RI

Colors

I do not have much to say,
But this is how I feel in my own little way.

Some days I am in trouble
And I feel like a big blue bubble.

Other days are happy
And I feel like pink Laffy Taffy.

Other days are funny
And I feel like a white bunny.

Sometimes when I am mad
I feel like a brown paper bag.

On days that are mean
I feel like a pen that writes in green.

This is how I feel on different days
All in my own little way.

Grant Campbell, Grade 5
Clover Hill Elementary School, VA

Ice Cream

Ice cream is soft just like a cloud.
When I see ice cream it means more to me than,
A frozen dairy treat in a cone.
Luscious is a word I would use,
But savory is better to describe the ice cream.
Many things you can do with ice cream,
Make a delectable smoothie with a tiny cherry,
Sprinkles, and an umbrella on top.
Put some in your mouth and, feel a cold chill
On your teeth while eating the frozen dairy treat.
What an appetizing dessert on a hot-hot summer day.
Tasty ice cream is good.

Adebodunrin Keku, Grade 4
St Thomas More Catholic School, NC

Old Piercing Eyes

As I walked outside,
I could feel the piercing eyes
Of the old abandoned house across the street.
Sitting in school,
I imagined the eyes
That were so mysterious to meet.
At the end of last period,
I sprang out of my seat,
And sprinted out of class with a cry.
When I finally reached my haven,
I reluctantly looked over,
At the old, piercing eyes.

Charlie Lawrimore, Grade 6
CrossRoads Middle School, SC

Craig Park

My dad, sister, and me
went to Craig Park exploring you see.
We heard birds singing like a beautiful choir.
We watched them fly higher and higher.

The flowers were blooming
and their fragrance was in the air.
They smelled so wonderful,
I did not have a care.
We played in the park
and climbed hills.
Going to the park is a great thrill!

Paiten Rivers, Grade 4
Edwards Elementary School, SC

Terrible News

I haven't seen you in several days
I'm tired of hearing about it every day
Some people don't believe in our cause
But they've never felt such a loss

Ever since you died in the war
I keep thinking about you more and more
You served our country, you served it well
You made many sacrifices and now, no one else can tell
Wherever you are, I know you would want me to know
You'll always watch over me, even though you had to go

I keep thinking that it was a dream
That you will come back to me
But I guess that's not how it was supposed to be
I want to see your beautiful angel's wings
Flying through the heavenly stream

I got one more word to say
I will care about you every single day

Karima Muhammad, Grade 5
Manchester Elementary School, NC

Basketball

Basketball's my favorite sport
All around played on a court
Light gleams from the gym
Gee I hope we win.

Basketball's my favorite sport
All around from port to port
As we walk to the court
It's just like the Olympic sport.

The ball is tipped over to me
When we score we're filled with glee.
Two minute left in the game
When we win we feel the fame.

Jared Flamm, Grade 5
Courthouse Road Elementary School, VA

Teddy

My hamster's name was Teddy
We stayed up late to watch Freddy
She would roll down the hall
In her big yellow ball
When I would call,
She stood up tall
When I gave her a treat
She looked so sweet
She passed away
I still cry to this day

Samantha Zincone, Grade 6
St Rocco School, RI

What the Wild Used to Be

Buffalos you used to see
Running wild, running free

Cougar cubs used to play
Tumble over rocks all day

The bald eagles used to soar
You hardly see a bear anymore

Wild horses used to run wild
Each prancing like a child

Now you can really see
What the wild used to be

Jessica Prince, Grade 5
Queen's Grant Community School, NC

Slow

Slower than the slowest slug,
Slower than a tortoise walks,
Slower than a snail slimes,
Slower than an anchor moves,
Slower than a penguin walks,
Slower than an ant climbs Mt. Everest,
Slower than the slowest slug,
Slower than an empty shell,
Slower than a dirty grub,
Slower than a worm eats dirt,
That's how slow my sister showers!

Spencer Seward, Grade 4
St Christopher's School, VA

School

I do not understand rules.
I do not understand teachers.
I do not understand work.
I do not understand school.
I do understand recess!

Robbi Qualls, Grade 5
Blaney Elementary School, SC

Animals

A lways talented
N ice to people
I n different habitats
M any different species
A re smart
L et people watch them
S ome are protected

Matthew Marquis, Grade 5
Good Shepherd Catholic School, RI

My Meme

Stubborn and bright
Even if she was wrong, she was right.
You did what she said
Or you better watch out.
She was the best
She was sincere.
Time's the shortest
With people who are dear.

Ashley LeBlanc, Grade 6
Northwood School, NH

Growing

Happy
Joy, excited, thrilled, gay
I was so happy I screamed hurray.
Strong
Muscular, bold, tough, buff
In the mirror I looked so tough.

Colin McGinty, Grade 5
Olde Providence Elementary School, NC

Hunting Dogs

Hunting dogs, hunting dogs
What do you see?
Whatever it is,
Will you show me?

Through the eyes of a wolf
Your fangs sharp as a dart
I know what you'd do
You'll fight to the last part

Deep in the tranquil forest
Finally, there's something you hear
Run quickly, attack quickly
Take down the King Deer

Crouching in the tall grass
I call to where you roam
As you trot to my side
It's time to go home.

Sofia Landry, Grade 6
Northwood School, NH

Martin Luther King

Martin Luther King
Led blacks
Through civil rights
To victory for African Americans
And to stop segregation
Once and for all.

Skylar Salem, Grade 6
Forestbrook Middle School, SC

Patches and S'mores

Patches and S'mores
Pitter patter goes their feet
Begging all day on their feet
When night comes they go to sleep

Pitter patter goes their feet
Crawling through their log
When night comes they go to sleep
They love getting spoiled all day long

Crawling through their log
Getting loved all day long
They love being spoiled all day long
Nibbling on salt and minerals

Getting loved all day long
Begging all day on their feet
Loving like the sisters they are
Patches and S'mores

Sara Crain, Grade 4
Riverside Elementary School, VA

Is It Love

He said he "loves" me but is it so
He said he'd "kiss" me but can he show
He broke my heart
But won't admit it
Because I ended it first
But no matter what he finds a way
To leave me broken hearted
Every day
I really loved him
I truly did
But he hurt me way back when
I still loved him even then
He hurt me in many ways
But none worse than
What I'm about to say
He hurt my heart
He hurt my soul
I'm nothing without him
Let it be told

Skylar Ondrick, Grade 6
Monelison Middle School, VA

Where I'm From

I'm from Orangeburg
Home of Edisto Gardens
Roses are red, violets are blue
I'm from Orangeburg,
How about you?
At Edisto Gardens
The flowers are yellow,
Pink, purple, gold, and red
So many flower beds
All beautifully spread

The grass is green on each side
The water is cold, dark and without a tide
In December the Christmas lights are merry and bright
Reindeer, frogs, ducks, and Santa Claus lights
Oh, what a marvelous sight!

We sang songs to wonderful people
We hold dear
At Christmas, just once a year
At our home, we thank God when we pray
For everyone on Christmas Day

That is where I'm from

Zachary Sampson, Grade 4
Whittaker Elementary School, SC

So What Do You Think About Black?

So what do you think about black?
Black is my talent to talk about
Black is the meanness, in rumors you hear
Black is danger
Scary enough, for superman to fear
Black is a giant, an evil one
Wearing a tuxedo, at a night prom
Penguins are black as well as a sharpie marker
Black is a crow, soaring through the sky.
Or the top hat on Frosty, saying "hi, hi, hi"
Black is the mask on a raccoon or ashes too
Goth people wear black, their clothes and makeup
They don't wear pink, that's not black
Black is the color of most pens' ink
Black makes me angry, black makes me mad
Black is the color of a trash bag
There are more black things than just crayons
You don't believe me? Ask anyone!

Kailyn Burke, Grade 4
Atkinson Academy Elementary School, NH

Kids

K ids are beautiful.
I nside.
D on't you think that their
S ouls speak for everyone and everything?

Savannah Talley, Grade 6
Forestbrook Middle School, SC

Big Ideas

If I ruled the world
There would be no war.
There would be houses for the homeless.
The world would be at peace.
The zoos would let animals walk free.
Everyone could fly!
And dogs would rule the White House!

Eva Kamman, Grade 4
Vergennes Union Elementary School, VT

Is It True

Is it true,
That Hurricane Katrina really blew through?
Is it true,
That there are homeless people wanting to be like you?
Is it true,
That soldiers in Iraq don't even get a thank you?
Just think about that,
Because they are all facts.

Justin Cain, Grade 5
Queen's Grant Community School, NC

Colors

Red is the rusty old bicycle.
Blue is the new tricycle.

Yellow sun shines on the grass and makes it glimmer.
White light shines on the water and makes it shimmer.

Green pops out at you.
Gray is the color of my tennis shoe.

Rachel Scardina, Grade 5
C Hunter Ritchie Elementary School, VA

Color Days

Some days are orange some days are white
Those days I feel like a nice cool Sprite

Some days are bright sunny yellow
Those days I feel very mellow

Electric lime green is the best day
Those days I feel like shouting hooray

Other days are café brown
Which makes me feel like a cranky mad clown.

Some days are midnight blue
Those days make me feel like a cow's low moo!

And that is my many color days
In my many color ways!!

Alice Brooks, Grade 5
Clover Hill Elementary School, VA

The Phantom

The phantom is in my house.
I know he is there
but no one can see him but me.
He sits in the large blue chair in my room.
He is a friend not a scary phantom
he does not hurt me.
He protects me.
He loves me
He is there for me.
He lurks around my house at night
not hurting a fly.
He just walks right by.
He has a pet a cat, a black cat.
You cannot see him either.
When you see him
he just stares at you with his big yellow eyes.
The phantom is still in my house.
He never hurts me.
He is the best.

Davis Lupold, Grade 5
St Christopher's School, VA

Character

Character grows from a little seed,
Helping you do many good deeds.
You can say nice words or help a pal —
Having good character, you will never fail.
Kindness, responsibility, and respect are number 1 at Riverview
They are important to me and you.
Mrs. Croyle, Mrs. Clark, and Mr. S. say,
"Don't do what's easy, do what's right every day!"

Vincent Mallardi, Grade 4
Riverview Elementary School, VA

Snow Dog

One cold snowy day in late February,
Something happened that was a bit scary.

Our dog got off his leash as quick as a flash,
When he realized he'd done it, he made a mad dash.

Just when I thought he was gone,
He ran right back to our snowy lawn.

When I saw him running home, I thought, "He's safe now,"
His black and white spots made me think of a cow.

My sis' saw what happened as he came to the house,
And to this day when I walk him, she's as scared as a mouse.

So, if you want to freak your sister out,
Just have your dog run away from your house.

Julia Guyer, Grade 5
Trinity Christian School, VA

A Best Friend to Me

I will never forget you
sunny, rainy, overcast too
your laugh, your smile, and your cry.
Now don't forget me
forgive me,
help me,
thanks
for being my friend.
In the dark you looked for me,
in the sun you didn't leave me.
Thanks again for being my friend.

Lauren Hickman, Grade 5
Rosemont Forest Elementary School, VA

Red

Red is the taste of a cherry
Red is a strawberry
Red looks like a firework booming in the fresh air
Red moves very fast in the air
Red speaks out like pride
Red is the color of anything
Red is a mighty lion
Red rides like a mad bull
Red runs in your body
Red is the color of the flag
Red is the color of Valentines

Justin Snow, Grade 4
Tabernacle Elementary School, NC

Laughter

Laughter is yellow like when you are in
a big, yellow school bus driving to school and
also like a yellow apple that when you take
your first bite you laugh because you
forgot you were allergic. It comes out
of my mouth and in to someone else's. It
reminds me of when little kids are
playing on the playground. It makes
me feel happy when I run down the
field playing soccer. It makes me want
to be a kid forever and ever.

Samantha Vest, Grade 6
Eagle's Nest Christian School, DE

The Sun

The sun that shines in my brunette hair
That makes my barrette sparkle everywhere
The sun that warms me in the cold
When the weather is icy and bold

The sun that warms me on the street
That makes my hair frizzy from all the heat
The sun that calms me when I'm mad
After the horrid day I know I have had

Sierra Pelino, Grade 6
Mater Christi School, VT

Seasons

I love the sea
It is like a sparkling pool of crystals
Dancing with the stars
In the whistling breeze.
And the sky is a deep pool of blue
Outdoing the stars in glee.
The clouds are like soft pillows
Floating above the grass
That is Earth's surface.
The trees are dancing in the breeze
With happiness and joy forever.
The breeze is like a bull
Knocking me off my feet.
The dirt is a big pool of chocolate
Where the insects live.
Summer is like a fresh new life.
Fall is a change of leaves
Starting a new tree.
Whether it's winter, autumn or summer
It's like a new start for you
So cherish it forever.

Tyrone J. McConnaughey, Grade 5
East Mooresville Intermediate School, NC

Flight

A large jumbo jet roars as it —
Takes off down the runway —
All four jets turn on and launch the plane —
Up-up and away —
All the passengers marvel at the phenomenon.
A little bird takes off for the first time
and is so happy —
People ignore it.

Alexander Davis, Grade 4
St Christopher's School, VA

School

School is a long journey.
There are some ups and downs,
you don't always know what is around the next bend.

School is a temporary job.
You have to wake up every day of the week
and go there to do work that may be fun or boring.

School is a book.
You cannot judge it
and its people by what they say.

School is a second home.
You have a second family
who cares for you and about you.

Andrew Stant, Grade 5
Holy Cross Elementary School, DE

Green

Green looks like my car that shines in the sun.
Green sounds like leaves rustling in the trees.
Green smells like fresh plants after a rainstorm.
Green tastes like a crunchy salad that my mom makes.
Green feels like soft grass growing in the field.

Connor Driscall, Grade 5
Holy Cross Elementary School, DE

My Dog Buddy

Every day I go out and feed and water my dog.
Every day I go out and play with my dog.
Yes, I do!
Yes, I do!
I hear his bark every night,
Woof, woof, woof!
Yes, I do!
Yes, I do!
My dog Buddy,
I love him.

Ethan James Pecoraro, Grade 4
Cool Spring Elementary School, NC

Dog

As she sits and watches with her long black hair.
She sits and grins with that evil little stare.

Soft as a feather and nice to all.
When you trip she will help you from your fall.

When the mail comes she gets it with her teeth.
When she's wet she shakes down to her feet.

Bobbie Albright, Grade 6
Fairforest Middle School, SC

Life

Life is a highway.
You can travel far and near
From New York City to San Francisco Bay
Cross the continent in just one day.
There are two roads to take:
The one you want
Or the one you make.
The one you chose could be your fate.
Look to the left,
Look to the right;
Make your decision.
Make sure it's right!

Mia Jasmine Jordan, Grade 6
CrossRoads Middle School, SC

Summer

Summer is awesome.
Going to the beach and play.
Fun every single day!

Jack Larson, Grade 5
C Hunter Ritchie Elementary School, VA

Snow

Snow
Cold, wet
Leaks in hands
I need my gloves
Ice

Esther LeVine, Grade 4
Trinity Christian School, VA

Skiing

Swerving
through oncoming trees,

Going
off jumps,

Shifting
back and forth like a pinball,

Screaming
as I helplessly tumble,

Speeding
past other skiers like I'm dodging traffic,

Skidding
across the base of the mountain,

Racing
my brothers over bumps and ridges,

Rag dolling
down a steep hill uncontrollably.

Ryan Rose, Grade 5
Daniel J Bakie School, NH

Flags

Flags are raised so very high
It seems like they can touch the sky
They wave and dance to the wind
And to the flagpole they are pinned.

Ryan Kampfmueller, Grade 5
Clover Hill Elementary School, VA

Dance

Sunsets go down after sunrises,
Dance as much as we can,
And we share our happiness,
So let's dance to our music —
The song of birds,
Dance away,
Nature is the dance floor.
I am the flower,
Dancing in the wind.
Let's dance.

Megan Newbern, Grade 5
Central Elementary School, NC

Spots!

Spots can be anywhere — you name it!
They could be on your body or on an animal,
Like a cheetah or a Dalmatian dog.
They can even be on your clothes,
Stains — oh gross!
The worst kinds of spots are chicken pox,
Ouch, they really hurt and itch!
There are sun spots and spots in the universe that are strange and mysterious.
Some spots make you feel sad and ill,
They can tell you that you better stay away — danger — like poisonous fish.
My favorite spots are polka-dots.
They are very colorful and pretty.
Everybody pays attention to spots.

Hannah Belawske, Grade 4
Chesterfield School, NH

Isy, My Puppy

The first time I hold my Chihuahua,
holding her in my arms until she gently falls asleep,
looking into her small, beautiful eyes, I smile.
She falls asleep on my lap, like a baby with its mom.
When she wakes, she laps up some water, then falls asleep again.
As I am holding her, I myself fall asleep.
She awakes me in the night sweetly licking my face.
As if all worries in the world have gone, I laugh.
I laugh until the first sign of light peeks over the horizon.
I realize that we have bonded and love each other.
As we sit in the dark I think of all the new doors that have opened,
Yet none have closed…life is good with my Chihuahua, Isy.

Corey Shaver, Grade 6
Chapin Middle School, SC

The Tooth and the Bud

I am a tooth.	I am a taste bud.
We're part of the mouth.	We're part of the mouth.
I chew.	
	I lick.
Together we taste.	Together we taste.
	My taste.
My roots.	
Together we function.	Together we function.
When I get pulled	
the human howls.	
	When I get bit
	the human cries.
I get brushed.	
	I get rinsed.
We unite again clean.	We unite again clean.
Crackers, apples, and carrots.	
	Yogurt, apple sauce, and salsa.
Together we eat,	Together we eat,
and together we are,	
	the mouth.

Benjamin Burnette, Grade 5
North Windy Ridge School, NC

Christmas Time

Colorful packages under the glowing tree
Speeding down the snow-covered hill on a sled
The sound of jingling sleigh bells
The smell of sweet gingerbread baking
"Is that Santa?"
Yummy red and green sprinkled sugar cookies
Festive woolen stockings hanging in the firelight
Hoping for lots of presents.

Nicholas Edwards, Grade 4
Hope Valley Elementary School, RI

A Little About Me

I want to tell you something just a little about me.
I'm filled with a bit of happiness and a bit of glee.

It's kind of complicated when I'm in school.
And when we get to math I start to drool.

When I get home I jump so happily.
And when I hug my mom it's like she's always with me.

It's always nice to tell someone about your life.
It's a good way to express yourself.
It's easy as cutting with a knife.

Deja Jones, Grade 5
Riverview Elementary School, VA

Papa

Papa's hands are like a wrinkly, veined, soft, autumn leaf.
Papa's hair is like an alabaster, puffy, white cloud.
Papa's face is like an American Indian's.
Papa's voice is like a gentle, kind shepherd.
Papa's smile is like a warm hug.

Katelyn Jensen, Grade 5
Lighthouse Christian School, DE

Barbie in Graceland

Goin' to Graceland for Elvis today
Though many other Barbie dolls I meet
I'm a die-hard fan, to Elvis I stay
He is my idol, that no one can beat

Oh! How many trunks will I have to pack
I'll have purses, shoes, and cute outfits too
There must be enough until I come back
Whatever am I now going to do?

My striking blonde hair blowing in the breeze
All the hair products I must bring with us
I must bring a sweater so I won't freeze
How will they bring all my stuff on this bus?

I cannot wait to see Elvis' home
Where did I put that stupid old hair comb?

Olivia Antonakos, Grade 6
Beck Academy, SC

Secret Places

Passing by the beautiful wedding chapel,
under the colorful, autumn trees.
The sun is creeping through the crack in the falling leaves.
Listen to the birds chirping
the cool breeze on my face
splashing water in the distance
All on a warm, fall afternoon
Relaxing
Relaxing
Relaxing

When was this amazing place discovered?
Let's keep it a s
        e
          c
        r
         e
          t.

Casey Langmaid, Grade 4
Maple Wood Elementary School, NH

I Am

I am the sun! I'm bright
I am a four leaf clover, I am full of luck
I am a snake, I can slither through problems
I am a horse, I am free
I am a bee, I am always busy
I am a rabbit, I eat lots of carrots

I am a cheetah, I am fast
I am a koala, I am wise

Gloria Almanza, Grade 5
Four Oaks Elementary School, NC

His First Winter

As winter is found.
He sees a white ground.
What is this he sees?
Is it some type of disease?
He steps outside he slips, he falls!
He sees a white ball.
It is soft and cold.
The size of a toad.
He rolls it.
He throws it.
He hits a tree.
Maybe he should let it be.
But wait it is fun.
And dinner is not done.
So maybe he'll stay longer.
So he can wonder.
His first winter.

Samaria Moss, Grade 5
Courthouse Road Elementary School, VA

Life/Dead
life
live, long
running, crying, smiling
happy, nice, sad, mean
shouting, screaming, worrying
gone away
dead
Taylor Tretick, Grade 6
Floyd T Binns Middle School, VA

I Am
I am a book without words,
I am a spark of shining light.

I am a melody in a song,
I am a title of a play.

I am a bird with no wings
I am a singer who can't sing.

I am a boat without a sail,
I am a bright blue pail.

I am me, that's who I am
An eleven year old girl.

I am myself ready for the world.
I am, I am, I am
Azjah Clark, Grade 5
Woodlawn Elementary School, VA

The Flute
Under the light,
It glistens, sparkles
So lovely, petite
I walk over, fascinated
The instrument sits there
So many shiny keys
I touch it; cold, smooth
I pick it up, somewhat light
I lightly blow
A sweet, beautiful sound rushes out,
Harmonic.
I move my fingers swiftly from key to key
As if I was typing,
A song begins,
Ends.
I look up
I put down the instrument
I smile
I just played
The flute.
Elizabeth Maguire, Grade 6
Main Street Middle School, VT

Teacher
Clashing, ripping, and screeching,
As the victim is torn.
Paper bleeding,
With bloody red gore.
The hawk is disappointed,
Because it's not what it expects.
Its prey is a failure,
Another F.
David Szalai, Grade 6
CrossRoads Middle School, SC

God Bless America!
Red and white
bright stars of gold,
this great wavy flag
never gets too old!

With millions of people
and more every day,
what's the total?
It's hard to say.

Republican, democrat,
No one knows for sure
what to do or say
or which is the right door.

Fifty states.
Many towns.
One country.
Zero frowns.

Many people
want to live in this place
and want to join
the American race!
Erin Murray, Grade 6
Forestbrook Middle School, SC

Starry Skies
Sensitive travelers are
Resting sleepily
Never knowing
What's on
The 'morrow.

Staying comforted by
Young souls.
Thoughts flying to
The heavens
Spirits soaring to
Far off lands.
Mason Cashman, Grade 4
Maple Wood Elementary School, NH

DC Shoes
DC shoes are the best
they beat all the rest
They come in white,
red and black as night.
You can buy them at Wal-Marts
not at Advanced Auto Parts.
DC shoes are the best
they beat all the rest.
Gunner Tootle, Grade 5
Queens Creek Elementary School, NC

My Cat Atticus
I have a cat named Atticus
We love him and he loves us
He's black and white and quite fat
I wouldn't want any other cat!
He loves to sleep and play with mice
When he is in the barn, it can be nice
He is my best friend
And he will be 'til the end.
Scott Simpson, Grade 5
Mary Walter Elementary School, VA

Trust
Trust is super glue.
Once you apply it,
it's hard to break the bond.

Trust is a boomerang.
Once it comes back after you throw it,
it's hard to catch.

Trust is a piece of rope.
If you pull it too hard,
it untwines.

Trust is a penny.
If you leave it out to sit,
it rusts away.
Nicholas Reyes, Grade 5
Holy Cross Elementary School, DE

If I Was…
If I was a crack in the sidewalk
I would be the Grand Canyon
If I was a blade of grass
I would be a gigantic redwood tree
If I was a small stream
I would be Niagara Falls
If I was a small pebble
I would be a mighty boulder
But I'm me…
Max Dodge, Grade 5
St Christopher's School, VA

October

October is dark orange
Just like the leaves falling to the ground
It feels like spiders crawling down my back
It sounds like leaves crunching beneath my feet
It smells like sweet pumpkin pie
October tastes like a tasty bag of Halloween candy
October is a delicious, scary month.

Dusty Uhrig, Grade 5
Vienna Elementary School, NC

Search

Art is fun.
Art is creative.
You use your imagination for art.
Most of all, you need to picture it in your head.

Keziah Lebron, Grade 4
Homeschool Plus, VA

Trees

Swaying back and forth in the breeze
In the summer you are green
In the autumn you are yellow, brown
Orange, and red

In the winter you are bare
Waiting for your hair, the leaves.
You're like an apartment in the city
You stand tall and high and a
Home to everybody

You're everywhere we can see
In the park and some cities
You're the colorful plant we call
Trees, oh trees

Audriauna Bryant, Grade 5
Manchester Elementary/Middle School, VT

My Dad Is My Hero

My dad is my hero.
His job is touch and go.
I miss him saying he loves me.
He wants to set the Iraqis free.

I love my dad, he's the best!
I'm glad he's home, he needs the rest.
Although it's only for a short while,
the memories we share will always make me smile.

My dad is my hero and my friend.
Iraq, he wants to mend.
My pride will always attend
because our country he will defend.

Savanna Lachica, Grade 6
Camperdown Academy, SC

Brandi

A twitching tail,
A wet sloppy kiss
All features of Brandi; that's who she is.
She makes me so happy all the time
I'm ever-so-grateful she is all mine.
Her wet nose sniffing my ear
Sends a chill up my spine
But I couldn't be happier when I'm with her.
She makes my heart sing
Unaware though she is.
My little puppy,
Now a big girl who I love so.
'Til the end of time, she is mine.
There could never be another
Brandi
Who makes me ever-so-happy
Takes a nap beside me
And fulfills my dreams
of a companion just like her
"My Brandi"

Tiana D'Acchioli, Grade 6
St Rocco School, RI

Where I'm From

I'm from a place
Where I love to go
A place that is peaceful
And the noise is low
I have a loving family, I love them so much
We get together to have lunch
We like to go to different places
Where it is a lot of spaces
We like to sing, "Take a bow"
No one don't ever frown
We eat foods like seafood, Chinese and Japanese
We eat so much; it makes you want to sneeze
At times it starts thundering and lightning
It can be very frightening
But Grandma makes it all better
I like to write her letters
I am from a family
That is made of gold
A family that you want to hold
I am from a family of God
That is where I am from

DaShawn Dukes, Grade 4
Whittaker Elementary School, SC

Love

L ove is life.
O h, love is great.
V ibrating hearts put together
   equals love.
E xtreme is love.

Lloyd Hightower, Grade 5
C Hunter Ritchie Elementary School, VA

Ode to the Wii

As the school day ends, I rush home to play the Wii.
But first, my parents make me do my homework.
Faster than a speeding bullet, my math is done.
Quivering with excitement, I move quick as lightning
Up the stairs to the game room.
I stop breathlessly as I stare at the gaming system
that makes this country great.
I reach slowly for the power button, cherishing the moment.
As the Wii is loading, I eagerly consider the countless games with which I will honor it today.
My choice made, I gather the controllers and begin my play.
Hit the road, Evil!
Here comes Lego Batman (with Robin) to save the day.
As my palms grow sweaty battling the villains,
I drop the Wii remote. Oh, No!
Luckily, the wrist strap prevents a disaster.
I quickly grab the remote and resume the struggle between good and evil.
Exhilarated, I save Gotham City from falling to pieces.
Dinnertime comes and I sadly turn off the amazing Wii.
As I watch the screen go dark like a moonless night,
I hope that tomorrow will come soon.

Daniel Hudson, Grade 6
CrossRoads Middle School, SC

Decks and Wheels

Skateboarding O skateboarding I'll have fun with you.
I'll go to the skate shop and buy a deck 4 wheels 4 bearings and two trucks and griptape.
I'll go get my friends and I'll tell you what we'll do with our skate shoes on and our skate pants too and our skate shirts.
We'll go to the skate park and ride the half pipe and the quarter pipe too.
The grind rail I'll grind that too falling is okay. All kinds of tricks are okay. It's dark, it's time to go home!

Nicholas Adolfo Vasquez, Grade 4
Courthouse Road Elementary School, VA

Bailey's Life Lessons

I've learned that doing what you want isn't always a good choice.
I've learned that taking a bath with a cat won't get you clean at all.
I've learned never to kiss a baby squirrel when it's asleep.
I've learned that you should think before saying the first thing that pops into your head.
I've learned that when there is an opportunity open, you should ask your mom before saying yes.
I've learned that reading 2 books at a time makes my head spin around like a merry-go-round.
I've learned that a snake isn't a good pet unless you like being bitten all the time.
I've learned that playing football with rough, tough high-school boys is not a good idea.
I've learned that you should actually hang out with a friend longer than 2 days before you invite them over.
I've learned that you should know a person before you text them back.

Bailey Goodine, Grade 5
Northside Elementary School, SC

Lavender

Lavender looks like pale lilac flowers fluttering in the breeze.
Lavender sounds like the ticking of the clock announcing the new seconds, minutes and hours.
Lavender smells like the wafting fragrance of the potpourri nestled in a vase.
Lavender tastes like the chocolate goodness of a lavender wrapped Easter egg.
Lavender feels like my lavender colored silk Easter dress which I wear to church.

Brinley Knopf, Grade 5
Holy Cross Elementary School, DE

Colors

Orange is a basketball.
Yellow is a butterball.

Blue is the sky.
Green is Easter egg dye.

Red is blood on your hand.
Peach is sandbox sand.

Bryan Reinaldo, Grade 5
C Hunter Ritchie Elementary School, VA

Daddy

Why did you leave me?
I was thinking about how you used to
Call me your baby. Now I'm all sad
Thinking I did something bad.

But you made your decision of life.
Now mommy cannot be your wife.
Daddy you know what you did is not right
But now you are in the peaceful light.
I hope you still love me.

I wish you could reincarnated into a bee.
So that you could still watch me physically.
But I guess that is pretty silly of me.

Remember in the first grade
I would tell everyone about you ever day?
Saying my dad is a great guy.
But I don't know what I'm going to do.
I mean I didn't know much about you.
All I knew was what you look like
And that you bought me a little banana seat bike
When I was a little girl. But that didn't matter
Because you left the world in a whirl.

Anna Caldwell, Grade 6
Barre City Elementary/Middle School, VT

Beach

The beach is a mesmerizing place
crabs snipping at seaweed
sailboats hunting for sharks
in the gleaming sun along the shore
open space to look for shells
your dark shadow
no clouds to obstruct your view
thundering waves smacking against the shore
people laughing
seagulls popping out from behind boats
squawking people splashing in the water.
How can the beach differ on a snowy day?
Feels so relaxed
people excited, excited, excited.

Tanner Fortier, Grade 4
Maple Wood Elementary School, NH

A Sweet Dream

In my dreams,
I visit a place,
where there are tons of candy,
floating in space.

In my dreams,
there are beautiful flowers,
and always yummy chocolate rain showers.

I go there and forget all my troubles,
and while I'm there,
swim in an ocean of bubbles.

When I wake and see the morning light,
I hope I have the same dream tonight!

Julia Pezzullo, Grade 6
St Rocco School, RI

How I Wish

How I wish the world would just take a break
    from the fighting and the bickering
        like we all wish.

How I wish the sickly would be like the healthy
    and become better
        like we all wish.

How I wish the bad would be like the good
    and do good deeds instead of bad
        like we all wish.

How I wish, that my wish
    would come true.

Lizzy Kunz, Grade 6
Wyman Elementary School, RI

Unknown Beast

It lurks in darkness not to be seen,
It waits till dark to hunt for prey,
And if it is seen, it gets mean,
If it gets mean, you need to find the day,
Once day is found, it needs a key,
The key must be found for you to be free,
And when you find the key, all is reborn,
Everything happy as if once before,
Peace is made and hearts are open.
So if you see the beast beware,
Look only on the good side if it is there,
Make sure that nothing has gone wrong,
For this creature will find all along,
The key to "day" may be found,
In the deepest part of us all.

Devin Vallejo, Grade 5
Clover Hill Elementary School, VA

Sorry About Your Rat

I'm sorry about your rat,
When I went by in my car he went splat,
And then over came my cat,
There is no more splat of your rat.

Emily C. Brown, Grade 5
Rye Elementary School, NH

Which Fruit?

Oranges offer good protection,
Mangos taste the best.
Apples are most popular,
Don't know about the rest.
Us worms are very picky,
'bout where we want our home.
Maybe in a coconut,
Is where I want to roam.

Soledad Green, Grade 4
Trinity Christian School, VA

Book and Bacon

I had a good book,
But then it was took.

I also had bacon,
But it was not taken.

The cook made the book,
But then it was took.

The writer wrote bacon,
And then he was achin'.

David Nall, Grade 4
Trinity Christian School, VA

The Watcher

I am
the Watcher
I see your every move
from the shadows,
I know you.

I watch
as you
create the theme
Narcissus,
and fulfill it.

I am
you
I can fill your place
because you
exclude me,
so I content myself
with watching.

Camille Testa, Grade 6
Archer Elementary School, VA

Caroline Pearce

Caroline
Daring, hyper, crazy
Owner of a dog
Who loved Edward Cullen
Who hated annoying people, loved her friends, liked egg rolls
Who feared bridges, wasps, and running with scissors
Who passed fifth grade with a nice grade
Who wanted to meet Barney, have a real party in her tummy, and live at Target
Born on Earth
Pearce

Caroline Pearce, Grade 6
Floyd T Binns Middle School, VA

Bow Legged

Running at the speed of light, sprinting up the field,
Ponytail flying behind her, jersey stuck to her wet skin,
Her skinny, bow legged figure, glides through everyone like butter.

Looking to pass, she sees no one,
Trapped by defenders surrounding her,
Stabbing at the ball, trying to get it loose,
Determined to get the ball past the jumble of players,
Someone bumps her nose hard,
And she feels the rush of pain crawl up her nose,
Shaking it off, she quickly pulls a move,
Her skinny, bow legged figure glides through everyone like butter.

Now, it's between her and the goalie,
Taking one more touch, she plants the left foot and swings the right,
Whoosh!
As the ball hits the back of the net, the goalie hits the ground,
And her skinny, bow legged figure glides through the cheering crowd, like butter.

As she stands in her team huddle, she wipes the sweat off her nose with the jersey,
There is suddenly a bloodstain on the neckline of her shirt,
The color of a rose bush,
It soaks in.

Daisy Sullivan, Grade 6
Manchester Elementary/Middle School, VT

January

January is the beginning of the year
January is the smell of hot chocolate
January is when I see the fresh crystal snow on the ground
January is the sound of little chimes
January smiles because it is first
January is the time for winter
January is hot cocoa rushing down my throat like a river
January is the time to roast marshmallows
January is when you feel warm from coming inside from the snow
January feels peaceful
January is when you see crystal clear snow falling from the sky

Delaney Cox, Grade 4
Tabernacle Elementary School, NC

Elizabeth

E ven though we fight I love her a lot
L oving and caring without a thought
I s the greatest friend I could ask for
Z ainy and cool all at the same time
A lways show integrity when no one is watching
B oth helpful and thoughtful to everyone
E very day she makes me smile
T eamwork is something she always can do
H onest to me and everyone

Emma Zalecki, Grade 5
Queen's Grant Community School, NC

In a Different World

If you were ever to look
In even the smallest of books,
You'd find whole different worlds,
Full of all different things,
Like,
Lizards with sox,
Chickens with pox,
Fairies with berries,
And mooses with gooses,
Fish that can fly,
And monkeys with pies,
Tricksters and kicksters,
And candy men too,
Books, I like to read,
'Cause they bring places to you,
Oh how I love books,
I love them,
I do!

Aerin Gilday, Grade 4
Courthouse Road Elementary School, VA

Let Out Your Inner Self

You walk down the path
There is nothing but that
You look a little depressed, and so misunderstood
Just seem worried, and so curious
I start to wonder if you could
Believe in yourself
Know how to be alive
Don't be afraid, start to realize
You're not much different
You are bright
If you just take each step at a time
And go be kind
Don't act like someone else that isn't you
Someone will have something in common with you
Go be outgoing
But no need for a new trend
Just be yourself and people would be your friend

Jessica Martineau, Grade 6
Dr Edward Ricci School, RI

Bronzed

never knew you
dumped on the floor
like a pile of junk
a bowl that's painted
in citrus
two old dolls
of holidays vanished

never knew you
bronze luxury
pick you up
and stare
name date birth
shoes from your childhood

never knew you
those shoes are
memories
never lived

never knew you
grandpa but always
love you

Joanna Jorgensen, Grade 6
Manchester Elementary/Middle School, VT

A Dog

A dog is a friend
because it's always there for you.

A dog is trust
because you can tell it won't abandon you.

A dog is an ocean
because your friendship with it never ends.

A dog is a toy
because you can play with it.

Danny Minshall, Grade 5
Holy Cross Elementary School, DE

The Sun

Is the sun tired when it hangs low in the sky?
When it thunders does it hide away in fright?
When it rains or snows does it stay dry?
How does it like never sleeping at night?

Sammy Powers, Grade 5
Trinity Christian School, VA

Twilight

The book *Twilight* makes you excited,
When the vampire and human world collided,
One vampire's name is Rosalie Hale,
And all of the vampires are pale.

Rhi Banks, Grade 5
North Windy Ridge School, NC

Nature

The sun is falling behind the mountains
The moon is almost here
The wind whistles an odd tune
The crickets chirp at me
My dog sleeps at the end of my bed
The hamster runs his wheel
My parents tell me to go to sleep
I start to hear a rhythm
An unlikely sound at night
It was nature rocking me to sleep

Holley Stinnett, Grade 6
Monelison Middle School, VA

Cats vs Dogs

Cats just sit around all day
While dogs are up and love to play
Cats are so relaxed and sweet
While dogs just want to eat a treat
Cats will never swim with you
While dogs will always play with you
So now it's up to you to choose
If cats are the best or
if dogs are just so neat
    Cats vs Dogs
    Who will win?
I love dogs but that's just me.

Mary Allman, Grade 4
Angelus Academy, VA

Monkeys

What's a monkey? Is it cute?
Can you put this thing on mute?
Does it crawl? Does it fly?
Can it jump up and say hi?
Does it squeal? Does it scream?
Is it something in a dream?
Is it brown? Is it cool?
Yes! It's a monkey! Don't they rule?

Courtney Snyder, Grade 5
Clover Hill Elementary School, VA

Lightning

Lightning comes after thunder
Like the boom of an explosion
It answers the call of thunder
By striking into the ground
Far somewhere in the clouds
Somewhere in a dark place
An unknown call
Leaves without knowing
Without any existence
Except in people's heart

Kristen Jay, Grade 5
Blaney Elementary School, SC

Red

Red is a Ferrari
a pepperoni pizza
red is a feather from an arrow
a crackling fire
red is heat on a winter day
the anger in your face
red is the eye of the tiger
the fur on a fox blowing in the wind
red is a sunset in the summer
red leaves falling in autumn
the smell of a warm apple pie
red is a hot iron sword
a Valentine day heart
red is the nose of a clown
the sound of the red robin singing

Jack Ferrell, Grade 5
St Mary School, RI

I Am Fire

I am fire…
Burning up stuff
Blazing like a hot summer day
Flowing like blazing heat waves
Fiery like firewood
Flaming like flame throwers
Steaming like volcanic ash
Crackling like fire sparks
Warm and hot, lit up matches
I'm a little blazing fire in a lighter

Jason Nguyen, Grade 5
Wakefield Forest Elementary School, VA

Smelly Feet

If I take off my shoes
It's sure to clear a room
It'll be a lose-lose
'Cause you'll be in a tomb

If I take off my shoes
Your face will melt
I'll sit back and snooze
When your nose has a welt

If I take off my shoes
You'll run away
You'll try to sue
But I'll deny everything you say

So when I take off my sneakers
Be sure to know
The warning you've received
And away you will go.

Wyatt Kolb, Grade 5
Pocalla Springs Elementary School, SC

The Amazing Winter

The snow is deep.
Birds chirp in the distance.
Sweetness fills the air.
The freezing wind stings my face.

A log is covered with powdery snow.
A rabbit lives under the log.
Life can be so happy.
When you find such beauty.

Ethan Devlin, Grade 4
Bethlehem Elementary School, NH

Mrs. Beach

Mrs. Beach is kind and fun
Her hair is shaped like a bun
But more importantly than her hair
About the students she does care

Jonathan Joseph, Grade 5
St John Neumann Academy, VA

Dragonfly

The dragonfly,
Is the king of the sky.
You may want to back off,
Because for lunch he eats a moth.
If you cross his way,
Forever you will lay.
He will grab you as fast as light,
With all his arm's might.
He'll smash you,
He'll mash you.
Until you are dead,
Then his tummy will be fed.
Fear him!

Rebecca Prymak, Grade 5
Old Bridge Elementary School, VA

Pool

The pool has a lot of water,
And people like to bring their daughters.

The pool is so cool
But I have to go to school.

When it is so sunny,
I really want to waste that money.

I like to buy food,
Don't look at that mean dude.

There are a lot of boys,
I like to bring my toys.

Antonio Carvajal, Grade 5
Woodlawn Elementary School, VA

Where Am I?

Where is this place I stand?
It is different and unknown,
Who are the people around me?
I feel like I don't know them,
Everything has changed…
I am so confused.
What happened to the place I know and love?
It has disappeared.
It is gone with the wind.
Everything and everyone has changed.
Why?
Why do I feel so,
Alone?
I can't place exactly,
What,
Has changed…
But something has changed,
And it will,
Never,
Ever,
Be the same.

Molly Cathryn Holt, Grade 6
Main Street Middle School, VT

The Heart

Your heart is the control center of emotion.
The ace in the deck of life.
like the ace it cannot be beaten.
Most of the time it will cause pain.
But none of it is in vain.
It is impossible to hide it.
For your heart cannot be denied.
Emotion, like Armageddon is inevitable.

Afnan Ali, Grade 5
Old Bridge Elementary School, VA

My World

My world is a place I made.
My world is all about me.
My world is me, myself, and I.
My world is filled with happiness.
That's all it is day or night.
And boy, is it a beautiful sight.

Taylor Jordan, Grade 5
Courthouse Road Elementary School, VA

Allison

A llison is smart
L oves her family
L oathes spiders
I s always trying to help her mom and dad
S ings to her sisters…sometimes
O utstanding with little kids
N ow can cook pastries

Allison Rose Schwartz, Grade 5
Courthouse Road Elementary School, VA

Skateboarding

A wesome action **B** ack flip
C aveman, **D** arkside grind
E nd over, **F** ackie ollie
G rind, **H** eel flip
I 'm goofy footed, **J** ump
K ick flip, **L** ean left to turn
M anual, **N** ollie, **O** llie
P ogo, **Q** uick reactions
R ed rolling wheels
S ome skateboards have unique shapes
T ail grab, **U** sually hardcore skaters live in L.A.
V arial flip, **W** et Willy is a skateboard character
X games have skateboarding in it
Y oyo plant
Z Boys are a skateboard team.

Andrew Leal, Grade 6
Wakefield Forest Elementary School, VA

I Am Thankful for My Family

My family —
Bright, shining
Like the stars in the sky
From Dad's delicious cooking
To Mom's tasty meals
To how much they love me to how much they care.
How they hug me!
How they make me laugh!
One day we will drift apart,
But our love will always show us the way home.

Olivia M. Marcello, Grade 6
Wyman Elementary School, RI

Broken Glass

Astounding,
To see,
Broken glass.
The truth,
Is,
Inconceivable
Incogitable.

The broken glass,
You may set eyes on,
Was painted with life.
It is not truly broken glass.

Broken glass,
Is a faded soul,
That could have been salvaged,

That soul,
Was mine.

Maggie Oliver, Grade 6
Manchester Elementary/Middle School, VT

Just a Twig

A twig is just a plain ol' twig
In the average head
But it could hold a bird's nest
That may also be a baby bird's bed

It might be a sword
Trying to fend off a snake
Or maybe a common kitchen knife
Cutting a birthday cake

A twig could be a fife
Playing a popular tune
Possibly a safe hanging place
For a growing cocoon

It may be a still snake
Waiting for its lunch
Maybe a giant pencil
With which I wrote this written bunch
Robbie Freeman, Grade 5
Rye Elementary School, NH

Dolphin

Dolphin glides through the water,
As fast as a jet,
He dives through the water.
To the bottom of the ocean floor.
Then comes up for a breath of air.
His eyes staring at me.
Dolphin says
"As I jump into the water.
I do a dive, I crash through the water
To the bottom of the sea,
The water, it's so crystal clear."
Durk Steed, Grade 4
St Christopher's School, VA

Fish

Fish so beautiful
Shark so man-killing yet cool
Squids pointy sharp heads
Joseph Payne, Grade 5
North Windy Ridge School, NC

Months

June
Summer, fun
Playing, swimming, biking
Cookouts, beach, presents, icicles
Skating, sledding, caroling
Cold, windy
December
Kevin Coderre, Grade 5
St Helena Elementary School, SC

The Fish

The fish have stage fright
So they hide from all others
Behind all the plants
That act like the stage curtain
Hiding all who want to hide
Jack Jacobs, Grade 6
Wakefield Forest Elementary School, VA

Go to Sleep Dog

The dog is barking
He is too loud, I can't sleep
He needs to shut up
Joseph Newsome, Grade 5
Manchester Elementary School, NC

It's Time for Tea

Tea
Cupcakes
Small sandwiches
Pinky up
It's time for tea.
Megan Westmoreland, Grade 4
Grace Miller Elementary School, VA

I Am

I am air
Light and easy on my feet
I am fresh with new ideas
I have essential energy
I am never rushing
Always breathing and blowing
Dry but wet
Light though dark
The birds in me sing
Blowing with wind
I am
AIR!
Hannah Curran, Grade 5
Wakefield Forest Elementary School, VA

At the Park

On Monday I went to the park
I played on the swing until it got dark.

Then I went down the slide.
I built a sandcastle for Clyde.

We played a game of kickball.
I ran to the bases with my baby doll.

I enjoy going to the park.
I can run, jump and play until dark.
Diamond Duncan, Grade 4
St Helena Elementary School, SC

The Bridge

As you walk across the bridge
The old weathered bridge
You hear the clicks and clacks
Beneath your feet
Of the old weathered bridge

You hear the splashes of the stream
Hit the poles holding you up
As you walk across the bridge

You see the fish swim by
Leaping out of the water
And falling back in
With a splash

Soon the bridge will come down
But now
It lived the true test of time
It's been here for a lifetime
Just sitting.
Tyler Quattlebaum, Grade 6
Chapin Middle School, SC

Swinging

steadily
powerfully
happily
gleefully
frequently
swinging
because of the hot day
without care
under the tree
before dinner
without a parent
swinging
since she was bored
where they had built the swing
when they had free time
although the swing was old
because she liked the adrenaline
swinging
Kelsey Yeager, Grade 6
St Mary's School, SC

A Day in the Life of a Cat

Pad, tap, tap
I just woke up, from my nap.
Here I come, down your driveway,
your cat food is the best, eat it I may?
This is normal, a day like this for me,
no work at all, a great day you see?
Carol Kowald, Grade 5
Immaculata Elementary School, NC

Waiting

Suspended,
On a forlorn hook,
Collecting dust,
The coat sits there.
Waiting.
Anticipating a wearer,
Not too big,
Not too small.
Dangling on a lone hook,
A musty maroon jacket waits.

Quinnlyn Murphy, Grade 6
Manchester Elementary/Middle School, VT

Basketball

Up the court and down the court
We all pass the ball around
Make a shot and miss
But get the rebound

It goes to the other team
You get back in a flash
Dash, dash, dash
Defense, defense

The ball goes out
You throw it in
You run down the court and make a pass
Shoot and swish

The fans yell and scream
And the other team is shocked
We clap and cheer but they shoot and score
We get back to offense and make a 3!!!!!

The game is over
The buzzer goes off
And we are very proud
This is the beginning of a winning season

Paige Whitehurst, Grade 6
Chapin Middle School, SC

Grandma and Papa

Sweet, kind, nice
She's the best cook ever,
I love her, she's the best,
She's confident, trustworthy, respectful
She's the best!
Papa's funny, kind and wise,
He'll tell jokes
And make you choke with laughter.
A nice little couple that will give you a chuckle
That's why I love them so.

Persia Poteat, Grade 4
Appomattox Elementary School, VA

Snow

Snow is white and fluffy.
It is like cotton balls on a winter day.
Snow is fun.

You can jump and play.
It is just like jumping into whipped cream.
Snow is soft.

You can make snowballs.
You can fight and watch gentle flutters
from the sky.

That is what snow is all about —
As long as you arc having fun.

N'Dya Carpenter, Grade 4
Bensley Elementary School, VA

Be Glad Your Mouth Is on Your Face

Be glad your mouth is on your face
not in another place
if it is in another place
it wouldn't be on your face
you wouldn't be talking
that's so sad
then you would get mad
so be glad your mouth is on your face

Amari Byrd, Grade 5
Courthouse Road Elementary School, VA

Army

The tracks squeak as they go into battle.
The ground shakes like an earthquake is happening.
Everyone gets ready for battle.
Boom! The shot is fired.
People fall to the ground like raindrops as they are killed.

Jeffrey Hayes, Grade 4
Waller Mill Fine Arts Magnet School, VA

Bong, Bong, Bong!

My head is aching bong, bong, bong!
The kids are talking all day long!
My ears are popping, pop, pop, pop,
I wish they could stop, stop, stop.
My head is aching bong, bong, bong!
This day is so long, long long!

Ehndé Howard, Grade 5
Courthouse Road Elementary School, VA

Best Friends

Here's a story of my two friends,
They have four paws and tails on their ends.
One is big, one is small
They're both lazy but come when I call.
They're my best friends after all!

Foster Wallace, Grade 4
Grace Miller Elementary School, VA

A Girl

A girl who is walking
A girl who doesn't like talking
A girl who was reading
A girl who is pleading
A girl who brightens your day
A girl who helps you on your way
A girl who makes tears go away
A girl who will not say
A girl who makes the sun come out
A girl who never pouts
A girl who makes the rain stop
A girl who always reaches for the top
Brendan Walker, Grade 6
Dr Edward Ricci School, RI

Claire

I have a friend named Claire,
She likes to play with her hair,
Claire is very very smart,
And she loves art.
Riandra Wykle, Grade 5
North Windy Ridge School, NC

Shoes

I have a collection of shoes.
Sometimes I count my shoes by twos.
I do not have heels.
The color is teal.
My shoes are a really cool view.
Tatasiana Cheatham, Grade 4
Battlefield Elementary School, VA

Octopus and Bumble Bee

Octopus and Bumble Bee
Swimming in the ocean blue
Buzzing around the flowers
Happy as can be

Swimming in the ocean blue
Pink and true
Happy as can be
My baby bumble bee

Pink and true
Yellow and black
My baby bumble bee
Tommy and Grandma

Yellow and black
Buzzing around the flowers
Tommy and Grandma
Octopus and Bumble Bee
Corbin Hawk, Grade 4
Riverside Elementary School, VA

Candy

If you're cravin' something
Sweet to eat,

You don't have to go far,
Just grab a candy bar.

It's definitely not nutritious,
But certainly sweet and delicious.

Don't eat a lot,
Or your teeth will rot.

You shouldn't eat one for dinner,
But it's definitely a winner!
Rachel Iudiciani, Grade 6
St Rocco School, RI

Pitcher to Catcher

Pitcher
Perfect, pretty
Winding, throwing, striking
Focused, thoughtful, protected, worried
Squatting, throwing, signaling
Strong, powerful
Catcher
Andre Wright, Grade 5
Northside Elementary School, SC

Spring

Spring is warm,
Spring is fresh,
While snow is melting into slush.

Spring is sunny,
Spring is bright!
Just look outside and see all the light.

The flowers bud,
and the flowers bloom.

The winter freeze,
becomes the gentle spring breeze.
Emma Bareihs, Grade 5
Wakefield Forest Elementary School, VA

Blue

Blue
Blue is the color I feel when I'm sad,
Blue is the color of the sky,
Blue is the color of the ocean,
Blue is the color of loneliness.
Blue
Morgan Soulia, Grade 6
Main Street Middle School, VT

Stinky Feet

I have stinky feet
my grandma calls me sweet
I clean up neat
but I have stinky feet.
Shatorey Bell, Grade 5
Pocalla Springs Elementary School, SC

The Baseball Game

Sizzle goes the sun
The game has begun.

He hits the ball-clink
He runs as fast as a blink.

Sun flower seeds go crack
He eats the whole pack.

Whiff, he falls at home base
Crunch there's dirt on his face.

It's the baseball game!!!
Molly Creel, Grade 5
Pine Tree Hill Elementary School, SC

The Barking Dog

My dog is sweet
But barks all night
He will bark all day
Until I'm in sight
Latrica Long, Grade 6
Benjamin Syms Middle School, VA

A Man Without Freedom

A man in shackles is a man in misery
A man without spirit
A man without hope is a man with
No freedom!
Jaren Michael Burford, Grade 6
Children's Studio School, DC

Sunset?

Pinks
Purples
Yellow sky
With a streak of white
Swirled
Twirled
Mixed together
Sunrise?
Or sunset?
Will we never know
Or will we?
Emma Caswell, Grade 4
Maple Wood Elementary School, NH

Hope

Hope, a simple word but it means a lot to me.
Dr. King had a dream that we would all live peacefully together.
I share the same dream,
but some different ones as well.
I dream of an America where whether you are
Hindu, Muslim, Jewish, Christian, or Buddhist,
people are respectful of
who you are and your right to be so.

I dream of a community in which people do not hate,
But, instead embrace each other's differences,
Black, White, Hispanic; we are all one people.
United, together, One!
I am a kid who wishes away all hatred and disrespect.

I am a student who dreams of a school
where kids can put aside differences
and learn together as friends.
Together we can do so much. Apart, we cannot.
"Yes, we can."
Very powerful words
They mean so much.
Teamwork, unity, but most of all, HOPE.

Martin Allen, Grade 6
Main Street Middle School, VT

What If*

Last night as I lay thinking here
Some whatifs crawled inside my ear
And pranced and partied all night long
And sang their same old whatif song:
Whatif I die before I wake?
Whatif I get eaten by a snake?
Whatif I lose all my money?
Whatif I slip and fall on honey?
Whatif I never get a date?
Whatif I cost my team the game?
Whatif everyone thinks I'm lame?
Whatif I lose my dog?
Whatif I trip on a log?
Whatif I fail a math test?
Whatif a baby bird falls out of her nest?
Everything seems swell and then the nighttime
Whatifs strike again…

Kennedi Meadows, Grade 6
East Mooresville Intermediate School, NC
*Patterned after "Whatif" by Shel Silverstein

Simon

Simon
Black, white, cute
Running, playing, jumping
Simon is cool and funny too
Awesome

Nicholas Krusz, Grade 4
Atkinson Academy Elementary School, NH

The Mess of a Pup

My mom had to prepare for the day
Two months before the month of May
She went out to clean a window for success
She went inside then came back out to a mess
Lizzy the dog had a new roll of paper towels
And was tearing them up and it was stretching her jowls
My mom ran after
But the dog was faster
And behind fluttered little bits
While my mom didn't want to make a fit
She threw a plastic horse shoe
And Lizzy ran after. Whew!
She cleaned it all up
And scolded the pup.

Will Braun, Grade 5
Trinity Christian School, VA

Change

Change is coming
Change is here
Change is on our minds

We live for it
We die for it
We prepare for the day it arrives

Cree Parris, Grade 5
Courthouse Road Elementary School, VA

The Waterfall

You can feel the water rush past you,
Peaceful and scary together,
With the wind rushing by like a whip,
So violently loud, you just might fall over the edge.

A big collage of colors,
All dance through the blue.
If you watch for too long,
Then you will get lost,
In a world of daydreams and memories.

You feel small, by the roar,
But more courageous too.
You are the one in this place,
And it's never too late,
You can one day be like this spot.

With so much to learn,
You can learn it all here.
Just come to this place and relax.
If you listen, the falls will speak.
The waterfall may terrify you,
But it's a place for dreams to come true.

Sarah Amatruto, Grade 5
Manchester Elementary/Middle School, VT

Basketball

Basketball
Strength, teamwork
Playing, bouncing, scoring
He dunks the ball
Shooting, passing, blocking
Practice, fast
Sport

Yong Ju Lee, Grade 6
Wakefield Forest Elementary School, VA

Dog

Dog
Furry, fluffy
Run, sniff, bark
Makes me feel better
Pet

Gigi Vaccaro, Grade 6
St John Neumann Academy, VA

Baseball

Walking out of the dugout
It is as if the day
starts over
as if a load has been taken
off my shoulders
and stepping onto the mound
feels like no other
like the world is in my hands
and before the ball is released
from my fingers, I am already
thinking about what to do next
waiting for the pitch to be thrown,
seems to take forever
with bright lights all around
it is hard not to be anxious
but the best part is hearing the crack
of a bat, and feeling the eyes shift
from one place to another

Connor Enright, Grade 6
Chapin Middle School, SC

Wonderful Friendship

Olivia is my friend
Friends are kind
Friends are special
Friends keep promises
If you want a friend be a friend

They're always there for you
Can trust them
Play with them sometimes

Can keep secrets
They help you

Elvie Guilmette, Grade 4
Hope Valley Elementary School, RI

Summer

Summer smells like fresh roses picked from my garden
Summer tastes like chocolate ice cream running down my throat
Summer jumps into the pool after putting on its sunscreen
Summer feels like a smooth dolphin dancing in the water
Summer looks like the sun beating down on the sea
Summer is like surfers surfing on the ocean

Deana Stiltner, Grade 4
Tabernacle Elementary School, NC

Wade Erwin

W illiam Swadley Erwin the 4th, Wade for short.
A Hungarian and Scottish child on my Mom's side.
D rewer is mother's maiden name and current middle name
E rwin, from my Dad's side of the family.

S wadley is my middle name from my Polish side of the family.

E qually German and Polish on my Dad's side of the family.
R eally politics run in the blood, I'm related to the first Governor of North Carolina.
W illiam the 4th, that means my great Grandfather was William the 1st.
I n the future I hope to keep the William tradition going.
N o turning back now.

4 generations of a great tradition.

Wade Erwin, Grade 6
Wakefield Forest Elementary School, VA

What Are You?

I see you hanging upside down in my tree. What could you be?
You're wrapped in silk, is that the key? What are you doing in my tree?
I hope you're ok upside down all day. Why don't you want to play?
I really just want to lay watch you hang there and grow all day.

I'll let you be, but I finally see, wow you're a butterfly, as beautiful
as can be, you are just for me, why butterfly you are as beautiful as a rainbow!
One rainbow in every wing.
You, butterfly look perfect!
A perfect shape,
A perfect color,
And a perfect place to be.
You are my butterfly.

Why butterfly, maybe we could have tea.
We could talk and be happy as can be.
What butterfly you can talk?
You talk like a machine.
But butterfly please stop you are making me dizzy!

Butterfly I must go to sleep.
Maybe you could come with me.
But no I must go I will see you next week!
You will return and be with me.

Cydney Jeffrey, Grade 5
Manchester Elementary/Middle School, VT

Dreams

Why do dreams have to end?
The world you escape to is perfect.
Every dream is a new form of hope.
If only unconsciousness lasted forever.
The endless fairytale of a handsome prince,
Or the ocean you've been longing to see.
Maybe a person you admire.
But then again, nightmares could haunt your dreams.
is that why dreams have to end?
To save you from the horror?
I guess it would be fair to live in an imaginary world
For eight hours.

Raven Furber, Grade 6
Boiling Springs Intermediate School, SC

If I Were a Spoon

If I were a spoon, I would do what spoons do.

I wouldn't cut a board like a saw.
I wouldn't sweep a floor like a broom.
I wouldn't write words like a pen.
I would do what spoons do.

What do spoons do?
You may ask?

Why spoons do all the hard work.
Spoons have the responsibility to transfer
liquids such as soup, ice cream, stew,
and sometimes Mountain Dew to our mouths.

Spoons do what forks cannot.
Our mouths appreciate what spoons do.
Do you?

If I were a spoon, I would like to be a sugar spoon.
How about you?

Spencer Saunders, Grade 5
Courthouse Road Elementary School, VA

A Day at the Lake

I can smell the lake water crawl up my nose,
I feel the shallow water on my bare feet,
I eat a popsicle.
I hear my cousins laughing and playing,
A painted turtle head pops up.
I taste the ice cream as it slithers down my throat.
I feel the hot sun creep onto my skin.
I can see a turquoise fish jump out of the water.
I smell the campfire as it starts to burn.
As the day comes to an end,
A bird sings a lullaby.

Laurel Wade, Grade 4
Crestwood Elementary School, VA

Beautiful Morning

Today is a beautiful morning.
The birds chirping,
the squirrels quirking,
morning glories blooming with joy.
There are smells of wonderful breakfasts,
pancakes, eggs, bacon.
There are smells of fresh air,
flowers, fruit, and grass.
Oh, what a beautiful morning,
perfect, wonderful, sweet.
But on this beautiful morning,
I'm going back to sleep!

Tessa Waddell, Grade 5
Old Bridge Elementary School, VA

Where I'm From

I am from a loving family peaceful and gentle
They love me in every way and I do too
They even worry when I am away
Where I'm from the food is great
I eat everything off my plate
My grandmother makes the best ribs
I get so messy; I need to wear a bib
Every gathering is the best
We gather up and have fun
We love when we have to run
I wish we can stay
But we can't always play
We all enjoy ourselves and have
A tremendous time
This is my family, they are all mine
The boys love playing football
And the girls, not so much
When I throw the ball
The crowd loves me a bunch
This is my life and that is
Where I'm from

Javin Ammonds, Grade 4
Whittaker Elementary School, SC

Laugh

The important thing about laughing is that
everyone has a different laugh.

Some people snort
or giggle softly.
Different laugh bubbles go to different people.
Special bubbles go to people that laugh every day,
not always will the bubble pop,
but it will be waiting to pop at the funniest moment of your life.

But the important thing about laughing is
people are the same,
only they have a different laugh.

Noah Mailloux, Grade 5
Daniel J Bakie School, NH

A Calling to the Sea
The first step I take, I take with pride.
I hear the water calling my name
The birds singing,
the starfish inviting me to play.

The palm trees sway with the swift summer breeze,
as if dancing a Spanish flamenco.
I put my pale white toe into the freezing, sapphire blue water.
I was shocked, surprised as if being poked by a thousand needles.

Next thing I knew I was in the water, eyes open wide,
wondering how I got in there.
I was as cold as the Antarctic, as frozen as an ice cube in the freezer.

Yet something called to me saying stay, you were meant to be in the water,
In the ocean, around Mother Nature, earth and sea.

And at that very second the water, starfish, and birds all stopped calling me.

Kate Cottrell, Grade 5
Manchester Elementary/Middle School, VT

The Sweet Game of Baseball

The sweet game of baseball
A place to bond
That sweet glove

Always open to me

Comforting me with plush leather

Rescuing me from the cold, hard ground
The sweet game of baseball
A place for laughter
That funny glove

Squeezing me with its tickling leather fingers

That sweet, caring, funny, kind,
cute, thoughtful glove

Looking out for an old waterlogged ball like me.

The sweet game of baseball
A place to bond

That sweet ball

Joining me when I'm lonely

Always pop-flying to my rescue

The sweet game of baseball
A place for laughter

That funny ball

Tickling me when it rubs my tummy

That sweet, caring, funny, kind,
cute, thoughtful ball

Looking out for a raggedy glove like me.

Matthew Bryan, Grade 5
North Windy Ridge School, NC

Brooke Newhouse
Brooke, funny, helping, caring, loving. Daughter of Anita N. Who loves cheerleading, chocolate, and cats. Who loves to help others. Who is caring. Who is shy. Who fears spiders. Who fears a crowd. Who accomplished all A's and B's on report card. Who got 100% on AR test. Who is in extended English, which is an honors English. Who wanted to win 1st at a cheerleading competition. Who was asked to cheer at the pro-bowl. Who always wore her hair down. Born in Virginia and living in Virginia, Newhouse.

Brooke Newhouse, Grade 6
Floyd T Binns Middle School, VA

The Sky's Emotions

When rain falls we get rain,
I think the sky is in pain when it rains

When the sky gets angry so we get thunder,
So I really wonder why we get thunder

When the sky gets cold we get snow,
I don't quite know why it gets cold

When the sky is happy it reveals its sun,
My son and I have fun in the sun.

P.S. If I had a son,
I wish for one.

Bryan Cotellese, Grade 4
St John Neumann Academy, VA

Trash Can

Inside a trash can are old things nobody wants.
These things could help people; there are batteries
you could recycle, old food people would love to
have, perfectly good toys that you just got
tired of, clothes that don't fit you, old glasses,
a bad grade, a necklace, an earring, pens, and
pencils. There are all kind of treasures in a trash can.

Amanda Atkinson, Grade 6
Eagle's Nest Christian School, DE

I've Learned That…

I've learned that Mrs. Sullivan can lead you to water,
    but she can't make you drink.
I've learned that I'm not the only one that suffers.
I've learned that teachers care about your feelings,
    not only your work.
I've learned that money can't buy you happiness.
I've learned that friends won't stay with you forever.
I've learned that your life isn't a fairy tale.
I've learned that my mom is doing the best that she can.
I've learned that you don't need everything your friends have.
I've learned that money is like a bomb;
    it'll destroy everyone.
I've learned that God is my light that guides me through my life.
I've learned that everything in your life can't be perfect.

Norah Mendoza, Grade 5
Northside Elementary School, SC

A Reader's Adventure

The reader's eyes are an explorer,
                l
            i   l
Running through the h   s
And ∧ valleys ∧
And over the seven seas of a story
To find the holy grail of a
climax.

Liam Buschel, Grade 6
East Mooresville Intermediate School, NC

Enchanting Rain

As rain falls
it trickles off roofs of lonely houses.
As rain falls
it hits the ground like thunder.
As rain falls
it dances through the sky like a ballet dancer on stage.
But all of a sudden it stops.
Enchanting rain…
Enchanting rain…
Enchanting rain…

Abby Suchocki, Grade 5
Rye Elementary School, NH

Washington

I remember the summer in Washington.
I remember the long car ride.
I remember the long empty plains.
And the empty blue sky.
I remember the sudden little town.
I remember the gust of warm air.
I remember the trees touching the sky.
Even now that it's April.
I remember the sound of the radios blaring.
But my favorite memory is yet to come.

Drew Peden, Grade 6
Boiling Springs Intermediate School, SC

Sam and I

Sam and I do everything together.
We have so much fun doing whatever.
We tell each other everything
and never tell anything.

Sam and I have never had a fight.
We're such good friends, and we're real tight.
We will always be there for each other.
Did I mention, she has a little brother?

Sam and I set lots of trends,
and we made lots of friends.
Sam would never dress-up,
and she would refuse to wear make-up.

Sadly, Sam, she had to move.
If I could choose, I'd disapprove.
I didn't get her address.
I'll never see her again, I guess.

Well, I know I have to move on.
It is so sad that she is gone.
Before she left we made a promise,
and Sam, I will always miss.

Marissa Swenson, Grade 6
Camperdown Academy, SC

The Beach

The place I like to go,
The place I like to be.
It's beyond Mooresville,
It's at the everlasting sea.
It is at the beach,
Where the trees grow of peach.
The sand is like wet cement that never is to dry,
Engraving the footprints of all who walks by.
I stand by the sea with my arms spread wide,
Where my feet are washed with the water from the tide.
Waiting for the waves to wash over me,
Waiting to be sprayed by the salty sea.
The gulls like airplanes, hover over me,
Looking for a meal to fish out the sea.
Then, I dive into the ocean to explore,
To see all the fishes and much much more.
I see the jellyfish dance through the sea,
I see the fishes swim so free.
The colorful coral is all around,
Making no movement, making no sound.
O please let us go back some day!

Shaniya Turner, Grade 5
East Mooresville Intermediate School, NC

African Plains

In the African plains
A lion stalks his prey.
He sneaks up,
It does not suspect it.
A lion stalks his prey,
Silently, stealthily,
It does not suspect it,
It gets closer
Silently, stealthily,
It strikes,
It gets closer,
In the African plains.

Hunter Smith, Grade 4
Vergennes Union Elementary School, VT

The Hunter

He stalks through the grass,
His eyes unmoving from his target,
His tail swishing back and forth,
Making not a sound as he slowly
Closes in.

He leaps through the air,
Back arched, paws outstretched,
And lands with his claws unsheathed,
Enveloping his prey in his mouth,
Success in his eyes.

Lea Knapp, Grade 6
East Mooresville Intermediate School, NC

Swimming My Last Race

"Beep!" I dove into the pool,
And the water was cool.
I tried to go faster,
But the water felt like plaster.
When I tried to speed up,
The crowd started yapping like a pup.
I was winning my last race,
And I didn't have to pace.
That second felt so dear,
As I swam near,
And touched the touch pad.
But I began to feel sad,
Even though I had won,
I was done.
I didn't know if to laugh or cry.
All I knew was that 25.10 seconds had gone by.
The score boards read:
C. Clifford Winner 25.10.

Colleen Clifford, Grade 4
St Thomas More Catholic School, NC

Dogs

Dogs
Silly, nice
Cute, funny, active
Man's best friend
Puppy

Geneva Doores, Grade 5
C Hunter Ritchie Elementary School, VA

Froggy

I saw a frog hop
Over a rock,
It hopped so high
Over the fly,
It hopped on each lily pad
'Till he got to the fly,
But the fly
Went too high.

Dmitri Stertz, Grade 4
Courthouse Road Elementary School, VA

Help Us Please

As the Nazi troops come marching in and yell and scream
All we can say is come help us please
As they put us in these nasty camps
We yell and plead come help us please

We are Jews, that's what we are
But Hitler cannot see that far
He kills all of our wives and kids
And stuffs their hair in pillows and beds
Help us please is what we say
Every day after day

Avery Hutton, Grade 5
West Hartsville Elementary School, SC

A Poem…

A poem is something so vivid and cheery
A poem is a light in the dark
A poem is a thought
A poem captures your mind and soul
A poem calls to ones heart
A poem is soft and delicate
A poem is sugary sweet
A poem is also tart
A poem is bold and strong
A poem has words and words have power
A poem is lively and full of life
A poem expresses your feelings
A poem is something that cannot be described with a few words
A poem is like silk
A poem is a challenge that must be overcome
A poem is a gem among a horde of treasure
A poem is an art a thing that must be practiced
A poem is as good as you want it to be
A poem is a song without a chant
A poem is as fluid as a stream

Jerry Forman, Grade 6
The Compass School, RI

The Maybe Safer

I dream that one day the whole world
Or at least half of the world would get saved
So there can be less fighting, gunshots, and other stuff.
Anyway that is my dream
And this is how I'm going to do it.
Ask questions in school if needed
Get great grades
Study the Bible
Learn different languages
Travel around the world

Jay McEntyre, Grade 6
Kannapolis Middle School, NC

The Sweet Smell of Flowers

The smell so sweet and tender
it's like it just makes you remember
how love so sweet and soft,
and how beautiful it is.
It's just as if you can touch it.
Those flowers you just want to love,
like you wanted to love some one before.
oh the smell of those sweet flowers
as you walk along the walk way
you can see all those beautiful colors.
oh it's just the smell of those sweet smelling flowers
just remember that no matter how beautiful something is
it's never as beautiful as…
the smell of sweet flowers.

Jaelyn Samboy, Grade 6
School of International Studies at Meadowbrook, VA

My Place

My place
Way down low
Is quiet
You know
Freedom is soaring like an eagle
Dreams are dancing in my mind
Happiness is a ray of sunshine
My place
I'm alone
By myself
Reading, dancing
My place
Happiness and loneliness
Surround me
My place
My place
My place
Way down low
Is quiet
You know.

Ashley Davis, Grade 5
East Mooresville Intermediate School, NC

Cartoons

Cartoons, cartoons, you are so fun.
All I ever see is Cartoon Network, Nick and so much more!
Cartoons, my favorite show is *SpongeBob*.
When my sister turns it, it's not much fun.
I wonder when I could get out of this TV!

Sarah Abigail Louk, Grade 4
Courthouse Road Elementary School, VA

Santa vs the Easter Bunny

Surely you have heard the tale
On that very frightful night
When the cherished Easter Bunny
Fought the cheery Christmas sight

Who was loved more was how it started
Givers to children finally parted
Easter fought hard but Santa won
And that's how the feud of the holidays begun.

Matthew Poling, Grade 4
Angelus Academy, VA

My Cats

Two fun cats with annoying meows,
Amazing, striped fur,
They never say "BURR!"
They are very rambunctious,
That means that they act monkeyish,
They sleep in the sun and love to run.
We bring them to the vet, they hate to get wet…
These are my pets!

Eric Link, Grade 5
Trinity Christian School, VA

Christmas Day

Christmas lights are gleaming
Singing Christmas carols
The bluebirds are singing
Waffles with the thick scent of syrup

Singing Christmas carols
"It's Christmas! It's Christmas!"
Waffles with the thick scent of syrup
I always leave cookies for Santa

"It's Christmas! It's Christmas!"
Hot chocolate steaming
I always leave cookies for Santa
Celebrating Christmas with relatives

Hot chocolate steaming
The bluebirds are singing
Celebrating Christmas with relatives
Christmas lights are gleaming
Domenic Ciringione, Grade 4
Hope Valley Elementary School, RI

Fishing

Better than being a baseball star,
More fun than playing video games,
Better than football,
Better than climbing a tree,
Better than swimming in the ocean,
Better than rock climbing,
Better than basketball,
Better than the TV.
That's how fun fishing is!
Brent Mistr, Grade 4
St Christopher's School, VA

'Ol Socs

Socrates was very unpleasant,
He looked a lot like an old pheasant,
He taught very well,
His voice like a bell,
But some didn't like him,
Some men became grim,
Some men held a grudge,
They took Socrates to a judge,
Ugly Socrates questioned the law,
He was to die, the men thought, "Ha!"
Socrates knew it!
He sure blew it!
But he didn't care,
He thought this quite fair,
Good 'ol guy,
Good-bye!
Lauren Osterhoudt, Grade 5
Trinity Christian School, VA

Jake's Chore

There once was a boy named Jake
Whose chore was to go out and rake
He hated the chore
Because it was a bore
And it gave him a back ache.
Connor Collins, Grade 4
Memorial School, NH

My Precious Box

I will put into my precious box
The love of my mom
The entertainment of video games
The sound of country music
The happiness of children
The care of my cat
And special, warm memories.

I will not put into my box
The violence of others
The misery of harmed people
The nuisance of misbehaved kids
The sadness of people crying
The unhappiness of hungry children.
Antonio Anton, Grade 5
Four Oaks Elementary School, NC

Lion

Lion
Very awesome
The king of the jungle
The lion is the furriest
Awesome
Austin Shope, Grade 4
Waller Mill Fine Arts Magnet School, VA

Starz

When the comets fly at night,
The stars are such a beautiful sight,
But as the light of dawn draws near,
They all begin to disappear.
Kate Nezelek, Grade 5
Clover Hill Elementary School, VA

Winter

Winter is white
like a flock of sheep
snow is falling down
like crystal diamonds
and snowflakes are swaying
from side to side,
dancing with
peace and harmony.
Huriyyah Chaudhry, Grade 4
Oak Grove Elementary School, NC

My Precious Box

I will put into my precious box
The sweet taste of chocolate,
The sound of country music,
The love of my family,
A great mystery book
The smell of a good supper,
And special, warm memories.

I will not put in my box
The sadness of hungry people,
The bad dreams people have,
The fear of war,
The sadness of someone dying,
And the meanness of my brothers.
Wynter Autry, Grade 5
Four Oaks Elementary School, NC

Love

Love is pink
Love is red
Love sounds like a heartbeat
Love feels smooth
Love tastes like candy hearts
Love smells like a sweet lollipop
Love is peaceful
Love is crickets chirping at night
Love is watching the sunset
Love is watching the stars
Dakota Staples, Grade 4
Tabernacle Elementary School, NC

Letters

L ooking at this paper
E ither
T yped or written
T aken to you
E xtra fast for a
R eason that is
S pecial
Emanuel Lirag, Grade 5
Sanford Creek Elementary School, NC

How Can It? How Does It?

How can a bird fly
so high up in the sky?
How can a snake crawl
with not any legs at all?

How does a fish swim
with the water so dim?
How do the animals know
where they need to go?
Damien Keene, Grade 5
Four Oaks Elementary School, NC

Seasons

Spring is a season full of joy
Kids running around playing with each and every toy
Flowers are blooming with buds spread out
All I can do is scream and shout!

Summer is a season full of sun
What anyone can do is play and run!
Then sun is out, with beams of heat,
All I can do is eat my ice cream treat!

Fall is a season full of leaves.
All those different colors that fall from trees,
Making a pile of red, orange, brown, and yellow
This scene is perfect while playing the cello.

Winter is a season with white, puffy snow
Filling each plant garden, row by row
Playing in snow, having a snowball fight
Those are all the seasons, I hope I'm right!

Naima Muminiy, Grade 5
Swift Creek Elementary School, NC

Chalk

I am a piece of chalk.
I sit on a tray all day.
My legs have been scratched away,
and so have my arms and hair.

When I am picked up
I feel like a feather
scratching up against the side of a tree.
It doesn't fill me with any glee.

My friend's name is CeeCee.
She always uses me.
I have other friends,
like Bobby and Connie.
With them the fun never ends.
It fills me with so much glee.

Sierra Frazier, Grade 5
Courthouse Road Elementary School, VA

Music

Music is colorful
because there are so many different kinds of it.

Music is a ride
because it takes you away.

Music is a feeling
because it can be emotional.

Music is calming
because it makes you calm down.

Claire Kolakowski, Grade 5
Holy Cross Elementary School, DE

Love Spring

I can feel the cool spring breeze tickling my body.
My hair dancing with the wind.
I stand on the dew damp grass.
Listening to birds sing in my ears.
My nose sniffs a sweet smell from the flowers.
Every day I'll be here.
Hoping to see such wonderful excitement.

Justine Tran, Grade 5
Oak View Elementary School, VA

Yes, Our Victory Is Near!

Will my heart go on?
When everyone says no
When life takes a turn
Yes! Give me courage to move on!
I will break free from the cage!

Or will I just lose
Will this battle defeat me?
Will my courageous ways fall behind?
No! The battle is not over till I have won!
Victory is near! Freedom has come!

Taylor Tyson, Grade 5
W G Pearson Elementary School, NC

My Wonderful Uncle Russell

I had an uncle.
He was part of my heart.
He had two sons, one daughter, and a wife.
They loved him larger than life.

My dad and I were in his truck for the call.
His brother was in a car wreck?
In the morning the kids were asking, "Is he here?"
The mood was quite drear.

Then Aunt Caroline started to talk.
She told us he died!
Then everyone started crying.
But Pitts told a message that hit with a sting.

My Uncle did not die in a wreck…
he shot himself.
He had died the next morning,
the kids not knowing anything.

This tragedy happened the summer of 2008.
Roses are red…violets are blue
Never do suicide for it doesn't fit you.
I wish you knew I loved you!

Ashlynn Powell, Grade 6
Camperdown Academy, SC

Aquarium

I arrived here at school,
And started to wait.
We finally began,
Yet students were late.

We got on the bus,
Some by some,
And later arrived,
At the aquarium.

We saw stingrays and sea horses,
Also the dolphins,
Turtles and monkeys,
Even the puffins.

We went to the gift shop,
And left at eleven.
We came back and had recess,
And I studied at seven.

Jodie Lee, Grade 5
Trinity Christian School, VA

A Thin Slice

Love is a treat
You have it now
Right when you meet
But when the song is sung
The nightmare has begun
A piece here
A piece there
Your love will disappear
One by one the killers depart
Leaving you with only one part
A thin slice
Happy Birthday!!!

Kenzie Kearns, Grade 4
Memorial School, NH

Lonesome

L ovable with nobody
O utside alone
N ever like someone
E nough of myself
S ad as light and dark
O pposed of love
M yself in the world
E mpty inside

Saikou Balde, Grade 5
Cooper Elementary School, VA

Spring Is Finally Here

Spring is finally here
now you can feel the breeze
go through your sweet hair.

Elise Williams, Grade 5
Pocalla Springs Elementary School, SC

Dad

Dad you are water
Always cleaning my mind just like water cleans my hands
But yet you are also earth strong as rocks and mountains

Brycen O. Walrath, Grade 5
Wakefield Forest Elementary School, VA

A Friend

A friend is like a book because you can't judge a book by its cover.
Friends are like animals because they love to party and go to the wild side.
Friends are like baskets because they carry you when you're down.
Sometimes friends are like money because they come and go.

Kendra Wyatt, Grade 5
Holy Cross Elementary School, DE

Messy

Messy describes my room, right now,
You might even find a cow!
A lot of toys
Are a little brother's joys.
A big sister's curly hair
Is found everywhere.

Dirty shirts and socks
And my long locks.
Pants and shoes
And maybe even Yoo-hoos.
Lipstick and lip gloss
To show you who's boss.

Purses galore
Now there's a score.
One clock that's broken
And socks that are soaken.
A soccer ball to squeeze
"Can I have my Ele please?"

My room is an atrocious mess, it's not very blessed.
Please don't let your room look like mine, for it won't look very fine.

Michaela Saunders, Grade 6
Linkhorne Middle School, VA

The Imaginative Umbrella

An umbrella is a shield to protect yourself from mortal danger
It is a parachute
A thin cliff that gets wide at the very top
An umbrella is a cheerful tree that lets in happiness
And prevents darkness and sadness from coming in
An arrow for a monstrous giant
It is a magical force field that keeps you safe from the elements
An umbrella harbors all living things
It is an upside down cereal bowl with a sturdy spoon supporting it
An umbrella is a mysterious balloon that you can only see the top of
It is a bird with a few flimsy bones
A sail of a mighty sailboat
An umbrella is a heavenly symbol pointing to the gods above

Jacie Lemos, Grade 5
Rye Elementary School, NH

Beautiful Bright Star

The bright star is the sun I know, it didn't take years to show,
It comes in a whoosh,
And doesn't ever need to be pushed,
It's bigger than a mountain
And larger than the sea, it's here for everybody,
The sun sways swiftly, and it sure does look nifty,
As I gaze at its golden face,
I squint my eyes with no time to waste,
Its glare is like a deadly flower,
It's pretty but has a lot of power,
And if you stand there and glare,
Your eyes would hurt and it's glasses you'd need
To keep up to speed,
Because the sun is a mighty thing,
And when it goes away it has time to sing,
As we come to a closing end,
I want to say goodbye my friend,
I hope you have time to spend,
With me and all my other friends,
So sleep away beautiful star, but don't you go too far.

Kayla Callahan, Grade 6
School of International Studies at Meadowbrook, VA

Little Bit

There once was a cat named Little Bit
Who liked to come inside and sit
She would drink her milk and eat her food
In a happy, happy mood
She would sit in her Daddy?s lap
To take a nice long nap

When it came time for her to go back out
She would always start to pout
So her Daddy would rub her fur
And this always made her purr
She went outside with no more sorrow
Because she knew there is always tomorrow

Zack Viar, Grade 6
Linkhorne Middle School, VA

Index

Author Autograph Page

Author Autograph Page

Author Autograph Page

Author Autograph Page

Author Autograph Page

Author Autograph Page

Author Autograph Page

Author Autograph Page

Author Autograph Page

Author Autograph Page

Author Autograph Page

Author Autograph Page

Author Autograph Page

Author Autograph Page

Author Autograph Page